The
Beartoot
Fishing Guide

by Pat Marcuson

Falcon Press Publishing Co., Inc.
Billings and Helena, Montana

Acknowledgements

The Beartooth-Absaroka Fishing Guide is largely a product of the persistent, yet kindly, urging of my daughter, Heather, and of Mike Sample of Falcon Press.

Without the pleasurable years of service to the State of Montana, Department of Fish, Wildlife and Parks, the work would have never been possible. Thanks in particular go to Clint Bishop, Fletcher Newby, Vern Waples, Roger Fliger, Art Whitney, and George Holton, all dedicated resource employees for the State of Montana. Thanks are also extended to Louis Pechacek and Ron Ken of Wyoming Game and Fish, Cody, Wyoming.

To the number of tough and able summer employees whose sweat and insect-bitten, tired, hungry bodies willingly gave endless weeks of underpaid effort, thanks. The support and partial financial assistance of the United States Forest Service, made possible by the likes of Gary Wetzston, Phil Jacquith, Gwen McKittrick, and George Schaller, were greatly appreciated.

Merci beaucoup to all who provided photographs and to my family, who went without vacations so that I could indulge in my incessant quest of surveying and enhancing over 1000 mountain lakes. Finally, to the many pioneers of the mountains for sharing the past and to all the folks in Cooke City, Red Lodge, Roscoe, Columbus, and Billings whose friendship and encouragement meant so much, thanks.

This book is dedicated to a lovely lady, my Mom.—*Pat Marcuson.*

Recreation Guides from Falcon Press

The Angler's Guide to Montana

The Beartooth Fishing Guide

The Floater's Guide to Colorado

The Floater's Guide to Montana

The Hiker's Guide to Arizona

The Hiker's Guide to California

The Hiker's Guide to Colorado

The Hiker's Guide to Idaho

The Hiker's Guide to Montana

The Hiker's Guide to Utah

The Hiker's Guide to Washington

The Hunter's Guide to Montana

The Rockhound's Guide to Montana

Falcon Press is continually expanding its list of recreational guidebooks using the same general format as this book. All books include detailed descriptions, accurate maps, and all information necessary for enjoyable trips. You can order extra copies of this book and get information and prices for the books listed above by writing Falcon Press, P.O. Box 1718, Helena, MT 59624. Also, please ask for a free copy of our current catalog listing all Falcon Press books.

Falcon Press Publishing Co.
P.O. Box 1718
Helena, MT 59624

Cover Photo: Bill Schneider

First Printing—May 1985
Second Printing—April 1989

Contents

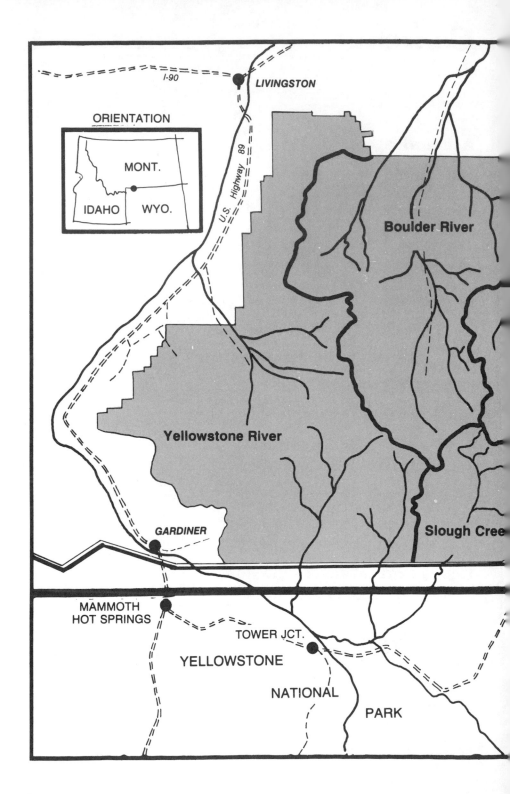

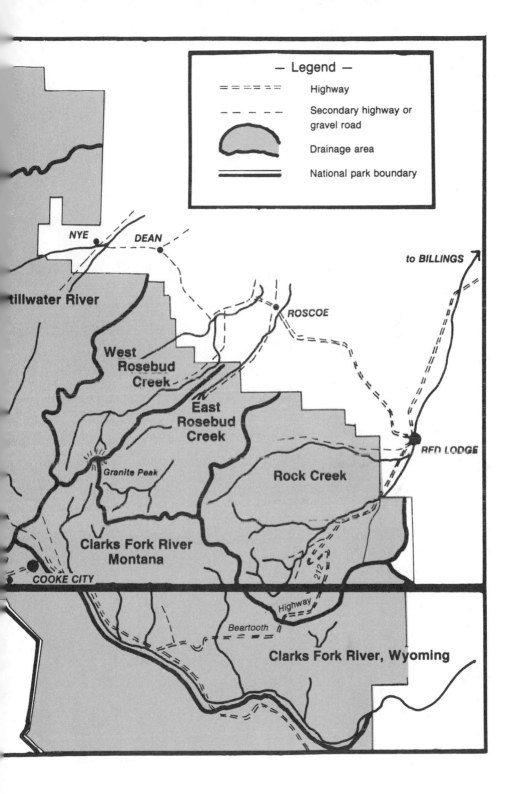

- Legend -

====== Highway

- - - - - Secondary highway or gravel road

Drainage area

National park boundary

NYE

DEAN

to BILLINGS

Stillwater River

ROSCOE

West Rosebud Creek

East Rosebud Creek

RED LODGE

Granite Peak

Rock Creek

Clarks Fork River Montana

COOKE CITY

212

Highway

Beartooth

Clarks Fork River, Wyoming

v

Wading the East Rosebud River puts this angler in waters draining more than 100 square miles of Custer National Forest. Michael Sample photo.

Introduction to Beartooth-Absaroka Country

The line spun off my reel as the largest golden trout I ever hooked made his last run for the depths of the cold, clear waters of Lightning Lake. I had caught numerous smaller goldens in the little outlet lake, but never one like this. For years I'd studied this brilliantly-colored wonder of the mountains, weighing, measuring, trapping, and stripping eggs for seeding other Montana waters. Finally, during the twilight hours of a beautiful day, it was my turn to outwit a large male golden trout. The evening was cool and the snow-capped mountains caught a lingering of evening light. Mixed emotions gathered about me: why had he taken the poorly-constructed ant imitation I was retrieving across the rocky lake bottom? It was true I wanted this fish, yet I felt sickened that a goal was about to end. But then, I had earned it. Who else had spent the years I had studying fish and their habitat in the Absaroka-Beartooth Mountains? Still, it didn't seem right. Had he eluded me yet another day, my goal would be prolonged.

The scene couldn't have been better. How fortunate I had been...the mountains I had crossed, the thrill of a close encounter, a slip on a seemingly endless snowfield fanning downward around an occasional lichen-covered outcrop of granite as it disappeared from view. The nights I huddled close to my campfire drying clothing soaked by a spectacular mountain storm. The ache of muscles straining under a load too heavy for common sense. A coyote running wildly through a bluebell meadow with a mountain lion methodically putting the fear of death into the wild dog's desperation. The spectacular stone arches, domes, glaciers, the careening waterfalls and shimmering lakes I beheld. Yes, I was indeed a fortunate person.

The force of the rod's steady resistance to the heavy fish woke me to the reality of the moment. The battle was swinging toward my advantage, but the fading evening light was on the side of the fish. It would take quick, precise action to beach him and finalize the victory. No doubt a fish his size could easily dislodge the small no. 14 hook, particularly during the wild struggle that was sure to occur anytime the fish approached the shallow shoreline.

Memories of becoming obsessed with surveying every lake—952 of them—in my management area of the Absaroka-Beartooth Mountains of Montana flooded my mind. The work started slowly with a survey of 20 lakes in 1967 and 50 or so in 1968. Then it started rolling, methods improved, and the number of "completed" marks struck across my tattered maps increased yearly. After shedding the feeling that the goal was beyond reach, my fever intensified. As the effort neared completion, the list of lakes surveyed each year approached 250. Lakes at the 5,000-6,000 foot elevation were visited in June and as the waters opened at loftier heights, I went after them with a backpack loaded with an echo sounder, a boat, nets, and an assortment of biological gear. In the process, I surveyed the highest lake in the State of Montana (at 11,200 feet above sea level) and the most elevated lake harboring fish (at 10,870 feet).

After completion of the Absaroka-Beartooth lake survey, I examined the lakes of the Crazy Mountains and then returned to the lofty Beartooths. A new goal emerged. Round two was aimed at optimizing the fishery by distributing fish of various species to barren waters and securing the welfare of certain threatened species. But more than anything, I believed that mountain lakes were capable of producing larger fish.

A sudden jerk of the rod again awakened me. In spite of the spectacular golden trout's reluctance, his tired body approached a rod's length from defeat. After disagreeing violently with the landing site I had chosen, the great fish turned heavily on his side. The hook held, the battle was won.

The *Beartooth Fishing Guide* includes lakes from the Clarks Fork side of the Beartooth on the east to the Absaroka Mountains bordering the Yellowstone River on the west. The

Guide also extends from the Beartooth Face on the north to the Clarks Fork River in Wyoming on the south. In total, 1,077 lakes, 435 with fish, are listed in this guide.

The country offers a variety of fishing opportunities. Cutthroat trout 18 inches and larger are scattered throughout the Montana real estate. Brook and smaller cutthroat trout are also readily available. A number of lakes support grayling and rainbow, golden, brown, and lake trout. A look through this book should assist you in locating a variety of fishing adventures.

Names of backcountry localities are curious. Some have persisted over the years, others fade away. The Absaroka-Beartooth Mountains are full of names of interesting pioneers, geographic descriptions, someone's wife, or a special meaning to someone, somewhere. They will probably change in times to come. I did a lot of snooping around in my effort to learn Beartooth history and, more often than not, a reason for a name became apparent. For purposes of this guide, I attempted to use historic names first. Other names I became aware of are listed in parentheses. A great number of lakes were assigned names during the lake surveys conducted by both Montana and Wyoming Fisheries Divisions. These names were merely a means of identification and record keeping for large numbers of fishable lakes. Without handles, management was in a state of disorder, fish were planted in unintended waters, and records were a mess. For your purposes, call them anything you like. Nameless lakes, mountains, and streams belong to wilderness.

The goal of this guide is to assist you in planning a good outing and a memorable experience. Enjoy the country, respect it, and treat it kindly. It's great country and fascinating fishing.

How to Use the Guide

The Beartooth-Absaroka area map provides orientation to the drainage boundaries used to distinguish the following nine chapters of alpine lake descriptions.

Code maps accompanying each chapter provide the numerical designation of the lakes in the text. The maps included in the *Guide* are not intended to be used as the sole reference for those planning to visit the Absaroka-Beartooth lakes listed here. The area is rugged and can be confusing even to experienced hikers. Rather, these maps are only provided as general locators. For more accurate, more detailed descriptions of terrain, trails, facilities, regulations, and distances, consult the complete Forest Service maps themselves or topographic maps available from the U.S. Geological Survey.

The lakes in each drainage were assigned numbers generally beginning with those on the lower left hand side of each drainage map and proceeding in a clockwise direction around each tributary stream, ending at the lower elevation lakes on the right hand side. The Wyoming portion of the Clarks Fork River (Chapter 8) is an exception to this scheme. Numbers begin on the lower right (SE) and proceed in a counterclockwise direction to the left of the drainage map (NW).

Those who browse through the lake descriptions and wish to locate a particular lake can refer back to the appropriate number on the chapter code map or use the legal land description.

Townships are located by a numbered grid of north-south Range lines and east-west Township lines. The block of land within the Township consists of 36 sections totaling 640 acres. Most descriptions break Townships into four 160 acre quarters, NE, NW, SE, and SW. Further subdivisions, the quarter-quarter sections, refine the location to a 40 acre plot, then to 10 acres, and finally to 2.5 acres.

This guide, however, uses a desirable modification reducing the lengthy quarter section method to a simple lettering system. The 160-acre subdivisions of each 640-acre section are designated as A, B, C, and D, in a counterclockwise direction beginning with A in the NE quadrant. For example, a lake in the NW1/4 of the NE1/4 of the SE1/4 of Township 8 N, Range 16 W, Section 16 would reduce to T8N, R16W, S.16 DAB. To be more precise simply requires further reductions of "B" by continued counterclockwise A, B, C and D lettered quarters. Lake locations take the simplest description. If lake boundaries are shared by a number of quadrants, the one most descriptive is used.

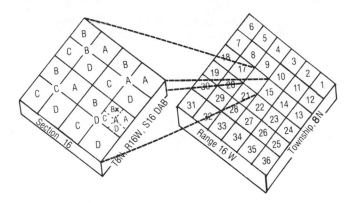

Fishing Tips

For those of you looking to increase your chances of a successful angling experience in alpine country, I offer the following suggestions: First of all, be prepared for the greatest of angling challenges. Fish can be extremely wary and have humbled many an angler in crystal clear mountain waters. Even lakes harboring large numbers of small brook trout sometimes become stubbornly unproductive. The old tale of fish hungry enough to take a bare hook is just that, "an old tale."

The biggest handicap for the alpine angler is weather. Surprisingly the bright, sunny, hot days are the most troublesome. Fishing usually improves at the day's extremes, both early and late. During still, warm days use the shadows cast by mountain ridges.

The best combination is a warm day with enough breeze to agitate the lake surface. This combination generates the best of both worlds: immergent insects and less than optimum external visibility for the fish. More severe weather slows insect hatches and sometimes promotes aggressive feeding behavior.

Consider mild wind a friend of alpine anglers. Use the prevailing wind to gain an advantageous position. Winds tend to windrow aquatic and terrestrial organisms to windward shores. Needless to say, concentrations of food attract concentrations of fish.

As a general rule, winds blow down-mountain in the evening and up-mountain in the morning, in response to changing air temperatures and air density. Inclement weather, though, overrules daily patterns. Take advantage of it.

If you're a bait fisherman, the old standby is the nasty earthworm. I personally find fish eggs superior bait. Fresh skein eggs, sprinkled with a borax or red jello mix and stored in the freezer make excellent bait. Fishing cluster eggs works best if the eggs are lifted slightly off the lake bottom. A small fluorescent float near the hook does the job. I suggest a setup of the type diagrammed:

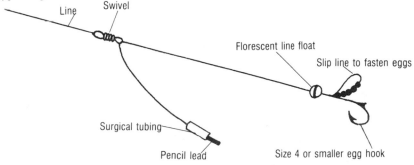

Slice small clusters of treated eggs, attach to hook, and slip a loop over eggs to secure. Fish the eggs on the rocks or gravels along deeper shorelines.

A variety of terminal tackle works well with a spinning rod. I found lures best in lakes with larger brook or lake trout. Otherwise, lures are generally a poor choice. A spinning rod also provides an effective means of fishing a fly. A teardrop casting float preceeding five feet of fine leader and a small fly makes an excellent trout weapon. A fast retrieve usually reduces the need to sharply set the hook, typical of conventional fly fishing technique.

Fly fishing produces the most consistent means of enticing alpine trout. Cutthroat and rainbow trout are particularly vulnerable. Most fly casters have a fly box full of feathered creations, most of which repel alpine fish. The avid fly fisherman knows his choice flies. I personally find the simplest *brown* and *gray hackle* patterns most effective. For variation and adaptation to specific situations, I fish a *Carey Special* in meadow-type lakes. Fish it near the bottom with a sinking line, using a slow retrieve and a short sporadic jerk every 10 seconds.

A gray or green *shrimp* pattern on a size 10 or 12 hook imitates the scud called *Gammarus*. The freshwater shrimp imitation should be no longer than three-quarters of an inch and is most effective where the real critters actually occur. They are fished deep along the shoreline with jerky retrieves. Imitate the real ones that skip quickly between hiding areas. Usually they inhabit weed beds and cobble beaches near weed beds.

The green *midge pupa* on size 14, 16, or 18 hook cast with 9—12 feet of leader is super during mid-summer. Present the fly well ahead of cruising fish. When the fish is five feet away, give it a single twitch to imitate the pupa's transformation to an adult midge.

Buffy-colored *caddis flies* flipped on the surface of an inlet stream are hunted by cutthroat and are even more deadly for rainbow. Real ones flutter a lot on the water surface, making considerable commotion. I rarely use caddis flies on quiet water. If I do, I try to imitate their habit of diving off shoreline brush, hitting the water hard. This is an excellent fly for stream fishing.

The ant, both brown and black, is a great underwater lure. Actual stomach analysis of alpine fish shows brown ants a common food item in late August and September. The ant is a real easy pattern to tie: I use a fine wire hook of size 12. The shank is wrapped with light brown thread to build up the body. Rib the fly with yellow thread. A short, brown hackle is optional. Shine up the body with head cement. I fish ants under the surface along windward shores.

More important than the selection of flies is the manner of presentation and the quality of leader. Learn to hunt alpine cutthroat. They cruise the shorelines usually in small groups. An effective fly presentation requires little lakeward casting distance. Fish parallel to the shore. Drape flies over rocks or use a dropper fly and tease fish to break water.

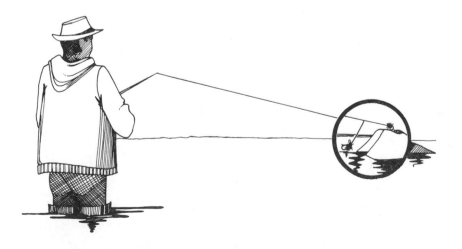

A raft can be effective in slough water with unstable or brushy shorelines. They are miserable to carry but handy for cruising shores. One great bonus of the life-raft is the relief they offer fragile shorelines. Increased human traffic has trampled permanent paths around vegetated shorelines, and rafts diminish the pressure.

Planning Your Trip

To those adventurous persons planning an extended trip through the Beartooths or northern Absarokas, I offer the following: *Have a plan and plot a course* that's realistic, and let someone know your intentions. A sketch of your proposed route and a dated listing of your companions' names eliminates a lot of confusion and concern. If you are a nonresident, leave your destination plans with the USFS Ranger Station in Red Lodge, Cody, Big Timber, Bozeman, or Gardiner. Don't forget to let them know of your return upon completion of your journey.

Planning your hike depends to a large extent on your objectives. Lots of folks intend to climb one or more of the numerous mountain peaks, others like to cross a segment of the range, while some go strictly to hit a number of fishing opportunities. A number of inquiries regarding the location of fishable lakes were received by the author from those seeking fishing opportunities while enroute to accomplishing a primary objective other than fishing. In other words, where can a meal of fish be found that would be a welcome culinary break from a freeze-dried diet and lighten the load? In this case, the *Guide's* listings of fishless lakes as well as lakes with fish should be scrutinized. Remember, however, that lakes with fish don't always guarantee a meal of fried fish.

Be realistic about choosing your routes. Study U.S. Geological Survey quadrangle maps. Those areas riddled with tight contour intervals are usually impassable. You may find a couloir that allows ascending or descending access past a vertical slope, but take care! You may become rimrocked. If you do choose a dead end, don't let your tired body influence your mind to take unnecessary chances. When traveling up or down a steep coulee, keep your party together to avoid the danger of a careening rock dislodged by your buddy furthest uphill.

How long will it take me to go from here to there? That, of course, is difficult to answer and depends on your abilities, conditioning, and objectives. If you're a nonresident living at elevations considerably lower than the 8,000 to 11,000 feet common in the Beartooth and Absaroka ranges, be realistic. Even well-conditioned bodies need some adjustment at higher elevations. Temporary headaches, nausea, hyperthermia, and a general listlessness may be common until your body adapts. Don't push it: plan an enjoyable, do-able trip.

There are those who can put a lunch in a small day pack and travel the 33 miles from East Rosebud Lake to the trail head near Cooke City in a long day. But such an itinerary is not advisable with a heavy pack unless you're going for physical punishment. Distance traveled per day depends on the weather, the terrain, and you. For the average family backpacker, I suggest you plan no more than 10 miles a day on trail systems and quite a bit less if you depart from major trails. Even those enjoyable plateau areas, though nicely suited to cross-country travel, are at elevations high enough to pull at body reserves. Extended travel across plateau zones is temporary at best, as most of the fishing and protected camping areas require a substantial elevation change.

In planning your trip, allow enough time to enjoy your stay. Travel the speed of the slowest member of the party. Leave notice of your intentions, and travel routes that are realistic and safe for the ability of *all* your companions.

Loading Your Pack

My advice is "keep it simple." Why go in the first place if all the comforts and conveniences of home have to tag along? A lot of over-zealous backcountry enthusiasts abort a fine trip because they didn't leave something behind. Why carry more than the body can comfortably handle?

The less you take, the happier you will be. Freedom to move, climb, or traverse a snowfield makes a genuine experience of your trip. Take in the whole grandiose scene, not just the next step in the trail.

As to how many pairs of pants, how heavy the bedroll, or how large a tent, I doubt I can be of much help. The main consideration for clothing is comfort. A loose fit, long sleeves, and pants that protect one from mosquitoes and sharp objects will adapt to all backcountry conditions better than a pack full of clothing options.

The weather rarely remains dormant in the high country. Be prepared for variable atmospheric conditions. Rain gear and a warm, hooded sweatshirt are highly recommended. During rest breaks, you will find it a bit cool until the perspiration dries following a strenuous hike. That sweatshirt will feel good, but take it off before you resume travel, otherwise you will wish you had another dry garment for the next break.

The market for lightweight bedrolls is adequate to fill your needs. Get one you can stuff into a water-resistant stuff bag. I found that a large nylon stuff bag allowed room for both my ground pad and sleeping bag. With the bedroll stuffed inside the hip-to-shoulder-length pad, I could count on a dry, comfortable bed. The stuff bag for my bedroll was off-limits to the laundry. Once the bag was water tight, I found myself much happier.

I had a habit of taking a large nylon tent fly for rain gear, tent, ground cloth, and even extra clothing during inclement weather. When traveling, I prespired so much I could equal the dampness of rain inside my rain clothing. I elected either to get wet and dry out after the hike or, if it looked to be a passing storm, I waited it out under the protection of the rainfly.

Make sure you have comfortable boots. If they are new, break them in before the trip. Sore feet have ruined many a good trip and alienated feelings among a party of friends. A good Vibram sole helps soothe the sharp rocks underfoot. If the boots are well greased, they will withstand a fair amount of water.

A hank of nylon cord is super handy for a variety of uses: shoe laces, dragging fuel, tying tents and tent flies, and securing packs, to name a few.

Camping Hints

Respect both the land and other campers. Take the time to choose a site that is not going to be impacted and scarred by your presence. Keep abreast of USFS regulations: their intent is to minimize land use abuses. When traveling main trail areas, it is probably best to use established camps rather than create new sites. The impact of camping can be minimized by choosing sites with healthy, well-established vegetation or heavy, armored soils. It's pretty difficult to leave any trace of your camp if you choose a rock to camp on.

If you need a campfire, carefully excavate top soil and vegetation for replacement upon departure. A pleasant fire can be enjoyed and left without a trace if properly constructed. Locating a small fire for maximum efficiency takes into account wind direction and a site enhancing heat radiation. A fire exposed to open wind provides little heat, while protective cover often allows recycling of the fire's warmth. Again, the nylon tent fly can be just the ticket to reflect heat for extra enjoyment. Downfall timber is usually plentiful in these areas, thus eliminating the need for packing a saw or axe.

The big disadvantage to camping in heavy use areas is the lack of fuel. Probably the most disgusting aspect of these camps is the appearance of sawed-off tree branches. A small propane stove is mighty handy and sure is a blessing to the landscape. Sometimes these propane units are temperamental during very cold weather,but if you warm the tank in your clothing or bedroll, it will usually fire right up. The same problem occurs with propane cigarette lighters in cold weather. I prefer stick matches. A waterproof container for stick matches can prevent a lot of grief. I carry them in a number of locations in my clothing and in my pack. Avoid carrying a bundle in the pocket of tight-fitting pants. I witnessed a nasty sulfurous burn on my son's leg from such a practice.

An ideal camp would be located near fuel, drinking water, and protective shelter. Don't take this advice lightly: a good camp selection could save your life during adverse weather. Campsite selection is most critical during the shorter days from September through the winter months.

Bears are rarely encountered in the high country. Where their presence is obvious, take the time to keep your food away from your sleeping quarters.

A good camp habit worthy of a dose of attention is keeping an organized camp. Knowing the whereabouts of your gear and finding it the next morning makes life much nicer. It is not unusual to wake up to a cold morning with a blanket of snow. A misplaced coffeepot, stove, or fork buried somewhere under the snow is not a good way to start day.

Be cognizant of other campers' territory. Part of the reason people go to the backcountry is to get away from it all. A camp spot sort of temporarily claims a piece of real estate and invasion of that space probably won't be appreciated. The area between a camp and the lake shore or stream is particularly regarded as off limits.

A conflict to be avoided involves dogs. There's nothing like puffing over the crest of a steep hill to find a snarling canine threatening your presence. If you take a pet, make sure you have it under control.

Rock Creek Drainage

If you're looking for a good conditioner trail, one that doesn't tear you apart but still gets you to some beautiful country, I'd suggest two of the three branches of what mountain men called the Rocky Fork. Just out of Red Lodge, beginning at Camp Bots Sots, is forest trail #1. This well-maintained trail begins at 7,863 feet in elevation and winds along the West Fork of Rock Creek past two scenic waterfalls to the foot of 9,600-foot Sundance Pass.

The trail parallels Quinnebaugh Meadows, a photographer's fantasy, where meadow and stream are backdropped by alpine grandeur. A climb north of the trail locates you in a position to view the mountain for which the Beartooths were named. Three side trips offer fishing opportunities at Lake Mary, Dude Lake, Senal Lake, and a group of five fishable lakes surrounding Ship Lake.

Another fine summer or winter cross-country excursion follows Lake Fork trail #1, with the option of a round trip over Sundance Pass and back to the trailhead by the route described above. Broadwater, Lost, and Keyser Brown lakes are easily accessible from the trail. An unimproved foot trail branches off to spectacular Black Canyon Lake. This is one fine fishing spot if the cutts are in the mood. The two Rock lakes and September Morn also provide fishing opportunities.

The forest road up the main fork of Rock Creek locates travelers at the Glacier-Moon Lake trail head. The gradient here is more taxing but distances are shorter and numerous fish species await.

That portion of the Rock Creek drainage within the forest boundaries includes 196 square miles of Custer and 15 miles of Shoshone National forests. Ninety-one lakes are scattered in this country: 63 in Montana, 26 in Wyoming, and two shared by both states. All but seven lakes are in the Absaroka-Beartooth Wilderness Area. Frosty Lake, at 11,020 feet above sea level, is the highest of the named lakes; however, two unnamed fishless waters occur at 11,180 and 11,110 feet. Wild Bill Lake, at 6,719 feet, is the lowest.

Lakes range from 0.6 to 176.7 surface acres and add up to a total of 1092.4 acres of lake water. Glacier Lake is the largest but not the deepest. That honor belongs to Sliderock Lake on Hell Roaring Plateau. Would you believe it is 245 feet deep? Black Canyon plunges to 185 feet, Glacier to 180, Emerald to 150, and Marker has a 115-foot hole.

Early exploits of O. J. Salo, Al Croonquist, Melvin E. Martin, Wild Bill Kurtzer, Ben Greenough, and employees of the State of Montana have filled each niche capable of harboring fish. The watershed has 23 lakes with brook trout, two with mixed populations of brook and rainbow, five with mixes of brook and cutthroat, and 13 with various sizes of cutthroat trout, for a total of 43 fishable lakes and meadows. The remaining 48 lakes are fishless and have little or no potential as future fisheries.

Let's take a look at the specifics of individual lakes. Remember to use the code map and numbering system to help you locate each lake. Only those lakes with fish, a fish history, or potential fisheries are described. All others are listed only for your reference. The number in parentheses expresses the number of lakes in the group.

1. HIGHLINE TRAIL LAKES (10)

Location: T58N, R104W, S. 23
Elevation: 10,000+ feet
Area: 20 acres total
Maximum depth: 15 feet

Near the headwater of Wyoming Creek on the south end of Line Creek Plateau are a group of lakes called the Highland Trail lakes. They are in Wyoming, about .75 mile south of the Montana-Wyoming state line. Only the largest and deepest of the 10 lakes supports fish and this population may be temporary. The lake will remain a fishery only if stocked by Wyoming Game and Fish on a periodic basis. The last sighting of numerous small cutthroat trout was in 1982. Wyoming Game and Fish would be happy to let you know when the lake was last stocked with fish.

2. FROZEN (fishless)

3. GREENOUGH LAKE

Location: T9S, R19E, S. 7, 8
Elevation: 7,280 feet
Area: .8 acres
Maximum depth: 9.5 feet

This small lake, named after the Greenough family, famous rodeo greats, is located about .5 mile from the Greenough Campground along Rock Creek. The original Greenough Lake was a small, spring-fed puddle containing a few brook trout. In 1965, the Forest Service constructed a dam and created the lake as it is today. Because of easy access and proximity to public campgrounds, many campers, kids, and even grown-ups enjoy an outing at Greenough.

Catchable sized rainbow trout are stocked two to three times per year and most are captured soon after planting. Greenough Lake is one of six Montana lakes in the Rock Creek drainage not located inside the Absaroka-Beartooth Wilderness boundary.

4, 5, 6 & 6a. TWIN AND UNNAMED LAKES IN THE TWIN LAKES CIRQUE (7)

Location: T58N, R104W., S. 21, 28
Elevation: 9,970-10,000 feet
Area: 31.1 acres; 44.3 acres; 5.1 acres; 12.7 acres; all others, 9.1 acres total, respectively
Maximum depth: 55 feet; 75 feet; 14 feet; 98 feet; all others, 1-8 feet, respectively

The Twin lakes are located in a scenic glacial cirque near the Montana-Wyoming state line: They are visible to the west of the Beartooth Highway 212 on the Beartooth Plateau. The lakes drain to Rock Creek Canyon via Chain Creek. The four largest lakes contain brook trout. These fish were originally stocked by O.J. Salo of Red Lodge, Montana. Ben Greenough, also from Red Lodge, was the capable packer and assistant. They secured the fish from the Bozeman National Fish Hatchery in 1924 and placed them in Lower Twin Lake. Two years later, Salo reported that he caught nine fish, 2.5 to 3.0 pounds each—excellent growth but not uncommon when a small population is stocked in a food-laden, fishless lake.

Upstream migration and possible transplants by fishermen probably account for the fish now occupying the upper lakes. I haven't seen any fish in these lakes as large as O.J. saw in 1926; nonetheless, darn good fishing can be experienced both summer and winter for nice sized brookies.

6b. MIRROR (fishless)

6c. QUINT (fishless)

6d. UNNAMED (fishless)

7. LITTLE GLACIER LAKE

Location: T58N, R105W, S. 15-WYO.; T9S, R18E, S. 32-MT.
Elevation: 9,812 feet
Area: 11 acres
Maximum depth: 30 feet

Some people might call Little Glacier part of Glacier Lake because only a small man-made barrier partially restricts fish movement from one lake to the other. The fish populations between these waters do differ, however. Little Glacier has an abundance of small brook trout which average 9.4 inches and 0.30 pounds, not big but fun angling and good eating. Glacier, on the other hand, has lots of larger fish. During spring run-off, no barrier exists between the lakes and fish from Little Glacier can add to Glacier's fish population.

Usually fish are readily caught in Little Glacier, a nice feature when fishing in Glacier Lake is slow. The shoreline is rocky on the south shore, with alpine grass and stunted pine on the remaining shores. Fuel and camping are good in the timbered areas away from the lake shore.

Access is via foot or horse on a maintained trail from Rock Creek Canyon. Don't take the wrong turn above the bridge over Moon Creek because you will be headed toward Moon Lake.

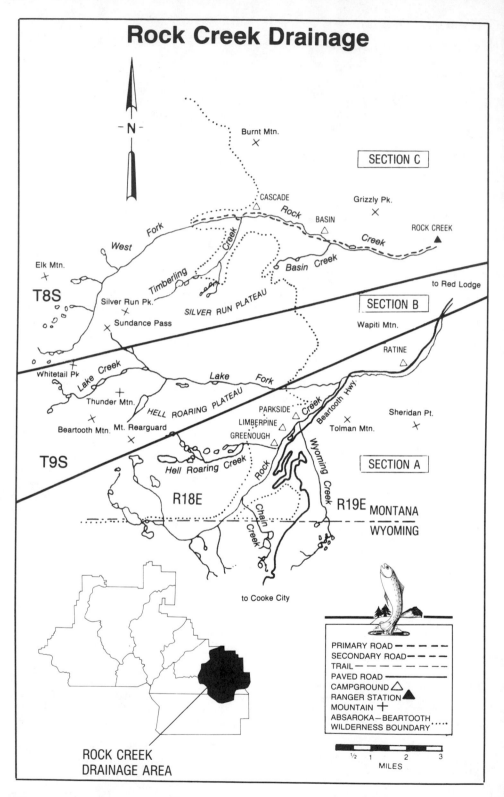

Rock Creek Drainage

- N -

Burnt Mtn.
×

SECTION C

CASCADE
Rock
Grizzly Pk.
×
BASIN
ROCK CREEK ▲

West
Fork
Timberling
Creek
Creek
Basin Creek

Elk Mtn.
×

T8S

Silver Run Pk.
×
SILVER RUN PLATEAU

to Red Lodge

SECTION B

Sundance Pass
×

Wapiti Mtn.

RATINE △

Whitetail Pk
×
Lake Creek
Lake
Fork

Thunder Mtn.
+
HELL ROARING PLATEAU
PARKSIDE △
Creek
Sheridan Pt.
×

Beartooth Mtn.
×
Mt. Rearguard
×
LIMBERPINE △
GREENOUGH
Beartooth Hwy.
Tolman Mtn.
×

T9S

SECTION A

Hell Roaring Creek
Rock
Wyoming Creek

R18E
R19E
MONTANA

Chain Creek
WYOMING

to Cooke City

ROCK CREEK
DRAINAGE AREA

PRIMARY ROAD — — — —
SECONDARY ROAD — — —
TRAIL — — — — —
PAVED ROAD ——————
CAMPGROUND △
RANGER STATION ▲
MOUNTAIN +
ABSAROKA—BEARTOOTH
WILDERNESS BOUNDARY ········

½ 1   2   3
MILES

10

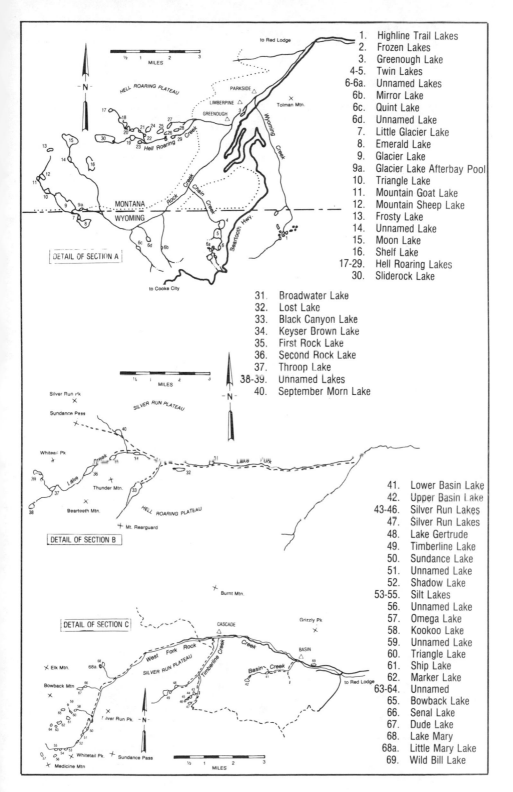

1. Highline Trail Lakes
2. Frozen Lakes
3. Greenough Lake
4-5. Twin Lakes
6-6a. Unnamed Lakes
6b. Mirror Lake
6c. Quint Lake
6d. Unnamed Lake
7. Little Glacier Lake
8. Emerald Lake
9. Glacier Lake
9a. Glacier Lake Afterbay Pool
10. Triangle Lake
11. Mountain Goat Lake
12. Mountain Sheep Lake
13. Frosty Lake
14. Unnamed Lake
15. Moon Lake
16. Shelf Lake
17-29. Hell Roaring Lakes
30. Sliderock Lake

31. Broadwater Lake
32. Lost Lake
33. Black Canyon Lake
34. Keyser Brown Lake
35. First Rock Lake
36. Second Rock Lake
37. Throop Lake
38-39. Unnamed Lakes
40. September Morn Lake

41. Lower Basin Lake
42. Upper Basin Lake
43-46. Silver Run Lakes
47. Silver Run Lakes
48. Lake Gertrude
49. Timberline Lake
50. Sundance Lake
51. Unnamed Lake
52. Shadow Lake
53-55. Silt Lakes
56. Unnamed Lake
57. Omega Lake
58. Kookoo Lake
59. Unnamed Lake
60. Triangle Lake
61. Ship Lake
62. Marker Lake
63-64. Unnamed
65. Bowback Lake
66. Senal Lake
67. Dude Lake
68. Lake Mary
68a. Little Mary Lake
69. Wild Bill Lake

DETAIL OF SECTION A

DETAIL OF SECTION B

DETAIL OF SECTION C

8. EMERALD LAKE

Location: T58N, R105W, S. 22, 23
Elevation: 9,750 feet
Area: 39.2 acres
Maximum depth: 150 feet

Emerald Lake shares the same country with Glacier Lake and is accessible by the same trail. The lake is in Wyoming but stocked by Montana State Department of Fish, Wildlife and Parks. It was originally stocked by persons working on the Glacier Dam in 1937. These original fish eventually aged and died out. I requested the lake be stocked in 1971 with cutthroat trout. They did superbly until their fifth year, producing fish to 18 inches and 1.75 pounds. This is one of those areas that need a fallow period between stockings to maintain a good food base and thus grow large cutts. Figure on seven year stocking frequency with the last plant in 1978, the next in 1986. This makes for good fishing between 1980-84 and again from 1988-1992.

9. GLACIER LAKE

Location: T9S, R18E, S. 29, 30, 31, 32
Elevation: 9,818 feet
Area: 176.7 acres
Maximum depth: 180 feet

The largest lake in the Rock Creek system is accessible by traveling a maintained trail approximately two fairly steep miles from the road's end. Glacier Lake was impounded by a 15-20-foot-high cement dam built by the Rock Creek Water Users Association in 1937.

According to O.J. Salo and other knowing persons, it was Melvin E. Martin, a prospector, who first stocked Glacier Lake in the 1920's. Then the Montana Fish and Game got into the act by stocking 7,600 cutthroat in September 1953, and again in 1971, 1978, and 1979, with plans for frequent plants on a continuous basis. Fish growth is phenomenal, but catchability is marginal. I went back to Glacier Lake nine times because of one super day of fishing. Winds of considerable intensity are not uncommon during the midday, making difficult fishing conditions.

Some of the largest brook trout in the entire mountain range inhabit Glacier Lake. The cutts also do well. Good growth is in part due to large populations of plus 2mm size zooplankton. One of these critters, a red zooplankton called *Diaptomous Shoshoni*, might suggest a lure or fly with some red coloration.

The largest lake in the drainage, Glacier Lake (seen here above Rock Creek) supports phenomenal fish growth. U.S. Forest Service photo.

9a. GLACIER LAKE AFTERBAY POOL

Location: T9S, R18E, S. 32
Elevation: 9,518 feet
Area: 2.4 acres
Maximum depth: 8 feet

This pool lies approximately 300 yards downstream from and 300 feet lower than Glacier Lake. Rock Creek tumbles out of Glacier Lake enroute to this pool, taking some finny survivors with it to this refuge. Fishing is usually good, with opportunities for numerous brook trout and an occasional large cutt. A nice feature of this depression is the shelter it provides from the winds typical upstairs at Glacier Lake. This is another of six Montana lakes in the Rock Creek drainage outside the A-B Wilderness Area.

10. TRIANGLE LAKE

Location: T9S, R18E, S. 30D
Elevation: 9,730 feet
Area: 7.9 acres
Maximum depth: 35 feet

A walk around the north shore of Glacier Lake and up the snowbank that hides the inlet of Glacier Lake puts you at Triangle Lake, one of my favorite fishing holes in the Beartooth Mountains. But be aware of the fish stocking schedule. Triangle Lake was last stocked in 1977 and is scheduled for restocking in 1986. There should be a few lunkers around, but won't be a real producer until '88. See you there.

11. MOUNTAIN GOAT LAKE

Location: T9S, R18E, S. 30BA
Elevation: 10,040 feet
Area: 12.5 acres
Maximum depth: 60 feet

Take the big snowfield which bridges the inlet of Triangle Lake (near Glacier Lake) about one-half mile to a pair of beauties: Mountain Goat and Mountain Sheep lakes. The higher of the two is Mountain Goat. If you need fuel for a comfortable camp, stay at Glacier Lake. Only snow, rock and alpine grass greet you at this site.

The fishery here is another good-this-year—poor-next-year type. Here's the skinny: stocking is alternated between these two lakes so one, or the other, should be producing. Mountain Goat was last stocked in 1982, due again in '87 and every seven years thereafter. Mountain Sheep will be stocked in 1986, 1993, and every seven years from then.

Look for some nice cutts from this program. Some fish escape from Mountain Goat to Mountain Sheep.

12. MOUNTAIN SHEEP LAKE

Location: T9S, R18E, S. 30BAC
Elevation: 9,985 feet
Area: 7.3 acres
Maximum depth: 18 feet

Remember, Mountain Sheep Lake is the lower, smaller, and narrower of the two. Some of its fish come from Mountain Goat Lake upstream (see #11). Because of the fish stocking schedule prescribed for these lakes, one or the other should produce good fishing most of the time.

13. FROSTY (fishless)

14. UNNAMED (fishless)

15. MOON LAKE

Location: T9S, R18E, S. 17 & 20
Elevation: 10,400 feet
Area: 82.2 acres
Maximum depth: 115 feet

Some walks seem to take longer than they should. The 3.5 mile hike to Moon Lake was always one of those for me. The trail is steep, rocky, and in the lower reaches

There's no fuel—just alpine grass—around Moon Lake, but regular stocking helps keep the fishing hot. Michael Sample photo.

often full of downed timber. Take the trail to the foot bridge over Moon Creek, but don't cross, and you will pick up the unmaintained trail to the shores of Moon Lake. Another route is cross-country via Hell Roaring Plateau. Moon Lake is in a cold valley, ice-covered most of the year. No fuel exists—just snow, rock and alpine grass.

Because of some key food organisms, cutthroat trout planted in Moon Lake grow really well. Three-year-old cutts from the 1975 plant produced fish exceeding one pound. Since 1981, fish are stocked every three years, and a variety of sizes should always be available to fishing adventurers.

16. SHELF LAKE

Location: T9S, R18E, S. 20D, 21C
Elevation: 10,120 feet
Area: 51.0 acres
Maximum depth: 55 feet

Well named, Shelf Lake is perched on a shelf on the east side of the Hell Roaring Plateau. You can arrive there by the Moon Lake route or via a journey across Hell Roaring Plateau.

Shelf Lake has a population of brookies, usually in robust shape, but this condition fluctuates from year to year. Several rechecks of the fishery have revealed a density subject to change. When the population was low, the size of the fish was typically 11 to 14 inches. Conversely, when the fish population was high, fish were smaller. A good day up here is a real pleasure. Watch out for the wind, though; it tends to blow the water clear out of the lake.

17-30. HELL ROARING AND SLIDEROCK LAKES (14)

Location: T9S, R18E, S. 13-16
Elevation: 9,510-10,900 feet
Better check the map on this group of 14 lakes so we're talking about the same lake. Ten of the 14 lakes harbor populations of fish, the dominant species being brook trout. These lakes are easily accessible by a short cross-country walk from the end of the Hell Roaring road. Some folks hike up Hell Roaring Creek from Twin Bridges rather than abuse their cars on the rough road beyond the bridges.

The Hell Roaring chain provides recreation reasonably close to an unmaintained road. I found it a nifty getaway, both summer and winter. The big plus was a mess of pan-sized brookies for the frying pan. All the lakes are in the Custer National Forest and plenty of fuel for camping is available, but please—stay 200 feet from the water.

17. HELL ROARING LAKE (fishless)

18. HELL ROARING LAKE (CLIFF, BAY, OR HAIRPIN)

Location: T9S, R18E, S. 15B
Elevation: 10,160 feet
Area: 32.9 acres
Maximum depth: 65 feet
Ask an old-timer from Red Lodge the name of this lake and he'll tell you Cliff Lake. Ask another and it becomes Bay Lake. Whatever you call it, it's the biggest, the deepest, and the best fish producer of the Hell Roaring chain—other than Sliderock.

Historically the lake put out some big brook trout. These fish were planted in the 1930s. More recent introductions have all been cutthroat trout. Since there were numerous small fish available in the Hell Roaring chain, I felt this lake should be managed for trophy concept. To accomplish this, 50 fish per acre were recommended every six years. This concept doesn't make for a fish every cast but does allow for some big prizes.

An occasional brookie can be also captured, but luckily their numbers haven't exploded like they often do. Fly fishing along the shoreline is the best producer. Find the fish in the shoals and give him your best presentation. Yes, I know, you want to know when the lake was last planted so you can figure the best time to fish—answer: 1982. So look for good fishing from 1984-88, then follow the six year stocking schedule for best results.

19. HELL ROARING LAKE (SNOWBANK)

Location: T9S, R18E, S. 15C & D
Elevation: 10,040 feet
Area: 18.8 acres
Maximum depth: 40 feet
Snowbank Lake needs fishing. Help it out and take mama home some nice little brookies. She will love it. Brookies here average eight inches with larger ones to 10.

20. HELL ROARING LAKE

Location: T9S, R18E, S. 15CA
Elevation: 10,100 feet
Area: 2.6 acres
Maximum depth: 4 feet
This small lake is just downstream from Cliff or Bay Lake. It has a few strays from the upper lake but nothing of real significance.

21. HELL ROARING LAKE

Location: T9S, R18E, S. 15DB
Elevation: 10,060 feet
Area: 2.7 acres
Maximum depth: 4 feet

Don't overlook this little lake. I've caught some nice brook trout here. Fish are in good condition. In a sample of 16, they ranged from 7.4 to 11.6 inches, averaging 10 inches, 0.39 pounds, but sizes vary with the numbers present in any given year.

22. HELL ROARING LAKE (fishless)

23. HELL ROARING LAKE (fishless)

24. HELL ROARING LAKE (CRESCENT)
Location: T9S, R18E, S. 14, 15
Elevation: 10,000 feet
Area: 13.6 acres
Maximum depth: 42 feet

Referred to as Crescent Lake, it is one of the more popular fishing holes in the chain. A sample of 29 brook trout averaged eight inches, 0.19 pounds. The population density has always been too high to allow good fish growth, but the fish are a good pan-size with excellent flavor.

25. HELL ROARING LAKE
Location: T9S, R18E, S. 14BD
Elevation: 9,660 feet
Area: 7.9 acres
Maximum depth: 30 feet

This is another popular lake in the chain, often referred to as Hell Roaring Proper. This is an especially scenic little lake with an interesting stocking history. It seems that a prospector from South Dakota had a fondness for this and several other Hell Roaring lakes. I assume fishing and eating were good diversions from the labors of searching for riches. According to O. J. Salo, this young prospector was named Melvin Martin. Mr. Martin obtained some cutthroat trout (source unknown, but a good guess would be Rock Creek), and stocked Hell Roaring Proper back between the years of 1901-05. Remnants of this stocking still remain. In fact, the next lake downstream has a fair number of cutthroat. Unique fish—very inbred, almost scaleless, slender and dark-colored—can be found in this lake.

Recent years have seen the constant invasion of brook trout. It's doubtful the cutts will be able to survive due to tremendous competition for food and space and to predation by adult brookies. I wish the aborigine cutthroat luck, and hope they have evolved into a lasting breed. If they actually were stocked in 1901-05, they are significant survivors, with a possible 20-plus generations behind them.

26. HELL ROARING LAKE (SMETHURST)
Location: T9S, R18E, S. 14DB
Elevation: 9,580 feet
Area: 4.6 acres
Maximum depth: 4 feet

More of the cutthroat described for lake #25 exist in this shallow little one. The only reason it doesn't freeze solid is that it has three flowing inlets that provide the spawning area for the historic cutts. Brook trout are also residents of this lake, sometimes called Smethurst Lake.

27. HELL ROARING LAKE (DALY)
Location: T9S, R18E, S. 14A
Elevation: 9,670 feet
Area: 7.4 acres
Maximum depth: 40 feet

This one was called Daly Lake by my old friends in Red Lodge. Brook trout live here—not big, but delicious. I like to ice-fish in this one during the nice sunny days of March. A few chub and suckers also eke out an existence here. I'd bet they came from Big Sand Coulee via a bail pail.

28. HELL ROARING LAKE (RYDBERG)

Location: T9S, R18E, S. 13, 14
Elevation: 9,510 feet
Area: 3 acres
Maximum depth: 2 feet
Known as Rydberg Lake, this is the lowest lake in the chain. It's not very big, but does offer a few casts at the brook trout readily observed from the shore.

29. HELL ROARING LAKE (fishless)

30. SLIDEROCK LAKE

Location: T9S, R18E, S. 16
Elevation: 10,480 feet
Area: 81.0 acres
Maximum depth: 245 feet
Instead of dropping off Hell Roaring Plateau in the Hell Roaring chain of lakes, head on up the plateau to Sliderock Lake. Don't camp here, but fishing is great. This lake has a good population of brook trout. Because of its vast amount of deep water (245' at its deepest), reproduction is limited and food production is good, making for big fish. The average length of a three-year-old brook trout was 9.4 inches; four-year-olds were 11.6 inches; five-year-olds were 12.2 inches; six-year and older fish were 13.1 inches and larger!

Remember, however, how sizes can change from year to year depending on how many brothers and sisters these brookies share dinner with. Be prepared for a little wind.

31. BROADWATER LAKE

Location: T8S, R18E, S. 35C
Elevation: 7,990 feet
Area: 1 acre
Maximum depth: 3 feet
My son Wade said "I wouldn't even write up this lake. It's just a wide spot on the Lake Fork of Rock Creek." He's right about the wide spot, but he must have missed out by not fishing the so-called wide spot. Nothing big, but a skilled angler can produce a little action for brooks, cutts, and an occasional rainbow.

In 1919, O. J. Salo and his boss, Al Croonquist, delivered rainbow trout to the lake. They did not temper the fish and they died. "Tempering" means they did not adjust the temperature of the water in the container of fish to that of the lake. It does not mean they failed to beat them prior to release. In 1927, O. J. hauled four cans of rainbow from the holding point at the Old Richel Lodge on Rock Creek and they were successfully planted. If you catch a rainbow trout in the Broadwater or the adjacent stream, look up to the heavens and give a nod of approval to O. J.

32. LOST LAKE

Location: T9S, R18E, S. 3
Elevation: 8,520 feet
Area: 11.3 acres
Maximum depth: 25 feet
About five miles up the Lake Fork trail #1 you will come to a trail leading southerly up the hill. Lost Lake is a couple hundred yards away. If you continue up trail #1 to the bridge over the Lake Fork, you have traveled about 300 yards past Lost Lake's turnoff. The north shore is mostly timber; the south has sparse timber with scattered rock.

Lost Lake was chemically treated to destroy rough fish and small brook trout in 1964, then rehabilitated with cutthroat trout. It was last stocked in 1982. The growth of the cutthroat was okay, but not sensational. I recommended Lost Lake as a future home for grayling. Hope the Montana Department of Fish, Wildlife and Parks (FW&P) tries it.

33. BLACK CANYON LAKE

Location: T9S, R18E, S. 5 & 8
Elevation: 9,280 feet
Area: 82.4 acres
Maximum depth: 185 feet

Black Canyon Lake is located on Black Canyon Creek, a tributary of the Lake Fork of Rock Creek. Access is served by an unmaintained trail that departs trail #1 just upstream from the Lost Lake trail. Black Canyon is approximately 7.5 miles from the trailhead.

The lake formation resulted from a large rock dike of glacial origin. Rock slides are common to the area; one large slide in 1971 caused heavy sediment loads in Rock Creek downstream as far as Joliet, Montana.

Black Canyon is a popular recreational area because it produces large cutthroat. The fish are healthy, with loads of pink fat, fluorescent air bladders, and rich pink flesh. The lake was well-stocked in 1973 with the McBride variety of cutthroat trout, which originated in McBride Lake in Yellowstone National Park. Since then, fish to 16 inches are common, with possibilities of a fish up to four pounds.

34. KEYSER BROWN LAKE

Location: T8S, R18E. S. 32 A & D
Elevation: 8,720 feet
Area: 9.5 acres
Maximum depth: 8 feet

Lots of folks around Red Lodge do not recognize the name Keyser Brown. Instead they call this lake First Rock, thus advancing the number of the two Rock Lakes upstream. Horses, backpackers, and several outfitters have left their mark on Keyser Brown's shoreline. The scars have started to heal in recent years, but users should recognize the fragility of the area and camp in appropriate areas and treat the area with care.

Keyser Brown is less than 10 feet deep but contains numerous brook and some cutthroat trout. Brook trout average eight inches, the larger ones about 12.5 inches. The cutts are progeny of a 1953 stocking in First Rock Lake.

35. FIRST ROCK LAKE

Location: T8S, R18E, S. 31AD
Elevation: 8,870 feet
Area: 17.5 acres
Maximum depth: 36 feet

About .5 to .75 miles upstream from Keyser Brown is a 17.5-acre lake called First Rock Lake on current maps. It's about 10 miles from the Lake Fork trailhead.

The fishery is dominated by cutthroat trout stocked back in 1953. A few brook trout can also be found. Really a nice spot.

36. SECOND ROCK LAKE

Location: T8S, R18E, S. 13C
Elevation: 9,110 feet
Area: 25.9 acres
Maximum depth: 50 feet

A good brook trout water with fish in excellent physical shape. It's only .75 miles upstream from First Rock Lake. Remember, some folks will call this lake Third Rock Lake—you just have to sort out which lake everybody is talking about.

The lakes beyond Second Rock Lake are all fishless.

37. THROOP *(fishless)*

38. UNNAMED *(fishless)*

39. UNNAMED *(fishless)*

40. SEPTEMBER MORN LAKE

Location: T8S, R18E, S. 29C
Elevation: 9,696 feet
Area: 10.3 acres
Maximum depth: 23 feet

September Morn Lake is located on maintained trail #1 just up the hill from Keyser Brown Lake. The lake, a great place to camp before heading over Sundance Pass to the West Fork, is below timberline, so fuel is available.

Brook trout are easily caught. O. J. Salo told me that E. Martin, the prospector from South Dakota, planted this lake in 1925 or 1926.

A large rock dike of glacial origin formed Black Canyon Lake, a popular recreational area because of its large cutthroat. Michael Sample photo.

Between towering peaks and beneath the blue Montana sky, Keyser Brown Lake provides beauty and tranquility. U.S. Forest Service photo.

41. LOWER BASIN LAKE

Location: T8S, R19E, S. 8
Elevation: 8,360 feet
Area: 2.5 acres
Maximum depth: 21 feet

The Basin Creek lakes are accessible via the trail up Basin Creek, which begins at Basin Creek Campground on the West Fork of Rock Creek. Don't look for loads of fish here but an occasional brook trout drifts into Lower Basin from the population at Upper Basin Lake upstream. These lonely brookies have nothing to do but eat.

42. UPPER BASIN LAKE

Location: T8S, R19E, S. 7A
Elevation: 8,960 feet
Area: 6.7 acres
Maximum depth: 5.5 feet

The route from Lower Basin to the upper lake is via a good trail dotted with numerous old cabins once occupied by prospectors and timber cutters. Look for brook trout in this lake and in the stream flowing out. These fish were stocked by the Red Lodge Rod and Gun Club in the 1930s. In 1953 and 1958 the State of Montana stocked cutthroat, but none exist in Upper Basin today.

43-46. SILVER RUN LAKES (4) (fishless)

47. SILVER RUN LAKE

Location: T8S, R18E, S. 14CB
Elevation: 9,600 feet
Area: 2.5 acres
Maximum depth: 10 feet

Just before you break out onto Silver Run Plateau from Timberline Creek, you'll come across five small lakes. Only one has fish so check the code map for the proper lake. It's the deepest of the five. A small sample of three brook trout averaged 10.5 inches and 0.39 pounds. Their origin is likely the result of a fisherman moving fish from Lake Gertrude.

48. LAKE GERTRUDE

Location: T8S, R18E, S. 10C
Elevation: 9,550 feet
Area: 6.1 acres
Maximum depth: 11 feet

A drive up the West Fork of Rock Creek approximately 15 miles from Red Lodge will put you at the Timberline-Gertrude trailhead (#12). The trail is good. Conifers, meadow, and some rock surround the lake, so camping in the area should have lots of comforts.

Gertrude Lake is just downstream from Timberline Lake. It is full of brook trout and they are easily caught. The lake was stocked in 1919 by O. J. Salo and Al Croonquist.

49. TIMBERLINE LAKE

Location: T8S, R18E, S. 15, 16
Elevation: 9,660 feet
Area: 31.3 acres
Maximum depth: 85 feet

Just upstream from Gertrude, you will find this scenic lake. Again, the fishery is loaded with small brook trout. O. J. Salo and Al Croonquist stocked it in 1917 by hauling in, in two trips, 10 pails with 100 fish per pail.

50. SUNDANCE LAKE

Location: T8S, R17E, S. 24
Elevation: 9,370 feet
Area: 2.9 acres
Maximum depth: 17 feet

Approximately nine miles up the maintained trail along the West Fork you will find a very green, glacial-silted lake. It was stocked, along with some of the lakes upstream, with cutts in 1976. I haven't found the fish yet from this plant, but it is scheduled again for the future.

51-54. UNNAMED, SHADOW, AND SILT LAKES (4)

Location: T8S, R17E, S. 26
Elevation: 9,560 & 9,800 feet
Area: 14.2 acres total
Maximum depth: 10 feet

At the foot of Sundance pass you will approach the headwaters of the West Fork. The stream, a lot smaller now, is also slower, and the valley bottom somewhat flattened by glacial activity. A series of glacial deposits has created a series of small lakes and the beautiful combination of flowing and still water, as well as the strategic camping locale, has invited a fish plant. In 1976 a batch of 450 cutthroat trout were introduced. Another 1,650 were injected into the system in 1980.

Whether these fish reproduce depends on their abilities to move the stream gravels possibly cemented by glacial flour. or, if the eggs do get into the gravel, they must get enough oxygen to incubate. Let's hope they manage. What an aesthetic scene for a nice mountain trout.

55. SILT LAKE (fishless)

56. UNNAMED (fishless)

57. OMEGA LAKE (fishless)

58-65. KOOKOO, TRIANGLE, MARKER, BOWBACK, UNNAMED LAKES (8)

The next lakes, 58-65, are on the bench surrounding Ship Lake, a very pleasant spot with access to the East Rosebud if you're into rugged cross-country travel. There are several ways to climb up to the fine bench lakes. I recommend camping on the West Fork Trail and hiking up for the day's adventure. The route from camp isn't bad, but it is easiest to take a hard right just beyond Sundance Lake, travel cross-country for about one mile—and you're in heaven. (See #58-65.)

Triangle Lake, dominated by Silver Run Peak in the background, has high densities of large zooplankton which permit good trout growth. Pat Marcuson photo.

58. KOOKOO LAKE

Location: T8S, R17E, S. 23 AA
Elevation: 10,200 feet
Area: 6.1 acres
Maximum depth: 30 feet

Kookoo Lake is not named on many maps except for the very old ones that D. M. Marino constructed and sold in Red Lodge in the 1940s. The lake is the last one on Ship Creek, nestled in a tight canyon. Sixty percent of the surface water of Kookoo is less than 15 feet deep.

Back in '72 a plant of 1,760 cutthroat was air-dropped into Kookoo. They took and are now self-sustaining. The fish are not big, but nice pan-sized.

59. UNNAMED (fishless)

60. TRIANGLE LAKE

Location: T8S, R17E, S. 33A
Elevation: 10,440 feet
Area: 6.3 acres
Maximum depth: 35 feet

This jewel is between Kookoo and Ship lakes. Watch the stocking schedule and fishing will be very rewarding. The lake was found to have high densities of large zooplankton, making for good trout growth and very pink, pink meat. The dope on stocking is as follows: 1977—630 McBride cutts; scheduled for a plant every eight years (1985, 1993, etc.). Fish two to six years after the plants with the best years being the fourth (1989 and 1997, etc.), but even the two-year-olds will be worthy of your fly.

P.S. Some fish escape to the little pool down the outlet.

61. SHIP LAKE

Location: T8S, R17E, S. 23
Elevation: 10,480 feet
Area: 28.9 acres
Maximum depth: 55 feet

The second largest lake in the West Fork of Rock Creek drainage, Ship Lake was stocked in 1923 or 1924 just after completion of the West Fork trail. Recent evaluations of the fishery suggest a brook trout density inversely proportional to the size of the fish—average fish, in other words, are about 10 inches. Expect an occasional cutthroat trout. Access is by foot, 1.25 miles from the maintained trail at Sundance Lake.

62. MARKER LAKE

Location: T8S, R17E, S. 23 CB
Elevation: 10,870 feet
Area: 15.5 acres
Maximum depth: 115 feet

About 400 vertical feet above Ship Lake is this 15.5 acre lake, one of my best achievements. No fish existed in 1972. I had it stocked at 199 fish per acre (or 3,080 cutthroat) in 1972. They went nuts—not the largest trophies, but loads of 13- to 16-inch fish with phenomenal catch rates like 18 fish per hour. It was stocked again in 1978. I thought too soon but it was not so. They did super. It's due for more fish in '86, so be prepared for lots of good fishing.

I love this place. By the way, this could well be the highest altitude in the State of Montana with a thriving fishery.

63. UNNAMED (fishless)

64. UNNAMED (fishless)

65. BOWBACK LAKE

Location: T8S, R17E, S. 23 BA
Elevation: 10,380 feet
Area: 6.4 acres
Maximum depth: 40 feet

This is the Bowback Lake with fish, and is in the Ship Lake area—not the Bowback over the ridge in the East Rosebud drainage. It is a very scenic lake, above timberline, with very rocky shores and no inlet other than snow melt. The outlet trickles underground at the lake's edge. Access is limited to foot traffic only with no trail present.

Cutthroat trout were stocked in Bowback in 1971 and rechecked again in '76, '77, '78 and 1981. The cutts did okay but not as well as the plant in Marker Lake. Why? Just didn't have those wonderful little guys called *Diaptomus Shoshoni* that were present in Marker.

Bowback Lake is one of those lakes whose fishery needs a little rest now and then. It was stocked in 1980 and will be every eight years thereafter. This appears to be the only way to make a decent fishery.

Dude Lake, just beyond Senal Lake, is within a hard day's hike of the trail head—if you aren't lugging a heavy pack. Michael Sample photo.

66. SENAL LAKE

Location: T8S, R17E, S. 12, 13
Elevation: 10,140 feet
Area: 3.1 acres
Maximum depth: 10 feet

Take off from the West Fork trail #1 by that little bridge where Dude Creek crosses the trail. Then go up, boy, go up. This is one of those: it's got to be just up on the next tier, but it's not. It's above timberline, the immediate shoreline is mostly boulders, and it's just a rockthrow from Dude Lake at the end of the line.

Mostly brook trout here with an occasional cutt. The cutthroat are drifters from Dude. I have caught some excellent brookies seven to 16 inches, all nice and fat. Occasionally this lake partially winterkills, meaning no oxygen under the dark ice and snow, which is very hard on fish. But winterkill holds the population down, giving more wiggly critters for the survivors to chew on.

67. DUDE LAKE

Location: T8S, R17E, S. 13, 14
Elevation: 10,180 feet
Area: 12.2 acres
Maximum depth: 20 feet

See #66: Dude's right next door. Altogether I'd estimate Dude is 6.75 miles from the trailhead at Bots Sots and can be visited in a day hike, though I wouldn't recommend a heavy pack.

Expect to find cutthroat trout. The program calls for fish intros every eight years starting in 1983.

68. LAKE MARY

Location: T8S, R18E, S. 6, 7
Elevation: 9,930 feet
Area: 8 acres
Maximum depth: 50 feet

Approximately 15 miles southwest of Red Lodge by road and 5.5 miles by trail will put you at Lake Mary. The last mile may seem like four, but you will get there. I was always impressed with this lake—pretty good fishing with a chance of seeing a mountain goat or two. The goats often hang out on the south slope of Grass Mountain.

Most of my samples produced brookies in the nine- to 12-inch category with a few smaller and some larger. Both the fishing and the area are enjoyable. From Lake Mary you can travel over the divide to Crow, Sylvan, and on down to the East Rosebud. Like a lot of brook trout waters in the Rock Creek drainage, Lake Mary was stocked first by—you guessed it—O.J. Salo and Al Croonquist of Red Lodge. They must have sneaked away from work at Camp Senia quite often. By the way, there's plenty of fuel for camping if you need it.

68a. LITTLE MARY (fishless)

69. WILD BILL LAKE

Location: T8S, R19E, S. 3
Elevation: 6,719 feet
Area: 3.2 acres
Maximum depth: 8 feet

Wild Bill Lake was named after Wild Bill Kurtzer, a man with big plans and a dream. It didn't all materialize for Wild Bill, but he did create a fishing hole that lots of people enjoy. The Forest Service completed the job, making a beautiful place where the handicapped could fish and enjoy themselves. This one is outside the wilderness, accessible by the West Fork road and close to Red Lodge.

Most of the fishing is for rainbow trout which are stocked two to four times a summer. Some brook trout occupy the inlet flows and the lake itself. The area gets lots of use and provides lots of fun, so let's keep it clean.

East Rosebud Creek Drainage

Spectacular East Rosebud is the land of plenty: plenty of waterfalls; plenty of blue glaciers; plenty of domes, arches, vertical walls, mountain goats. It has plenty of visitors, too, but it's a grand place nonetheless.

Three trailheads serve the canyon, all leaving the canyon near East Rosebud Lake. The major and most used trail (#15) crawls up the canyon to Fossil Lake and on over to Cooke Pass. Trail #17 follows Armstrong (Phantom, Shannon) Creek to Froze to Death Plateau and on to Mystic Lake. Trail #13 heads eastward to Sylvan, Crow, and onward to Lake Mary.

East Rosebud Lake and its nine tributaries drain 108.8 square miles in the Custer National Forest. Seventy-six lakes nestle in this beautiful country. If you add up the total area of lake water, it comes to 1,333 surface acres with the lakes ranging in size from less than an acre to 169-acre Fossil Lake. Only East Rosebud and Cairn lakes share the 100-plus acre distinction with Fossil.

The lowest lake is East Rosebud at 6,208 feet. The highest is Upper Granite Creek (Lowery) at 10,300 feet. The majority (83%) are between 9,000 and 10,300 feet in elevation.

Alice Lake on upper Falls Creek takes honors as the deepest pool at 202 feet. Other lakes exceeding 100 feet in depth include Froze to Death at 195; Rainbow at 180; Fossil at 150; Cairn at 125; Summit at 116; Upper Arch at 112; Martin at 108; and Upper Granite Creek Lake at 105 feet.

Fish flourish in 35 of the lakes; the other 41 are fishless. A good variety of species occupy the fish-filled 35. You can find brookies in seven lakes; three lakes with golden trout; two with 'bows; seven mixed populations of goldens and rainbows or cutts; and 16 with cutthroat.

Check the code map and let's go for it.

Lakes of the East Rosebud drainage, totalling 1,333 surface acres, support brook, golden, rainbow, and cutthroat trout. Michael Sample photo.

Spilling into Duggan Lake on the upper East Rosebud River, Impasse Falls creates one of the most stunning settings anywhere. U.S. Forest Service photo.

East Rosebud Creek Drainage

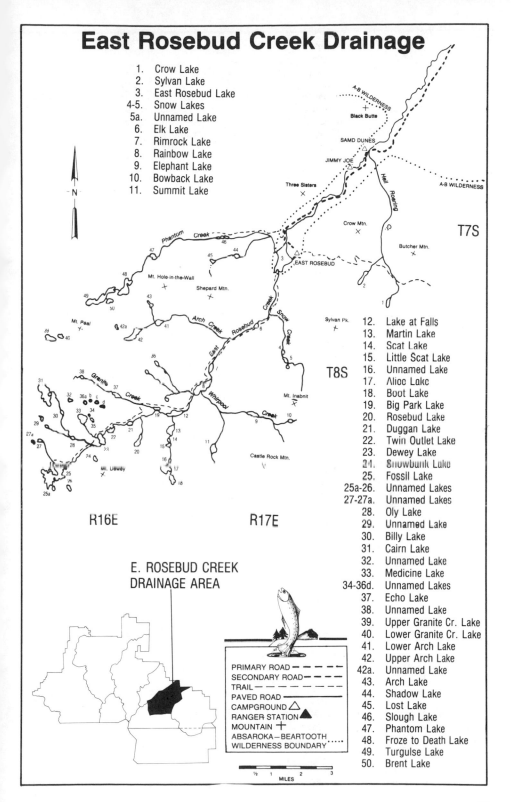

1. Crow Lake
2. Sylvan Lake
3. East Rosebud Lake
4-5. Snow Lakes
5a. Unnamed Lake
6. Elk Lake
7. Rimrock Lake
8. Rainbow Lake
9. Elephant Lake
10. Bowback Lake
11. Summit Lake

- N

A-B WILDERNESS
Black Butte
SAMD DUNES
JIMMY JOE
Three Sisters
A-B WILDERNESS
Crow Mtn.
T7S
Butcher Mtn.
Roaring Cr.
Hell
Phantom Creek
47   46   44
45
48   3
Mt. Hole-in-the-Wall   Shepard Mtn.   EAST ROSEBUD
49   43
50   Arch Creek   Rosebud   Snow Creek   2   1
Mt. Peal   42a   41   Sylvan Pk.
39   40   42   East   6   4   T8S
36   5
38   Granite   37   7
31   Creek   Mt. Inabnit
32   36a b c   Whirlpool   Creek   9   10
33   34   d   19   12
29   35   Creek
27a   22   23   13   11
27   28   21   14
24   20   15   Castle Rock Mtn.
25   16   17
25a   Mt. Dewey   18

R16E   R17E

E. ROSEBUD CREEK DRAINAGE AREA

12. Lake at Falls
13. Martin Lake
14. Scat Lake
15. Little Scat Lake
16. Unnamed Lake
17. Alice Lake
18. Boot Lake
19. Big Park Lake
20. Rosebud Lake
21. Duggan Lake
22. Twin Outlet Lake
23. Dewey Lake
24. Snowbank Lake
25. Fossil Lake
25a-26. Unnamed Lakes
27-27a. Unnamed Lakes
28. Oly Lake
29. Unnamed Lake
30. Billy Lake
31. Cairn Lake
32. Unnamed Lake
33. Medicine Lake
34-36d. Unnamed Lakes
37. Echo Lake
38. Unnamed Lake
39. Upper Granite Cr. Lake
40. Lower Granite Cr. Lake
41. Lower Arch Lake
42. Upper Arch Lake
42a. Unnamed Lake
43. Arch Lake
44. Shadow Lake
45. Lost Lake
46. Slough Lake
47. Phantom Lake
48. Froze to Death Lake
49. Turgulse Lake
50. Brent Lake

PRIMARY ROAD
SECONDARY ROAD
TRAIL
PAVED ROAD
CAMPGROUND △
RANGER STATION ▲
MOUNTAIN +
ABSAROKA—BEARTOOTH WILDERNESS BOUNDARY

½   1   2   3
MILES

1. CROW LAKE

Location: T7S, R17E, S. 36
Elevation: 9,064 feet
Area: 11.4 acres
Maximum depth: 72 feet

Crow Lake is located on upper Hell Roaring Creek, which flows into East Rosebud Creek near and Dunes Campground. Don't hike to Crow Lake this way, believe me. It is accessible via good trail up Spread Creek east of East Rosebud Lake. You can also visit Crow from West Fork Rock Creek, via the Lake Mary trail.

Good catches of brook trout await your visit. I haven't heard of any whoppers, but the combination of lots of fish and spectacular scenery make the trip enjoyable. Give Al Croonquist credit for stocking back in 1924.

2. SYLVAN LAKE

Location: T7S, R17E, S. 26
Elevation: 9,153 feet
Area: 18.5 acres
Maximum depth: 40 feet

Sylvan Lake is the second best golden trout water in the State of Montana. I wouldn't expect to beat the state record for golden trout, but plenty of fish up to 13 inches are available. These fish are absolute pure goldens from the Cottonwood Lakes in California. Many golden trout populations are hybrid forms combining with other spring spawning fish. Because of their pureness, however, eggs are periodically secured from Sylvan's female goldens for use elsewhere.

I undertook "egg-takes" to provide a secure future for the golden trout, "the most colorful of the trout family," and to enable its species to reside in several other Beartooth Lakes. Goldens arrived with the help of John Branger, Sr., in 1927. Vern Waples of Red Lodge and several fish and game employees took eggs in 1955 and 1956 for stocking in the lakes of upper East Rosebud Creek.

One fine feature of Sylvan is that, with work and an early start, one can travel there and back in one day. Sure it's six miles and a good climb but still an enjoyable trip during the long days of summer.

Please take care of the lake; especially avoid shoreline abuse. Always remember to pack out your garbage, and if fires are allowed, destroy them properly. Campers should stay on the bench located about 200 yards from the water. Good camping sites are available along the trail #13 near the lake.

Don't be afraid to take some fish home with you; the welfare of the entire population would be better off with fewer individuals sharing the meager food supply. Fishing strategies do not include minnows. Minnows for bait would be useless since golden trout don't eat fish. It would be devastating to this unique fishery if minnows took up permanent residence in Sylvan Lake.

3. EAST ROSEBUD LAKE

Location: T7S, R17E, S. 21, 28
Elevation: 6,208 feet
Area: 117 acres
Maximum depth: 20 feet

East Rosebud Lake is the lowest lake on East Rosebud Creek and is accessible by car. A public campground and picnic area are located near the lake as well as several trailheads. Much of the shore, however, is private property.

Along the west shoreline, brown trout reside in the boulders scattered on the lake bottom. They are tough to catch but I have caught browns up to 8 pounds; possibilities of rainbow, cutthroat, whitefish and an occasional brookie also exist for the patient angler.

4, 5, & 5a. LOWER AND UPPER SNOW LAKES (3)

Location: T8S, R17E, S. 4, 9A
Elevation: 9,160 feet; 9,265 feet, respectively
Area: 8 acres; 10.4 acres, respectively
Maximum depth: 53 feet; 25 feet, respectively

Lower Snow Lake could be called Memorial or Inabit Lake because of the memorial plaque mounted on a rock in memory of Fred Inabit (1866-1928).

These lakes are difficult to get to. As a possible hiking route, I suggest you try Five Mile Creek drainage, then swing back to the north to the lakes. The lakes are fed with glacial water and the fine "glacial flour" causes a very green water color. The lakes were stocked with rainbow in 1975 and they are beauties. If they fail to reproduce and become extinct, encourage your FW&P Department to restock.

The glacial pool (5a) is fishless.

6. ELK LAKE

Location: T8S, R17E, S. 6
Elevation: 6,780 feet
Area: 7.3 acres
Maximum depth: 5 feet

Elk Lake is the first lake upstream from the trailhead at East Rosebud Lake. The trail provides quick access and makes for a nice day hike. The Brangers who settled in the canyon at the TO Bar Ranch (a name no longer in use) would really like this lake's name changed to Elizabeth Lake in honor of their mother. The name, Elizabeth, would be more appropriate than Elk, a critter of rare occurrence in the vicinity.

The lake harbors a population of brook trout. Although not in significant numbers, the brook trout look to be in good shape. I used to marvel at the way they kept ice from forming around the shorelines by their aggressive spawning behavior in November. The biggest fish I have ever sampled in Elk Lake was 12.2 inches.

7. RIMROCK LAKE

Location: T8S, R16E, S. 12
Elevation: 7,540 feet
Area: 33.6 acres
Maximum depth: 25 feet

This pretty lake is squeezed into a little alpine box canyon. Don't count on a good camping spot. The shoreline already suffers from overuse. The Forest Service did a nice job constructing a trail in difficult surroundings. A bridge was constructed over the outlet for easy access. A big ice bridge blocks the trail from mid-November until spring. I've slid through the tunnel of ice and rock many times. Once I attempted a long jump which fell a foot short and nearly dropped me into the thin ice covered lake. My fingers caught a small rock protrusion and by sheer strength and luck I managed to withdraw myself from impending death. Please don't tell my wife, Renie, as I have always assured her that my late season travels were without dangerous incidents.

The possibilities of a mixed creel are probable since the lake contains a variety of species: rainbow, golden, and cutthroat. Fishing is usually best in the vicinity of the inlet.

8. RAINBOW LAKE

Location: T8S, R16E, S. 13
Elevation: 7,670 feet
Area: 58 acres
Maximum depth: 180 feet

Tent City (the area is logistically located for camping) and the meadow at the upper inlet provide the wide landmark tired bodies look for. Precipitation is usually high at this location, and while it remains in the shadow of Granite Peak, the meadow is not visible from the area.

Even though Martin Simmons, John Branger, Sr., M. Witham, and Al Newman stocked rainbow in 1915, there is little evidence of pure rainbow trout at the lake. Golden trout stocked in Lake at Falls (#12), and other lakes upstream in the mid '50s mated with the 'bows and produced the basic crossbreed common to Rainbow Lake.

Rainbow Lake provides an excellent opportunity to sit back and watch human behavior among fishermen and campers. Have you ever noticed how fisherman from one camp share fishing spots and bait suggestions while remaining secretively possessive of their spot and fishing techniques with members of other camps?

9. ELEPHANT (fishless)

Conveniently located for camping and blessed with a wide meadow, Rainbow Lake is home to rainbow-golden crossbreeds. U.S. Forest Service photo.

10. BOWBACK LAKE (fishless)

11. SUMMIT LAKE (fishless)

12. LAKE AT FALLS

Location: T8S, R16E, S. 13, 14, 23, 24
Elevation: 8,100 feet
Area: 49.8 acres
Maximum depth: 50 feet

Two large waterfalls tumble into this appropriately-named lake. Easily located, the lake is big and the trail parallels the east shoreline. Prior to 1970, the lake was a sanctuary for golden trout, until the cutthroat came filtering down the drainage from Dewey Lake. You can still catch both cutts and the "golden ones," but hybrids are increasingly common.

The state record golden trout was captured by Terry Cammeron of Billings at Lake at Falls in 1981. It was a beauty at 20.5 inches and 3.10 pounds, and caught on a gray dune assembled on a size 10 hook.

A serious fisherman should work this lake, because some lunkers still exist. I would try the outlet area since nobody fishes there and believe me, you may well see some trout that will make your wrist twitch, if nothing else.

13-18. FALLS CREEK LAKES (6)

See the code maps of these six lakes. A recent 1981 plant of golden trout was introduced to the lower three lakes of this chain. Lakes #13-15 are described in more detail below.

13. MARTIN LAKE

Location: T8S, R16E, S. 23
Elevation: 9,260 feet
Area: 30 acres
Maximum depth: 108 feet

The first lake encountered on lower Falls Creek is Martin Lake. You will find it perched on the first ledge above Lake at Falls, a sight well worth the climb for its scenery. Watch your footing: the climb up is steep and slippery when wet.

Fish were first introduced to the system in 1982 when 3,700 little, but healthy, golden trout were flown in by helicopter. These little fellows were the progeny of Sylvan Lake parents collected as eggs in 1981, reared overwinter at Washo Springs Trout Hatchery in Anaconda, Montana, and delivered to Falls Creek by the able navigation of Cliff Higgins of the Montana Department of Fish, Wildlife and Parks.

14 & 15. SCAT AND LITTLE SCAT LAKES (2)

Location: T8S, R16E, S. 23D & 26 AB
Elevation: 9,310 feet; 9,330 feet, respectively
Area: 7 acres; 5 acres, respectively
Maximum depth: 45 feet; 3 feet, respectively

Scat is the second and Little Scat is the third and upper limit of the recent golden trout plant. Golden trout tend to spawn in warmer outlet flows during the period of ice melt. Often the parents and usually the babies are flushed down the chain to the next lake in a series resulting in eventual evacuation of fish from the original upper lakes. Knowing this, I had the 3,700 golden stocked in Little Scat Lake so that the combination of Little Scat, Scat, and Martin Lakes would eventually all have golden trout. Look for good fishing from this trio.

16 & 17. UNNAMED AND ALICE LAKES (2) (fishless)

18. BOOT LAKE (fishless)

19. BIG PARK LAKE

Location: T8S, R16E, S. 14
Elevation: 8,276 feet
Area: 7.8 acres
Maximum depth: 3 feet

Big Park Lake is a shallow, wide spot at the confluence of East Rosebud and Granite Creeks. The golden trout, cutts and hybrids of the two are part of the lake and stream environment in this area.

Late one fall, I dropped down out of the high country to get some relief from the high winds aloft. To my surprise, an outfitter's camp was comfortably situated in the Big Park area. A lawyer and realtor from Atlanta, Georgia, had invested considerable money in licenses, air fares, guide service, new rifles, and gear in the quest for mountain sheep. They admitted they were not in good physical condition to climb the elevation necessary to find this quarry. The lawyer took me aside and told me that he had come a long way, and after telling his many envious friends in Atlanta that he was going to kill a sheep, he realized he didn't have it in him. When I told him that I had seen rams at 10,900 feet, he immediately offered me $4,000 if I would bring him and his hunting companion the two rams he had promised to show his friends back home. After a severe ear bending, he retreated to his tent with his head down and, for some reason, no longer enjoyed my company.

20. ROSEBUD (fishless)

21. DUGGAN LAKE

Location: T8S, R16E, S. 22
Elevation: 8,840 feet
Area: 4.4 acres
Maximum depth: 10 feet

The wide pool below Impasse Falls is referred to as Duggan Lake. Why Duggan? Well, when the forest service crews were blasting the trail along the lake, a few large "duggans" took to the air from the force of the blast. As these rocks splashed down into the big pool below, Chuck Martin of Red Lodge dubbed the pool Duggan Lake.

Look for goldens, cutts, and the resultant hybrid fish in Duggan Lake. A Mepps or black ant fly works well in this aesthetic spot.

22. TWIN OUTLETS LAKE

Location: T8, R16E, S. 21, 22
Elevation: 9,190 feet
Area: 29.5 acres
Maximum depth: 50 feet

Between Duggan and Dewey lakes is one of the few lakes on the mountain with two outlets. This irregularly-shaped lake was once exclusively a golden trout hatchery. However, since a 1968 plant of cutthroat in Dewey Lake upstream, Twin Outlets is another of the "mixed" type of fisheries and the lake doesn't get as much fishing pressure as it should. Some nice, colorful fish exceeding a pound await your presentation. I would advise fishing the shorelines with small flies.

23. DEWEY LAKE

Location: T8S, R16E, S. 21, 28
Elevation: 9,340 feet
Area: 37.3 acres
Maximum depth: 95 feet

The old Gallatin National Forest maps mistakenly had this lake named Medicine Lake, which is really one mile northeast of Dewey. Fish from Big Timber Fish Hatchery were scheduled for Medicine Lake, but due to the map error, were air-dropped into Dewey in 1968. This then became the source of cutts in the many lakes downstream. Until 1969, Dewey Lake had golden trout. These goldens failed to repopulate Dewey, however, and died out after 14 years of residency.

Cutthroats are easier to catch than stubborn old goldens and these cutts are of excellent Goose Lake stock. I would expect heavy-bodied, pink-meated fighters at Dewey.

24. SNOWBANK (fishless)

Fossil Lake, one of the most irregularly shaped lakes in the Absaroka-Beartooth Mountains, has a history of large fish. Tom Egenes photo.

25. FOSSIL LAKE

Location: T8S, R.16E., S. 29, 31, 32
Elevation: 9,900 feet
Area: 164.7 acres
Maximum depth: 150 feet

Fossil Lake is one of the lakes from which East Rosebud Creek originates. It is easily reached via trail #15 from Alpine, Montana at East Rosebud Lake, or from the opposite direction beginning at Cooke Pass. Fossil takes honors as one of the most irregularly-shaped lakes in the A-B Mountains. A perfect circle lake would get a score of one: Fossil rates a 3.74.

Fossil has a history of larger fish. In 1955 and for several years afterwards, it was the home of large goldens. Then Tommy Garrison, of Cooke City, made Fossil a home for brookies. They grew big but, thankfully, did not reproduce and later died out. The lake was planted with 10,115 cutthroat trout from Big Timber Trout Hatchery in September 1970, and was scheduled again in 1972, '77, '80, '83, and every three years thereafter.

Don't worry about counting the years after stocking because Fossil will always have a stock of a few good-sized fish. These fish cruise the shoreline, so a little hunting instinct is required.

25a. UNNAMED LAKE

Location: T8S, R16E, S. 31D
Elevation: 10,100 feet
Area: 1.8 acres
Maximum depth: 15 feet

This two-acre lake is near the Clarks Fork-East Rosebud divide. Access is by trail to Fossil, then by foot to the south side of Fossil Lake and up a small drainage. Usually the lake is fishless but an occasional fish from Fossil sneaks up this system of pools to this unnamed lake.

26. UNNAMED (fishless)

27. UNNAMED (fishless)

28. OLY (fishless)

29. UNNAMED (fishless)

30. BILLY (fishless)

31. CAIRN LAKE

Loocation: T8S, R15E, S. 13
Elevation: 10,186 feet
Area: 148.3 acres
Maximum depth: 125 feet

An enjoyable cross-country hike following the maintained trail near Dewey will take you up a pleasant valley to Cairn Lake. If you are unsure of the directions, just follow Cairn Creek.

Cairn Lake, unfortunately, is home for a small group of fat brook trout. If they escape down Cairn Creek, the whole series of lakes downstream will be crowded with stunted brookies. The Forest Service should make a Wilderness Area policy exception at Cairn to fly in the necessary dose of rotenone during March and zap these few brook trout to prevent a later misfortune of brook trout everywhere. Golden trout would be a great replacement.

32. UNNAMED (fishless)

33. MEDICINE LAKE

Location: T8S, R16E, S. 20, 21
Elevation: 9,960 feet
Area: 30.0 acres
Maximum depth: 127 feet

Medicine Lake is 1.5 miles northwest of Dewey Lake. It's a good place to isolate yourself from the gang of people along the main trail. Cutthroat are periodically stocked in Medicine. Fishing produced a few large fish in 1983-1984. It is scheduled for stocking in 1985 and should be productive again from 1988 through 1993.

34. UNNAMED *(fishless)*

35. UNNAMED *(fishless)*

36a. UNNAMED *(fishless)*

36b. UNNAMED *(fishless)*

36c. UNNAMED *(fishless)*

36d. UNNAMED *(fishless)*

37. ECHO LAKE

Location: T8S, R16E, S. 15, 16
Elevation: 8,486 feet
Area: 12.2 acres
Maximum depth: 21 feet

After passing Big Park Lake, you will come to a bridge over Granite Creek. Turn around, walk back down the trail, climb the bank and follow Granite Creek to the lake. You should be heading directly toward Granite Peak, not visible until you climb the rise just beyond Echo Lake.

This 12-acre lake has been known to put out some dandy fish. Since its original plant of cutthroat trout, it became self-sustaining. No additional stocking is necessary. If reproductive success is too good, the size of the cutts will probably diminish but they should be easily caught.

Look for mountain goats. The big ridge to the north is goat heaven.

38. UNNAMED *(fishless)*

39. UPPER GRANITE CREEK (LOWARY) LAKE *(fishless)*

40. LOWER GRANITE CREEK LAKE *(fishless)*

41. LOWER ARCH LAKE

Location: T8S, R16E, S. 2 BA
Elevation: 9,580 feet
Area: 24.3 acres
Maximum depth: 95 feet

Check out the code map to help your understanding of this lake group. Setting foot on the shores of these lakes requires determination and hard work.

The first problem is crossing East Rosebud Creek. Don't try it in early summer unless you luck out and find a new log jam. The most reliable route is to cross the split channels just upstream from Elk Lake, and if you proceed carefully up the creek, you will find remnants of the old trail to Rimrock. You will see the only feasible route. Arch Creek is not passable unless you're an experienced mountain climber. Even after ascending the first pull, you have lots more. Brownie, the friendly black bear, used to greet me in the vicinity of the falls.

Lower Arch provides the best camping area in the vicinity of the three lakes with plenty of fuel, cover, and water. It is also the most consistent fish producer; but trophy types could be landed in the other two lakes at appropriate times (see #42, #43 below). Lower Arch has a reproducing population of cutthroat.

42. UPPER ARCH LAKE

Location: T8S, R16E, S. 3
Elevation: 10,120 feet
Area: 46.9 acres
Maximum depth: 112 feet

Pat Marcuson stands beneath the granite arch which gave Arch Lake its name. Heather Marcuson photo.

The largest of Arch Lakes is at the foot of Phantom Glacier. Access is by foot only, without a trail. Don't expect to find fuel.

Watch the stocking frequency on this one. It was last stocked in 1980, and is scheduled for every eight years thereafter. If you try it during the four years after stocking, expect some big ones, but possibly slow fishing.

42a. UNNAMED (fishless)

43. ARCH LAKE

Location: T7S, R16E, S. 34, 35
Elevation: 10,120 feet
Area: 6.5 acres
Maximum depth: 54 feet

This is the northernmost lake of the group. Again, the goal at Arch Lake was to provide a few big cutts. It was last stocked in 1971, due again in 1985. Good growth should result if the schedule is adhered to. Follow the ridge on down toward East Rosebud Creek and you will see why Arch Creek got its name: it's a big, classy granite arch.

44. SHADOW LAKE

Location: T7S, R17E, S. 19, 20
Elevation: 8,400 feet
Area: 5.4 acres
Maximum depth: 19 feet

Shadow Lake is accessible via a very steep (one step up-slide down two) trail west of East Rosebud footbridge, or by traveling cross-country through conifer timber and talus rock.

Shadow has loads of prolific brookies: in fact, while I was sampling with nets once, a curious observer approached for a closer look-see. When he noticed I was fishing illegally with a net, he didn't even question me. Instead he just said, "Guess the lakes need a little thinning out. Set it again."

45. LOST LAKE

Location: T7S, R17E, S. 30 B
Elevation: 9,160 feet
Area: 3.5 acres
Maximum depth: 36 feet

Numerous Lost Lakes occur in the A-B Mountains. This one is just beyond Shadow Lake, not really that hard to find. Some people refer to Lost Lake as Hidden Lake. You might find a few cutts left over from a 1971 plant, but don't count on it.

Lost Lake was scheduled for grayling in 1983. This has all the cards for a good hand: ideal spawning, preferred foods, and a neat spot.

46. SLOUGH LAKE (3)

Location: T7S, R17E, S. 19
Elevation: 7,500 feet
Area: 5.8 acres
Maximum depth: 6 feet

A series of sloughs adequately describes Slough Lake, one of those wide spot situations in Armstrong Creek. Beaver find this a suitable meadow to generate ample fishing holes. Access is maintained by forest trail #17. Lots of brook trout, fuel, shelter, and all the comforts of home including an occasional mosquito.

47. PHANTOM LAKE

Location: T7S, R16E, S. 26, 17
Elevation: 9,320 feet
Area: 19.5 acres
Maximum depth: 56 feet

John Branger saw this lake as some sort of spooky woman and so named it Phantom. Most of the lake is surrounded by talus and rock walls; however, camp spots are good on the north and west shores. It is reached by trail #17, then cross-country over hill and dale, mostly hill.

The present fish picture is of cutthroat trout, ranging from 7 to 12 inches. I caught them at a rate of 2.5 fish per hour. You might run across some old literature proclaiming a lake full of grayling. They never materialized (see #48).

48. FROZE-TO-DEATH LAKE

Location- T7S, R16E, S. 27, 34
Elevation: 10,156 feet
Area: 74.5 acres
Maximum depth: 195 feet

Better check with your regional fisheries manager on the status of this lake. I had it stocked on August 24, 1978, with cutthroat trout of the McBride variety. I went back in 1981 and they ranged from 9.5 to 13.3 inches, and from .37 to .81 pounds. Average length and weight equaled 11.3 inches, .51 pounds. There should be some fishing until 1985, but then it will need another shot of fish because the lake is very green with glacial silt and no reproduction will occur. You might report your findings to the state Fish, Wildlife and Parks Department. Grayling were flown to Froze-To-Death years ago, but didn't take.

49 & 50. TURGULSE AND BRENT LAKES (2)

Location: T6S, R16E, S. 32, 33, 33 CB
Elevation: 10,206 feet; 10,216 feet, respectively.
Area: 82 acres; 13.3 acres, respectively
Maximum depth: 80 feet; 75 feet, respectively

Turgulse and Brent are connected to Froze-To-Death Lake in a cold glacial valley that penetrates Froze-To-Death Plateau. They are approximately 2.5 miles northeast of Granite Peak. Both are very green in color. The fish situation is the same as that in Froze-To-Death.

West Rosebud Creek Drainage

At one time, you could count the number of fish-filled lakes in the West Rosebud drainage on a hand with a couple of extra digits. It is still a rather fishless group of waters, even though the number of lakes with fish has more than doubled. Some of the "fishy" waters in the drainage are predominantly foothill environments in the mid-6,000-feet elevation zone. Examples of this type of lake include Emerald, West Rosebud, Crater, and Lost lakes. Most of the lakes are in the Custer National Forest; a couple are on State of Montana lands. Reeves Pond is on private land.

Two nearly distinct drainages exist in this watershed. West Rosebud Canyon and its accumulation of tributaries constitute one district. Island, Lost, Twin, and the Fishtail lakes area north and west of Fishtail Plateau on upper Fishtail Creek make up the other. Access to the canyon is confined to the Mystic Lake Trail #19, departing near the Montana Power Company plant. Trail #17 wanders into Mystic from the East Rosebud—not your direct route to fishing.

You have to watch your point of departure from the roads in the Fishtail Creek watershed because there are lots of private lands between road and public lands. Consult your maps carefully or get permission from landowners.

Come to think of it, if the FWP were to discontinue stocking in the West Rosebud Creek drainage (ouch), only five lakes in the mountain zone would have fish. To lessen the impact of such an event, I stocked a few areas where the fish should reproduce and hopefully abound for a long time. Grayling were scheduled, and golden trout were newly introduced into some prime virgin lakes.

The canyon has four lake groupings. The first group consists of the Mystic, Island, and Silver lakes: all of these lakes have fish. Second, the upper drainage containing Star Lake and all the headwater lakes south of Big Park Mountain is essentially without fish. Third is the Huckleberry Creek-to-Granite Peak area, mostly new fisheries. Fourth is the bench semi-circling Island and Silver lakes on the west. These waters are in various stages of experimental or developing fish populations.

The forest portion of the entire West Rosebud drainage covers 124.7 square miles and is administered by the Beartooth Ranger District in Red Lodge, Montana. The drainage is bordered by the East Rosebud to the east, the Stillwater on the west, and portions of the Stillwater and Clarks Fork to the south. Lakes in the headwaters below Grasshopper Glacier are mostly glacial, emerald green, icy, fishless pools.

Lake water in the drainage covers 1,164.3 acres, ranging from .3 to 434.9 acres in size, and from 1 to 235 feet in depth. Mystic Lake is the largest, but not the deepest; that honor goes to LaVella, at 235 feet. Mystic, with its 205-foot hole, is second.

The altitudinal distribution of the 84 lakes in the drainage ranges from Reeves Pond at 5,950 feet to an unnamed lake in Upper West Fishtail Creek at 10,600 feet above sea level. About half the lakes are distributed in the 9,000-foot elevation zone. Ram Lake, at a 9,580-foot location on the Chicken Creek area of Fishtail Plateau, is the highest lake with fish.

Even though the West Rosebud lacks fish, it makes up for it in scenic beauty and solitude. The high country has some nifty peaks, glaciers, pools, and a unique grasshopper-laden glacier. For climbers, the route to Granite Peak via Huckleberry Creek now has adequate fish to lighten the packer's food supply.

1. EMERALD LAKE

Location: T7S, R16E, S. 1
Elevation: 6,310 feet
Area: 28.5 acres
Maximum depth: 7 feet

Emerald is accessible by car with a graveled forest road along the north and west shoreline. Camping facilities are provided by the Forest Service. The lake is stocked annually with catchable-size rainbow trout which provide the bulk of the catch. With the rainbow are brookies, browns, and an occasional cutthroat. Beware of the outlet, especially during spring melt: it has been known to take an unsuspecting angler.

Accessible by car and complete with camping facilities, Emerald Lake offers lots of fishing with little fretting. Michael Sample photo.

From the shallows of Emerald Lake, this fly fisherman hopes to entice rainbow, brook, brown, or even an occasional cutthroat trout. Michael Sample photo.

West Rosebud Creek Drainage

1. Emerald Lake
2. West Rosebud Lake
3. Afterbay Pool
4. Mystic Lake
5. Huckleberry Lake
6. Princess Lake
7. Cold Lake
8a-8d. Snowball Lakes
9. Unnamed Lake
10. Lower Storm Lake
11. Avalanche Lake
12. Middle Storm Lake
13. Upper Storm Lake
14. Island Lake
15. Silver Lake
16. Star Lake
17. Grasshopper Lake
18. Wolf Lake
19. Unnamed Lake
20. LaVelle Lake
20a. Little LaVelle Lake
21. Kid Lake
22. Big Foot Lake
23. Eedica Lake

23a-24. Unnamed Lake
25. Nugget Lake
26. Beckwourth Lake
27. Frenco Lake
28. Unnamed Lake
29. Nemidji
30. Weeluna

31-31a. Unnamed Lakes
32. Arrapooash Lake
32a. Unnamed Lake
33. Little Face Lake
34. Ewe Lake
34a. Jaw Bone Lake
35. Ram Lake
35a. Unnamed Lake

36. Reeves Lake
37. Lily Pad Lake
38. Crator Lake
39. Lost Lakes
40-45b. West Fishtail Creek Lakes
46. Heart Lake
47. Twin Lakes
48. Island Lake

W. ROSEBUD CREEK
DRAINAGE AREA

PRIMARY ROAD
SECONDARY ROAD
TRAIL
PAVED ROAD
CAMPGROUND
RANGER STATION
MOUNTAIN
ABSAROKA—BEARTOOTH
WILDERNESS BOUNDARY

½ 1 2 3
MILES

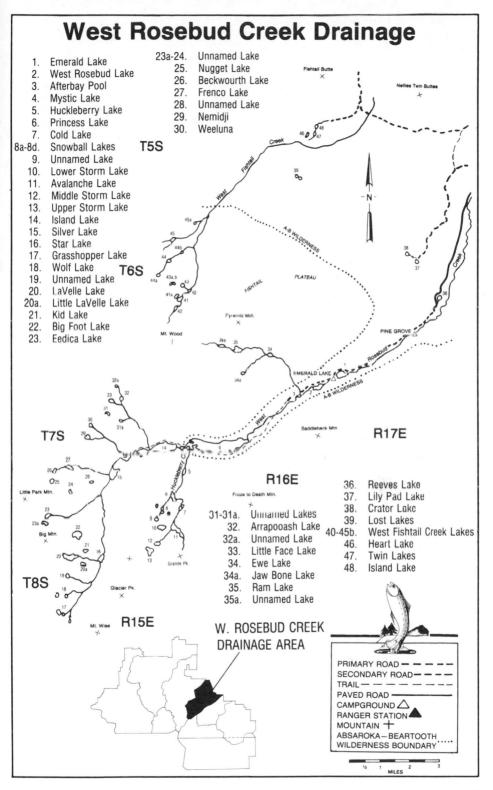

2. WEST ROSEBUD LAKE

Location: T7S, R16E, S. 2
Elevation: 6,387 feet
Area: 19 acres
Maximum depth: 6+ feet

This lake is just 1.25 miles downstream from the Mystic Lake Hydroelectric Plant owned and operated by Montana Power Company. The lake is accessible by car, and picnicking and camping facilities are available. West Rosebud is stocked with catchable-size rainbow trout—but, unlike Emerald, cutts, brookies, and browns are commonly captured in both the stream and lake. The outlet has a regulating dam controlled by the power company. The function of this dam is to catch the surge and release a steady flow downstream. Look for 8- to 12-inch fish.

3. AFTERBAY POOL

Location: T7S, R16E, S. 2C
Elevation: 6,480 feet
Area: up to 5.8 acres
Maximum depth: 3+ feet

This is just a small pool in West Rosebud Creek immediately downstream from Montana Power Company's Mystic Lake Power Plant. It has fish and can be a fun place to throw a fly. You can drive to this one.

4. MYSTIC LAKE

Location: T7S, R16E, S. 7, 8, 9, 16, 17, 18
Elevation: 7,683 feet
Area: 434.9 acres (when full)
Maximum depth: 205+ feet

Mystic is the largest of the lakes in the Beartooth and Absaroka mountains. The lake is surrounded by lands classified as wilderness, but the lake itself is outside the Absaroka-Beartooth Wilderness. Montana Power Company built a 314-foot dam, 30 feet high with 42-inch splash boards here in 1936 and a wooden flume in 1924. Water is delivered through the wooden pipe to a surge tank and dropped 1,116 feet to the turbine generators. The total drawdown capability of the lake is 86 feet. The dam adds approximately 40 feet of additional water storage.

The area is subjected to almost constant high winds, particularly in the afternoons. I tried three times to accurately sound the lake for depths, each time getting blown around like a bobber. Mystic gets lots of pressure: approximately 1,600 fishermen visit the lake between June and September. Ice goes out earlier here than on most of the lakes because of the power plant operation and the vast size of the lake.

In the winter, big chunks of ice all over the lake makes it look like an arctic ice breakup. What happens is this: the water is drained out from under the ice for power generation and the ice eventually collapses—quite a sight.

Fish found in Mystic are mostly rainbow trout with some rainbow-cutthroat hybrids. An occasional cutthroat trout is caught. The abundance of rainbow trout fluctuates annually, but, in general, good fishing is had by all.

Jim Annin of Columbus reports that rainbow trout were stocked in 1909 before a trail existed up West Rosebud Creek. The fish were packed over the mountain from the East Rosebud side to Mystic and Huckleberry lakes.

5-13. HUCKLEBERRY CREEK LAKES (12)

Location: T7S, R15E, S. 25, 26, 35, 36
Elevation: 8,380-10,550 feet

Twelve lakes lie in the Huckleberry Creek drainage; all except Huckleberry Lake were fishless. Recently, two more lakes have been introduced to fish and another is in the mill.

Huckleberry Creek is the most commonly used route for mountain climbers heading for Granite Peak. Since the drainage receives human use and the upper lakes provide campsites for those looking to tackle "Old Granite," it seemed logical to provide some angling opportunities along Huckleberry Creek. When I first traveled up the drainage, there was only a faint sign of a trail to Huckleberry Lake and a probable route on up; now the trail has been beaten out to Avalanche Lake, by many sets of Vibrams. It's all rock and snow thereafter.

A hiker pauses on a high plateau overlooking Mystic and Silver lakes. Michael Sample photo.

5. HUCKLEBERRY LAKE

Location: T7S, R15E, S. 24
Elevation: 8,380 feet
Area: 8 acres
Maximum depth: 8 feet

Huckleberry Lake is approximately six miles from Mystic Lake Power Plant, a mile from the little bridge over Huckleberry Creek at Mystic Lake. This lake is your basic widewater—only eight feet deep with a few aquatic plants along the shores. There are lots of rainbow trout, some extra nice ones. Most folks go right on by Huckleberry Lake. I caught rainbow up to 17 inches here—real fighters. And, yes, there are lots of huckleberries on the way.

6. PRINCESS LAKE

Location: T7S, R15E, S. 25
Elevation: 9,080 feet
Area: 25 acres
Maximum depth: 35 feet

Princess doesn't have any fish, but it does have potential. Look for grayling in the future; FW&P plans to start stocking them. This fish would provide some diversity to the West Rosebud system, and the lake is ideally suited to their needs. You'll find good camping here—lots of fuel and shelter—items that are rare further up Huckleberry Creek. This lake is a beauty; take your camera for one waterfall spilling into the lake and one downstream between Princess and Huckleberry lakes.

7. COLD *(fishless)*

8a. SNOWBALL *(fishless)*

8b. SNOWBALL *(fishless)*

8c. SNOWBALL *(fishless)*

8d. SNOWBALL *(fishless)*

9. UNNAMED (fishless)

10. LOWER STORM LAKE

Location: T7S, R15E, S. 35, 36
Elevation: 9,839 feet
Area: 17.8 acres
Maximum depth: 95 feet

All of the maps of this area have the words "Storm Lake" written across a bunch of lakes, including Avalanche Lake. If this baffles you, don't feel alone. In actuality, Lower Storm Lake is the closest lake to Avalanche Lake, and if you take the easiest route above Princess Lake, you will walk along the north shore of Lower Storm Lake. You might feel like a rabbit when you wade through the krummholtz (low, stunted fir and pine trees)—good old tanglefoot. I admire these trees' stubborn resistance to the elements and the rugged life they live.

To get to Lower Storm, I suggest heading up the old Avalanche scar southwest of Princess Lake, then straight south past Snowball Lakes. Climb the next gentle slope and you're there.

The other two Storm Lakes are fishless lakes. They are tucked up under Mystic Mountain. Lower Storm Lake was stocked with cutthroat of the McBride variety in 1979. They are doing fairly well. It will be stocked every eight years, so the next plant will be in 1987. Do the lake a favor: if you fish here and the fish appear snaky, tell a fisheries biologist. Perhaps the department will give the lake a little break by planting fish less frequently or by reducing the stocking density.

11. AVALANCHE LAKE

Location: T7S, R15E, S. 36
Elevation: 9,750 feet
Area: 62.2 acres
Maximum depth: 135 feet

From Avalanche, you can finally see Granite Peak—that is, its north face. If you're heading up that way, try fishing the far shoreline of Avalanche Lake. You'll have to do lots of big rock hopping, but the going is faster than traveling on the cliffy stuff on the southeast shore.

Avalanche Lake was stocked for your pleasure. The goal was to create a source of angling recreation for you while you eyeball Granite Peak. This provides hikers with tasty, pink, sizzling meat as an alternative to freeze-dry-yuck. The lake will be stocked every five years, so plenty of fish should always be available for your frying pan. Freeze-dry enthusiasts who don't carry frying pans can use a pinch of salt, a little butter if available, and a gentle wrap of tin foil, to snuggle fish down in the coals. As of this writing, the lake was last stocked in 1979.

12. STORM (MIDDLE) (fishless)

13. STORM (UPPER) (fishless)

14. ISLAND LAKE

Location: T7S, R15E, S. 13, 14, 15
Elevation: 7,717 feet
Area: 144 acres
Maximum depth: 40 feet

Another of the big lakes in the West Rosebud Canyon, Island Lake is located just upstream from Mystic. Access is easy by horse or foot on a maintained trail; however, the trail leads into a big log debris pile at the outlet of Island Lake. Horse riders have to find an alternate crossing (you might also check the Forest Service's regulations regarding horse travel; I believe it is open in the fall only).

A total of 76 percent of the lake is less than 15 feet deep. The shoreline is predominantly lined with conifers along with some rock talus and wet meadow.

Island Lake has plenty of rainbow trout with a touch of cutthroat slash on their throats. Catch rates are usually good: I figured it at 1.1 fish per hour. You take the .1 portion; I prefer the 1.

15. SILVER LAKE

Location: T7S, R15E, S. 22
Elevation: 7,820 feet
Area: 72.6 acres
Maximum depth: 21 feet

Fish in Silver Lake are not rod breakers, but they're nice. Most range from 6 to 14.5 inches. Like the lakes downstream, Silver contains lots of rainbow and cutts—mostly rainbow.

A good trail leads to Silver Lake but doesn't go much beyond. Camping is good, with plenty of fuel and other comforts of home available. You might catch an occasional grayling here someday if the Montana Department of Fish, Wildlife and Parks responds to urging that they plant some in Star Lake (see below).

16. STAR LAKE

Location: T8S, R15E, S. 4A
Elevation: 8,640 feet
Area: 23.5 acres
Maximum depth: 15 feet

Another 3.5 miles up West Rosebud Creek from Silver Lake is Star Lake. Fish the meadow waters upstream from Silver. The going gets bushy and very wet in damp weather.

The lake has always been fishless. However I have urged the powers at FWP to stock the Star Lake-West Rosebud Creek system above Silver Lake with grayling of a special variety—aborigines from the Red Rock system in southwestern Montana. These fish deserve the best—a system without competing fish and a place away from the threat of man-caused pollutants—the West Rosebud.

Star Lake has a big fan-shaped inlet delta providing excellent spawning opportunities for grayling on the sandy gravel. Star is really a large stream environment with one deep hole of 15 feet. It was scheduled for grayling in 1983. Let's hope—and urge—that it gets done as soon as possible.

Camping with ample fuel is possible near the outlet and along the west shoreline. The far shoreline is mostly talus rock. Star Lake was formed by a large rock slide across West Rosebud Creek.

Overpopulated, undernourished brook trout such as those in Lonesome Lake may be small, but they still provide endless fun for young anglers. Bill Schneider photo.

17. GRASSHOPPER LAKE *(fishless)*

18. WOLF LAKE *(fishless)*

19. UNNAMED *(fishless)*

20. LaVELLE LAKE *(fishless)*

20a. LITTLE LaVELLE LAKE *(fishless)*

21. KID LAKE *(fishless)*

22. BIG FOOT LAKE *(fishless)*

23. EēDICA LAKE
Location: T7S, R15E, S. 29 C
Elevation: 9,720 feet
Area: 8.9 acres
Maximum depth: 40 feet

Eēdica Lake is an isolated, scenic gem hidden between Big Park and Little Park mountains. The lake is in a glacial valley with good in- and out-flows of water. A fish venturing downstream from Eēdica can say good-bye—he won't be coming back.

The name Eēdica is a Crow Indian word meaning "far away." The lake was stocked with McBride cutts in 1979. Let your fisheries biologist know what you catch at Eēdica—trying, of course, to be honest.

23a. UNNAMED *(fishless)*

24. UNNAMED *(fishless)*

25. NUGGET LAKE
Location: T7S, R15E, S. 20 C
Elevation: 9,340 feet
Area: 8.3 acres
Maximum depth: 30 feet

Nugget is on the shady side of Little Park Mountain. To get there, amble up the slope near Island Lake toward Frenco and Beckwourth lakes. It's the next lake upstream. The lake is at timberline.

Professional fish chasers are known to do some experimentation. Action in Nugget was just that—an experimental fish plant. It was intentionally stocked with too many fish for the available supply of food. Then I visited the lake each year to document growth rates. Eventually, the cupboard went bare of certain food critters, and even though other foods were available, the fish didn't convert to less preferable food organisms.

It was stocked in 1976 and was rescheduled for another stocking in 1984—this time with a more realistic number of cutts.

26. BECKWOURTH LAKE
Location: T7S, R15E, S. 20 B
Elevation: 9,230 feet
Area: 6.2 acres
Maximum depth: 9 feet

This is one of several lakes on the west bench above Silver Lake. Some cutthroats are found here. They really belong downstream in Frenco Lake. An occasional wayward, adventuresome fish takes the trip to Beckwourth, but don't look for too many pans full of fish here.

27. FRENCO and PONDS (2)
Location: T7S, R15E, S. 20 AA
Elevation: 9,115 feet
Area: 13.9 acres; 2.4 acres total, respectively
Maximum depth: 28 feet; 1.4 feet, respectively

Not long ago, Frenco Lake was the only lake on "the bench" with fish. There are no clues as to how and when the fish arrived. It is suspected that the cutthroat in Frenco were the source of the hybrid types in Silver, Island, and Mystic lakes.

Access to Frenco is restricted to foot travel without a trail. Plenty of fuel for fires is available. The small ponds formed in the outlet stream near Frenco all have fish. Rumor has it that Frenco puts out a lunker on occasion. I witnessed lots of cutts, averaging 9.5 inches. The fish population in Frenco has lots of size classes, as is typical of lakes that are self-sufficient (no stocking needed).

Splendid scenery is mirrored on the surface of Frenco Lake, until recently the only lake on "the bench" with a self-sustaining fish population. Pat Marcuson photo.

28. UNNAMED (fishless)

29. NEMIDJI LAKE
Location: T7S, R15E, S. 16 B
Elevation: 9,595 feet
Area: 7 acres
Maximum depth: 25 feet

If the name of this lake doesn't roll off your tongue easily on the first try, don't feel alone. Pronounced Nehmidge'ee, it comes from the Crow Indian legend of how the Stillwater River, of which the West Rosebud is a tributary, got its name. Those familiar with the Stillwater River know it is anything but a still, gentle old slow-poke. The Crow story, best described by Jim Annin in "They Gazed on the Beartooths," tells of an Indian brave named Nemidji and his squaw-to-be, Weeluna. To make an extreme disaster of a beautiful epic, before the wedding took place, Weeluna became so ill that she died. She was buried under a huge fir tree, and as the tribe was mourning her death, a violent storm came and uprooted the tree, throwing Weeluna's body into the waters below. When Nemidji looked into the pool of water and saw her body, he jumped in and wrapped his arms around her. Suddenly, a huge boulder rolled into the water, taking them both under. After the storm ended and the waters calmed, the tribe named this the hallowed place, Stillwater, the same Stillwater we know today.

The lake that bears the star-crossed Nemidji's name shares the same glacial cirque with Weeluna Lake on "the bench" west of Silver Lake, close to the treeline. Both lakes were virgin, fishless lakes prior to 1979. Nemidji was loaded with large red zooplankton and therefore considered a prime candidate for a good catchable population of cutthroat trout. The cutts were planted, and were planted again in 1984, and will be every five years thereafter.

30. WEELUNA LAKE
Location: T7S, R15E, S. 9
Elevation: 9,494 feet
Area: 10.2 acres
Maximum depth: 30 feet

See lake #29, Nemidji Lake (#29), for "the rest of the story" on Weeluna Lake's name. Weeluna is the northernmost of the two lakes. It's the one adjacent to the talus rock slope. Again, there is fuel in the area but it's not in abundance at the lake's shoreline. You won't find any trails after you leave the West Rosebud Creek trail.

Contrary to the plan for Nemidji Lake which calls for stocking lots of fish at close intervals, Weeluna will be managed as a trophy fishery—with small numbers of cutts stocked less frequently. Take your choice. If you don't succeed in Weeluna, you'll probably catch a fish next door.

31. UNNAMED (fishless)

31a. UNNAMED (fishless)

32. ARRAPOOASH (fishless)

32a. UNNAMED (fishless)

33. LITTLE FACE (fishless)

34. EWE (fishless)

34a. JAW BONE (fishless)

35. RAM LAKE
Location: T6S, R16E, S. 33 BD
Elevation: 9,580 feet
Area: 14.4 acres
Maximum depth: 29 feet

Look for Ram Lake at the headwaters of Chicken Creek, a tributary that merges with the West Rosebud Lake. Ram Lake drains the Fishtail Plateau in a valley between Mt. Wood and Pyramid Mountain. It hurts to get there.

Ram was planted with cutthroat trout in 1975 as an experiment to see what fish do to a zooplankton population, how long the fish live without fishing pressure, and various other biological goodies. We call it biological puttering.

The fish grew to 15 inches in three years but didn't continue the same growth rate in later years. However, they're still nice fish if you're willing to go after them. Ram was scheduled to be stocked again in 1983, but you might want to check with the fish managers in Billings to see if they really did it.

35a. UNNAMED (fishless)

36. REEVES LAKE (fishless)

37. LILY PAD LAKE (fishless)

38. CRATER LAKE
Location: T6S, R17E, S. 16
Elevation: 6,660 feet
Area: 2.3 acres
Maximum depth: 36 feet

Crater Lake is located near the headwaters of Fiddler Creek west of the main West Rosebud. It's only 2.3 surface acres and 36 feet deep, with lots of aquatic weed beds. You can drive a four-wheel vehicle to it. It has some problems: the vegetation causes severe oxygen depletion during the winter, causing fish kills. Access is another problem: even though the state lands belong to the public, this area is locked up to all but the lease holders. Crater might be developed into an accessible rainbow trout fishery again someday. I only list it in the fish-filled lakes section because it did have fish once and might have them again.

39a-c. LOST LAKES (3) (fishless)

Ram Lake, below Pyramid Mountain, was stocked with cutthroat in 1975 as part of a biological experiment. Pat Marcuson photo.

One of the middle Snowball lakes of the West Rosebud drainage, all of them
fishless. Pat Marcuson photo.

40, 41, 41a, 43, AND 43c. WEST FISHTAIL LAKES (5)

Location: T6S, R15E, T6S, R16E
Elevation: 8,500 to 10,600 feet
Area: 1.1 acre; 7.3 acres; 2.0 acres; 4.2 acres; 4 acres, respectively
Maximum depth: 4 feet; 40 feet; 12 feet; 24 feet; 2 feet respectively

Look for the Fishtail water holes nestled in the canyon flowing out of the mountain between the Fishtail and Stillwater plateaus. Don't take a horse; plan on walking unless
you're the stubborn type in which case you can search out a route for a week with your
pony. My suggested route is to start at Chrome Lake area, break through the thick,
lodgepole jungle toward the creek drainage, and continue on up the creek. Moose like the
drainage and have beaten some intermittent paths between the lakes, but beware: moose
also go from bush to bush as well as to the lake.

I'm reluctant to tell about this spot. The last time I let the word out about a good fishery,
I felt guilty when seeing the subsequent garbage, campfire rings, and other general signs of
abuse. Please respect the area and practice no-trace camping.

Golden trout were introduced here in 1982 after considerable effort in removing the eggs
from the Sylvan Lake source, running the babies all over the State of Montana, getting
their health check-ups, and delivering the durable survivors to the appropriate lakes. The
effort would not have been expended if the fishes' future wasn't reasonably assured in their
new home.

The idea of the plant was to make a stream-like, reproducing, genetically isolated
population of pure-strain golden trout. To accomplish this, certain lakes were selected for
trout introductions with the knowledge that goldens would dissminate throughout the
liveable waters.

42. W. FISHTAIL CREEK LAKE *(fishless)*

43a. W. FISHTAIL CREEK LAKE *(fishless)*

43b. W. FISHTAIL CREEK LAKE *(fishless)*

48

Mt. Wood overlooks this West Fishtail Creek lake, where moose have beaten the only trails and where golden trout were introduced in 1982. Pat Marcuson photo.

44a. W. FISHTAIL CREEK LAKE (fishless)

44b. W. FISHTAIL CREEK LAKE (fishless)

45. W. FISHTAIL LAKE (fishless)

45a. W. FISHTAIL CREEK LAKE (fishless)

45b. W. FISHTAIL CREEK LAKE (fishless)

46. HEART LAKE (fishless)

47. TWIN LAKES (2)

Location: T5S, R16E, S. 26
Elevation: 6,050 feet
Area: .34 acres; .31 acres, respectively
Maximum depth: 11 feet; 8 feet, respectively

Twin Lakes, North and South, are small, connected bodies of water in the western portion of the West Rosebud Creek system. The outlet flows to Island Lake, then to Fishtail Creek. These small lakes are within the Custer National Forest boundary, but outside the Absaroka-Beartooth Wilderness Area.

I caught eight brown trout, averaging 11 inches and one-half pound, when I was there. The largest fish was 18 inches. Shorelines are not particularly conducive to easy fishing—lots of brush.

48. ISLAND LAKE

Location: T5S, R16E, S. 23, 26
Elevation: 6,030 feet
Area: 2.4 acres
Maximum depth: 26 feet

Located just inside the forest boundaries near the old 4-K Guest Ranch out of Dean, Montana, Island Lake is a semi-man-made lake with an outlet dam and a pipe delivering some water. The lake is inhabited by brown trout, 8-22 inches in length.

Stillwater River Drainage

I lay in my tent that early morning in the Stillwater country, knowing I had a big climb ahead of me and a load to carry. I had to set nets, sound for depths, map, and perform miscellaneous biological duties at two lakes. The night before it had rained cats and dogs; the ground would be cold and the wood wet—and I stalled. As I was mentally selecting my route over Mount Wood, a rush of wind filled the lower canyon, nearly unstaking my little tent as it shot by. I heard what seemed to be that same big blow turn around at the canyon head and start back. This time I took a grip on the nylon tent, pulled my head into my bedroll, and lay there in shock as the wind leveled the tent. Now I knew I had to get up. While making this miserable effort, I heard the wind again. As I struggled to get dressed, old mister wind got in its last "good morning"—straight down from heaven. The tent poles were trashed; one was broken, the other bent 18 degrees, and the whole wet mess clung to my half-dressed body. My companion finally woke up and commented, "Couldn't you be more careful when you get up?" Wish I could sleep like that.

The Stillwater watershed is the largest hunk of real estate in the Beartooth Ranger District of the Custer National Forest. It covers 342.9 square miles, plus that much more of private lands, stretching to the Yellowstone River. The National Forest section contains 151 lakes; three small lakes occupy private lands for a total of 154 lakes. All but 15 are within the Absaroka-Beartooth Wilderness Area of the Beartooth Mountain Range.

Sixty-three of the lakes lie in Park County, 48 in Stillwater County, 42 in Sweet Grass County, and one is shared by Stillwater and Sweet Grass counties. Towns within the drainage include Nye, Dean, Fishtail, Limestone, and Absarokee. Cooke City is the closest town to the drainage's southern end.

Lake water covers 1,194 acres of the Stillwater drainage. Lakes range from .4 to 102 acres in surface area, the largest being Goose Lake. The average size of the 154 lakes is 7.5 acres. Goose Lake is the only one exceeding 100 surface acres.

Only 205-foot-deep Courthouse Lake exceeds 200 feet in depth. Five lakes, including Goose (130 feet), Barrier (170 feet), Lightning (122 feet), Wilderness (120 feet), and Wrong (116 feet) have depths between 100 and 200 feet. Eleven lakes are between 50 and 100 feet deep; 44 are between 15 and 50 feet deep; and the remaining 93 are less than 15 feet deep.

The highest lakes in the drainage encompass Fox Peak near Goose Lake. The very highest is Unnamed (#41a) at 10,400 feet above sea level.

Both the Stillwater River and the West Fork are accessible by maintained trails. Other trails branch off these paths to areas on Lake Plateau and Lake of the Woods. Some headwaters lakes are most easily reached by the Goose Lake jeep trail out of Cooke City.

The latest count revealed fish in about 38 percent of the 154 lakes. The lakes contain almost every species of trout except browns and grayling.

1, 1a, 1b. CHROME, TURCO, AND LITTLE ROCKY (3) (fishless)

2. LAKE WILDERNESS

Location: T6S, R15E, S. 26, 27
Elevation: 9,481 feet
Area: 19.0 acres
Maximum depth: 120 feet

Lake Wilderness is located on upper Woodbine Creek near Mount Wood and Mount Hague. I don't advise the hike up Woodbine: lots of thick lodgepole timber and sharp rocks provide for tough going. A college kid from Texas destroyed a pair of boots just descending from the area. The best access is across Stillwater Plateau. One might find a way to take a horse this latter route; however, no trails exist.

Probably the wettest I've ever been was on one of my rendezvous with Lake Wilderness. I spent one of those all-nighters maneuvering around a big fire.

I had cutthroat trout air-delivered to Lake Wilderness in 1976. However, I doubt that it gets fished much. It was rescheduled for 1984, but you might check with the Montana Department of Fish, Wildlife and Parks before counting on it.

Anglers testing the Stillwater River have the benefit of a watershed covering more than 600 square miles. Michael Sample photo.

3. WOOD LAKE

Location: T6S, R15E, S. 26E
Elevation: 9,690 feet
Area: 12 acres
Maximum depth: 38 feet

The next lake, a half mile southeast of Lake Wilderness, is Wood Lake. Follow the rock-buried inlet of Lake Wilderness which is a climb of a couple hundred feet. Wood Lake will provide an excellent bivouac point for those desiring a climb up Mount Wood. The lake was stocked with cutthroat in 1976 and 1981, so it should be good. As two-year-olds, the cutts averaged 11 inches, one-half pound. Let your imagination work on the current size of the 1981 stock.

3a, 3b, & 4. UNNAMED (7) (fishless)

5. WOODBINE LAKE (fishless)

6. NIGHTMARE LAKE (fishless)

7. SIOUX CHARLEY LAKE
Location: T6S, R14E, S. 12 AB
Elevation: 5,630 feet
Area: 3.6 acres
Maximum depth: 3.5 feet

To get to Sioux Charley Lake, take trail #24 by foot or horse approximately 3.5 miles from the trailhead at Woodbine Campground. The arbitrary size of Sioux Charley depends on the imaginary boundary between it and the Stillwater River. My boundary makes this wide spot in the river 3.6 acres. In Sioux Charley you can catch brookies and an occasional cutthroat ranging from 6 to 11 inches in length. Sioux Charley makes a good day trip for some fly casting and a batch of good pan fish. Beware of wading the Stillwater during spring freshets; it can get tricky.

8. CATARACT LAKE
Location: T6S, R15E, S. 29
Elevation: 8,751 feet
Area: 9.7 acres
Maximum depth: 45 feet

Cataract Lake, or Falls Creek Lake, lies on a tributary of the Stillwater River near Twin Peaks. There isn't a trail, and access (foot only) is tough. You'll find trees and adequate camping on the north side near the outlet or by the inlet stream. The area is a good place for solitude seekers. On August 17, 1977, I had 1,000 cutthroat dropped into the lake by helicopter. I bet Cliff Higgens, the pilot, thought I was crazy to stock this one. He was right. Don't expect any more fish here for a while.

9. CORKSCREW LAKE (fishless)

10, 10a. UPPER CORKSCREW, UNNAMED LAKES (3) (fishless)

11. UNNAMED (fishless)

12. UNNAMED (fishless)

13. IMELDA LAKE
Location: T8S, R15E, S. 6 A & B
Elevation: 9,750 feet
Area: 32.4 acres
Maximum depth: 75 feet

Accessible from the Goose Lake area, Imelda has a self-sustaining population of brook trout. Like most brook trout they "rabbitized" and filled their niche with lots of fish. Thirty-five brookies averaged 8.5 inches when I checked them.

14. UNNAMED (fishless)

15, 15a. UNNAMED (2) (fishless)

16. UNNAMED (fishless)

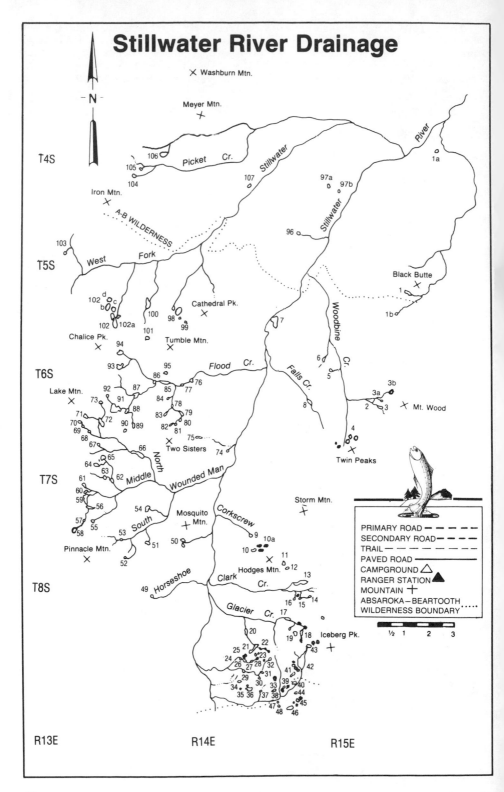

Stillwater River Drainage

X Washburn Mtn.

-N-

Meyer Mtn.
+

T4S

River

1a

106 Picket Cr.

105
104

Stillwater

107

97a   97b

Iron Mtn.
+

A-B WILDERNESS

103

West   Fork

Stillwater

96

Black Butte

T5S

1

1b

d
102 c
b
102   102a

100

98

Cathedral Pk.
+

99

7

Woodbine   Cr.

101

Chalice Pk.
+   94

Tumble Mtn.
+

93

95

Flood   Cr.

6

Falls Cr.

5

T6S

86   76

3b

Lake Mtn.
+   73

92   87   85   77

84   78

3a

2   3   X Mt. Wood

91

88

83   79

90 89   82   80

8

81

71
70
69
68
67   66

75

74

Two Sisters
+

4

Twin Peaks
+

64   65
63
61   62   Middle

North

Wounded Man

T7S

60
59
57   56
55   54
58   55   53   South

Mosquito
+ Mtn.

Corkscrew

Storm Mtn.
+

PRIMARY ROAD — — —
SECONDARY ROAD — - - -
TRAIL — — —
PAVED ROAD ———
CAMPGROUND △
RANGER STATION ▲
MOUNTAIN +
ABSAROKA—BEARTOOTH
WILDERNESS BOUNDARY ·····

51
50
52

Pinnacle Mtn.
+

9   10a

10

11

Hodges Mtn.
+   12

13

½ 1   2   3

49   Horseshoe

Clark   Cr.

16   14
15

T8S

Glacier   Cr.   17

20

19 18   Iceberg Pk.
+

22
25 21
24   28 23
26 27 32
31   41 39
34   29 33   40
35 36 30   44
37 38
47   45
48   46

43
42

R13E   R14E   R15E

1.	Chrome Lake	40.	Wall Lake	79.	Comet Lake
1a.	Turco Pond	41-41a.	Unnamed Lakes	80.	Asteroid Lake
1b.	Little Rocky Lake	42.	Goose Lake	81.	Lake Vengenance
2.	Lake Wilderness	43.	Little Goose Lake	82.	Hermit Lake
3.	Wood Lake	43a,b.	Ponds	83.	Lake Pieces
3a.-3b.	Unnamed Lakes	44.	Hilltop Lake	84.	Dryad Lake
4.	Five unnamed lakes	45.	Unnamed Lakes	85.	Cimmerian Lake
5.	Woodbine Lake	46.	Huckleberry Lake	86.	Lake Surrender
6.	Nightmare Lake	47.	Mutt Lake	87.	Raven Lake
7.	Sioux Charley Lake	48.	Jeff Lake	88.	Dreary Lake
8.	Cataract Lake	49.	Lake of the Woods	89.	Trouble Lake
9.	Corkscrew Lake	50.	Wildcat Lakes (2)	90.	Clam Lake
10.	Upper Corkscrew Lake	51-53.	Unnamed Lakes	91.	Lake Pinchot
10a-12.	Unnamed Lakes	54.	Aufwuch Lake	92.	Unnamed Lake
13.	Imelda Lake	55.	Mouse Lake	93.	Jay Lake
14-16.	Unnamed Lakes	56.	Favonius Lake	94.	Chalice Lake
17.	Glacier Creek Lake	57, 58.	Unnamed Lake	95.	Lone Ranger Lake
18.	Incisor Lake	59.	Pentad Lake	96.	Mt. View Lake
18a-18c.	Unnamed Lakes	60.	Unnamed Lake	97a.	Horseman Flats Lake
19.	Cavity Lake	61.	Sundown Lake	97b.	Zoeteman Lake
19a.	Unnamed Lake	62.	Jordon Lake	98	Saderbalm Lake
20.	Wrong Lake	63.	Cirque Lake	98a-99.	Saderbalm ponds
21.	Courthouse Lake	64.	Sunken Rock Lake	100.	Tumble Lake
22, 23.	Unnamed Lake	65.	Martes Lake	101.	Unnamed Lake
24.	Sourdough Lake	66.	Barrier Lake	102.	Lightning Lake
25.	Fly Lake	67-69.	Unnamed Lakes	102a.	Little Lightning Lake
26.	Spider Lake	70.	Pipit Lake	102b.	Okeepanokee Lake
27-28.	Unnamed Lakes	71.	Owl Lake	102c-d.	Unnamed Lakes
29.	Lake Aries	72.	Wounded Man Lake	103.	Divide Creek Lake
30-33.	Unnamed Lakes	73.	Diaphanous Lake	104.	S.Picket Pin Lake
34.	Beauty Lake	74.	Roosevelt Lake	105.	North Picket Pin Lake
35.	Puddle Lake	75.	Sienna Lake	106.	Castle Creek Lake
36.	Anvil Lake	76.	Bill Lake	107.	Unnamed Lake
37.	Stardust Lake	77.	Mini Lake		
38.	Panhandle Lake	78.	Needle Lake		
39.	Unnamed Lakes				

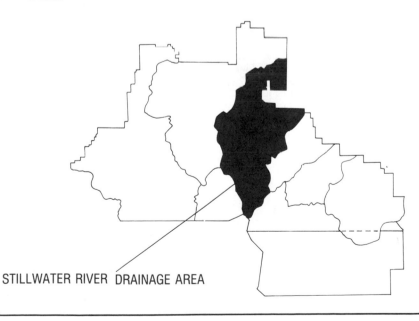

STILLWATER RIVER DRAINAGE AREA

17. GLACIER CREEK LAKE

Location: T8S, R14E, S. 12
Elevation: 8,920 feet
Area: 16.3 acres
Maximum depth: 47 feet

Glacier Creek Lake is surrounded by the Wolf, Sawtooth and Courthouse mountains. No trail exists; however, access is easy from Goose Lake. The lake lies in the timber surrounded by steep slopes, scarred by numerous avalanches.

The lake harbors a nice population of brook trout. The fish were fat and in good shape last time I checked in on them. You'll find good fishing around the inlet and outlet where the brookies average 9 inches in length.

18. INCISOR LAKE

Location: T8S, R15E, S. 18 CA
Elevation: 9,640 feet
Area: 5.9 acres
Maximum depth: 32 feet

This six-acre lake lies in the headwaters of Glacier Creek on the east side of the main Stillwater River. The easiest route is a short hike from Goose Lake, but don't look for a trail. Incisor Lake is the new home for 600 golden trout that were flown in during 1982. Wish them luck.

18a, 18b, 18c. UNNAMED (3) (fishless)

19, 19a. CAVITY, UNNAMED (2) (fishless)

20. WRONG LAKE

Location: T8S, R14E, S. 15A
Elevation: 9,000 feet
Area: 20.6 acres
Maximum depth: 116 feet

This is probably not the right name for Wrong Lake. I dubbed it "Wrong Lake" for two reasons: I had a lad working for me one summer who was directed to this lovely lake to do a job. He went to the wrong lake. To press the name even deeper into my life, when Courthouse Lake was scheduled for stocking some time ago, the fish went to—you guessed it—Wrong Lake. If I were you, I'd go to Wrong Lake because it's the right lake for you.

Situated in a beautiful locale on a small bench below Courthouse Lake and Courthouse Mountain, Wrong Lake is well worth the trip. It was last stocked in 1979, and the survivors should be worthy candidates for your angling skills.

I suggest starting at Goose Creek just downstream from Goose Lake. Follow the shorelines of Wall and Panhandle lakes to Anvil Lake. Press on to Beauty, through Sourdough Basin, to Courthouse Lake. Then pause, take a look down 1,000 feet, and "thar she blows." It will take most of the day to get there, according to my daughters. They elected to accept it as the wrong lake and stayed at Courthouse.

Look for healthy, big cutts in Wrong Lake. Fish the shoreline. I suggest putting a little red on your fly. Spin fishermen might try a casting bubble with five feet of leader, a fly, and a fast retrieve.

21. COURTHOUSE LAKE

Location: T8S, R14E, S. 23B
Elevation: 10,000 feet
Area: 18.8 acres
Maximum depth: 205 feet

This is a dynamite lake, with cutts in excess of two pounds. Watch the stocking dates, however. The last stocking was in 1979, and the lake is on an eight-year frequency. Thus, fishing will be best in '87, '95, etc. Give them three years after stocking for best results. Figure on slow fishing, maybe, after the sixth year, but hang onto your rod. What does bite could be of lunker proportion.

See Wrong Lake for access description. Another route is from the Lake Abundance jeep trail to Beauty Lake and on up to Courthouse. No trails exist. Bring your backpacking stove for camping at Courthouse Lake—fuel is in short supply here.

22. UNNAMED (3) (fishless)

23. UNNAMED (3) (fishless)

24. SOURDOUGH LAKE

Location: T8S, R14E, S. 22 DC
Elevation: 9,529 feet
Area: 2.6 acres
Maximum depth: 22 feet

Directly west of Goose Lake approximately three miles, or halfway to the main Stillwater River, is a group of 10 little lakes. One of them, Sourdough Lake, catches the flow of water from two small lake chains. Collectively these are called the Sourdough Basin lakes (see the code map). Lots of approach routes are feasible (see Wrong Lake for a suggested route). Brook trout are plentiful.

25 & 26. FLY AND SPIDER LAKES

Location: T8S, R14E, S. 22 D
Elevation: 9,760 feet
Area: 2 acres; 6.3 acres
Maximum depth: 38 feet; 61 feet

The northern tributary of Sourdough Lake includes Fly and Spider lakes. Spider is the larger of these two Sourdough Basin lakes which are separated by about 60 yards of stream and full of brook trout. The lake contains lots of quarter-pounders, 8-10 inches in length.

27. UNNAMED (3) (fishless)

28. UNNAMED (4) (fishless)

29. LAKE ARIES

Location: T8S, R14, S. 27 AA
Elevation: 9,570 feet
Area: 3.8 acres
Maximum depth: 32 feet

This one would probably win the beauty contest of the Sourdough lakes. In addition, a crowd of hungry brook trout swarms beneath its shimmering surface. A sample of 61 brook trout averaged 7.8 inches, .15 pounds. The largest was 9.5 inches.

30. UNNAMED (fishless)

31. UNNAMED (fishless)

32. UNNAMED (fishless)

33. UNNAMED (fishless)

34. BEAUTY LAKE

Location: T8S, R14E, S. 2 DBB
Elevation: 9,200 feet
Area: 5.9 acres
Maximum depth: 55 feet

I contemplated leaving Beauty out of the guide for selfish reasons. As it is, this is all I'm saying about it.

35. PUDDLE (fishless)

36. ANVIL LAKE

Location: T8S, R14E, S. 27 D
Elevation: 9,440 feet
Area: 10.1 acres
Maximum depth: 45 feet

Anvil Lake is not a bad hike from the Goose Lake jeep trail or from the Lake Abundance jeep trail. There are plenty of trees around the area.

If you're interested in fisheries investigations, read on; otherwise, go to the next paragraph. Not knowing the stocking pattern when I sampled Anvil Lake, I discovered two size groups in a catch of 37 cutthroat trout, neither very large. About 10 percent of the fish were deformed, as if someone had taken vice grips in front of the tails and given a squeeze and a twist that remained. The fish all proved to be two- and three-year-olds at 7 and 10 inches, respectively. Checking the records, I found that Anvil was on the stocking program for two years in a row and this had severely impacted the individuals in the population. Much later another bunch of cutthroat was planted; they did very well. Upon resampling, I caught some of the new, better shaped fish plus a couple of the original ten-year-olds. The old boys were 14 inches, a little over a pound, and still swam around despite their crooked tails.

Anvil's a good place to fish now. It gets a little breather between plants, so watch the stocking program. It was stocked in 1977 and is scheduled for another in 1986 and every eight years thereafter.

37. STARDUST LAKE (fishless)

38. PANHANDLE LAKE (fishless)

39. UNNAMED (3) (fishless)

40. WALL LAKE (fishless)

41, 41a. UNNAMED (5) (fishless)

42. GOOSE LAKE

Location: T8S, R15E, S. 19, 20
Elevation: 9,830 feet
Area: 102 acres
Maximum depth: 130 feet

Goose Lake provides hikers with a jumping-off spot for many areas, including Grasshopper Glacier. The lake is on the Cooke City side of the hill. Its outlet, however, flows out Goose Creek and around the corner to the north-flowing Stillwater River.

Goose Lake has a population of interesting cutthroat trout—interesting mostly because of the mystery of their origin. The most realistic explanation seems to be that of Bud Hart, who occupied what is now the remains of a cabin at the outlet of Goose Lake from 1906 to 1907. Mr. Hart apparently hauled cutthroat from the Clarks Fork of the Yellowstone River in lard pails to Goose Lake during his prospecting days.

Goose is an ideal fishing spot for cutts, which can reach trophy size. The lake is shadowed in a cold valley between Fox Peak and Mount Zimmer, so the weather can change suddenly. One time, while sampling Goose Lake in March, I found out what it feels like to be in a huge flour bowl. In an attempt to shovel a hole to the ice, I was continually engulfed with fine shifting snow until I had a hole large enough for my pickup. By the time my objectives were complete, I felt like a firmly-planted albino cornstalk. Pardon the corny scenario.

43 & 43a-b. LITTLE GOOSE LAKE AND PONDS

Location: T8S, R15E, S 19A
Elevation: 9,835 feet
Area: 8.1 acres; 1.6 acres; 8 acres
Maximum depth: 23 feet; 7 feet; 3 feet

Little Goose and the two small connecting ponds are up the inlet from Goose Lake. I captured 22 cutts ranging from 7.5 to 16.5 inches in these little lakes. Some of these cutts are probably residents, but then, nothing stops fish travel between Goose and these little lake appendages.

44. HILLTOP LAKE (fishless)

45. UNNAMED (5) (fishless)

From the rocky shores of Goose Lake, it's easy to understand how the Sawtooth Range earned its name. Pat Marcuson photo.

Beartooth country offers fishing fun for all anglers—regardless of how old or how skilled. Bill Schneider photo.

46. HUCKLEBERRY LAKE

Location: T8S, R14E, S. 36D
Elevation: 9,520 feet
Area: 15.3 acres
Maximum depth: 49 feet

Huckleberry Lake is another of those lakes on the Cooke City side. The lake is accessible via jeep trail (Goose Lake) and a short, half mile cross-country hike. Brook trout call it home. I doubt it would take much convincing to catch a 6- to 9-inch fish. It should be against the law to throw any back once removed from the water.

47 & 48. MUTT AND JEFF LAKES

Location: T8S, R14E, S. 36
Elevation: 9,200 feet
Area: 1.5 acres; 1.3 acres, respectively
Maximum depth: 3.5 feet; 4 feet, respectively

Mutt and Jeff lakes are a pair of small meadow ponds accessible by foot or horse from the Goose Lake jeep trail. The lakes are so close to and over such mild gradient from Long Lake, it seems senseless to drive a 4x4. Many ruts scar the landscape just so some can save their energy at the expense of alpine turf. The area around the lakes is timbered with rocky knolls. Brook trout are abundant; nothing large, but tender.

49. LAKE OF THE WOODS

Location: T8S, R13E, S. 1D
Elevation: 8,675 feet
Area: 7.9 acres
Maximum depth: 16 feet

Lake of the Woods is actually surrounded by meadow with timber on all sides. Outflows travel to the Stillwater River via Horseshoe Creek. Trail #34 either from the Stillwater or Horseshoe Basin parallels the southeast shore. Most of the fishing occurs during the early elk hunting season in Slough Creek drainage. The cutts in Lake of the Woods are of the Yellowstone variety. An inspection by fish identification experts revealed these fish as pure-strain aborigine fish. I suspect they were transported from either Slough Creek or the Stillwater River. The lake harbors lots of 6.5- to 11.5-inch fish.

50. WILDCAT LAKES (2) (fishless)

51, 52, 53. UNNAMED (fishless)

54. AUFWUCH LAKE

Location: T7S, R13E, S. 13, 24
Elevation: 8,650 feet
Area: 30 acres
Maximum depth: 28 feet

Aufwuch Lake (the name refers to a unique community of organisms attached to the lake's substrate) drains into the South Fork of Wounded Man Creek in the Stillwater River drainage. I've hiked into Aufwuch Lake from trail #23 on the Middle Fork-Wounded Man Creek and from the Pinnacle-Timberline Mountain divide. You will be done in by this country. It was stocked in 1969 and after that never again. I'm not guaranteeing anything, but I'd bet some reproduction occurs producing a few babies.

55. MOUSE LAKE

Location: T7S, R13E, S. 22 AC
Elevation: 9,650 feet
Area: 6.9 acres
Maximum depth: 30 feet

Look for Mouse Lake between Pinnacle Mountain and Favonius Lake on the Middle Fork-Wounded Man Creek. Since the lake was scheduled for a plant of cutthroat in 1984, you probably ought to wait until 1986 before even thinking about a fishing trip.

56. FAVONIUS (CROW) LAKE

Location: T7S, R13E, S. 15
Elevation: 9,140 feet
Area: 25.5 acres
Maximum depth: 15 feet

Favonius Lake is a peaceful alpine scene and provides a nice spot for an overnighter. Good fishing is almost a guarantee, with nothing too big but nice, colorful 10- to 13-inch fish. Everything with fins appears hybridized; cousins, aunts, uncles, the works, all have a little cutthroat blood and a lot of rainbow blood. Access to the lake is easy from the Columbine area west of Favonius. Another trail follows the Middle Fork of Wounded Man Creek from the maintained trail on the Stillwater River.

57, 58. UNNAMED (fishless)

59. PENTAD (CRAZY MULE) LAKE

Location: T7S, R13E, S. 15
Elevation: 9,362 feet
Area: 40.7 acres
Maximum depth: 58 feet

If it wasn't for a small rock outcrop, Pentad and Favonius would be one body of water. In other words, they're close neighbors. The lake is accessible by horse or foot and the terrain funnels one to Pentad from Jordan Lake, Middle Fork-Wounded Man Creek, or Columbine Pass; take your pick.

Pentad refers to five points around the shoreline; how you perceive the points depends on what you put in your coffee. A local packer lost a spooked mule which unfortunately drowned in the lake, thus the Crazy Mule handle. The lake is a favorite haunt for outfitters. It provides aesthetics, alpine grass, camp spots, and is logistically located—and yes—good fishing. Catches are much the same as in Favonius, with its cutts and 'bows at 9-14 inches, one-third to one pound.

60. UNNAMED LAKE

Location: T7S, R13E, S. 15 B
Elevation: 9,330 feet
Area: 3.6 acres
Maximum depth: U

Unnamed Lake is Pentad's northern neighbor. I'm sure some outfitters have tagged their favorite horse's name on this one. Again we have a fishery that clones the Pentad-Favonius type, hybrids averaging 10 inches with larger fish up to 14 inches.

61. SUNDOWN LAKE

Location: T7S, R13E, S. 10 C
Elevation: 9,500 feet
Area: 5.2 acres
Maximum depth: U

This is a beaut! The outlet of Sundown Lake spills over a small cascade as it escapes downstream. Sundown, like the other Pentad group of lakes, is in the Middle Fork of Wounded Man Creek. This is the second lake north of Pentad: kind of tucked out of the way in its own secluded valley. The lake had the biological clues to suggest trophy fishery potential, plus some opportunity to provide additional recreation. In an area where a lot of the same type of fishing prevailed, a cutthroat fishery was introduced in 1979 and will be again in 1987. Tell your Department of Fish, Wildlife and Parks biologist how good the fishing is or what you see.

62. JORDAN LAKE

Location: T7S, R13E, S. 11
Elevation: 8,790 feet
Area: 14.7 acres
Maximum depth: 35 feet

Access to Jordan Lake is possible through several routes from the numerous trails around Lake Plateau. The Middle Fork of Wounded Man Creek lifts one out of the

Stillwater Valley. You're looking at 20-22 miles from the trailhead at Woodbine. You could approach from Columbine Pass or Rainbow or Upsidedown Creek trails, another 16-20 mile trek. No wonder horses are a popular means of transport. However, for the hiker, lots of opportunities for numerous excursions await you once established on Lake Plateau. So don't count Jordan out.

Jordan Lake provides lots of cutts and is a fun lake to fish. Usually lots of fish action and a tasty prize for the pan.

63. CIRQUE (fishless)

64. SUNKEN ROCK LAKE

Location: T7S, R13E, S. 3 DC
Elevation: 9,250 feet
Area: 11.1 acres
Maximum depth: 30 feet

Sunken Rock Lake is a scenic lake in the Jordan Pass area of Lake Plateau. The name derives from the large submerged rock on the northeast shore. It probably has other handles as well. Access is by horse or foot and fuel is plentiful.

The lake has good summer feed for trout and has produced fish up to three pounds. However, one problem exists: the fish tend to spawn in the outlet stream and away go the babies when venturing out of the egg.

It could have a few fish by now, but I can't guarantee it. It was on the list as a potential golden trout lake but was dropped when better golden habitat was considered.

65. MARTES LAKE

Location: T7S, R13E, S. 2, 3
Elevation: 9,150 feet
Area: 17.5 acres
Maximum depth: 33 feet

The biggest cutts in the country were produced from the first plant ever made in this lake in 1969. It was restocked in 1979 and should contain some fish worthy of attention. It's on an eight-year stocking cycle, with the continued goal of producing trophy types. Martes Lake is one of those rare lakes with dual outlets. The lake is special for scenic value and pristine character. Treat it respectfully and everyone can enjoy the natural beauty.

It's on the Middle Fork of Wounded Man Creek and you have to cross-country from trail #23 through Jordan Pass to get there. It's worth it.

66. BARRIER LAKE

Location: T7S, R13E, S. 1
Elevation: 8,150 feet
Area: 42.4 acres
Maximum depth: 130 feet

Another high class scene: even the old fire scar has an appeal about it. The shoreline is predominantly large talus rock with little camping comfort except near the outlet and upper inlet meadow. The in-flowing water disappears under large rocks, so don't drop your cup.

Barrier Lake is on the North Fork of Wounded Man Creek, north and east of Jordan Mountain. It's easy walking or riding country from trail #23.

Look for very colorful rainbow and golden hybrids. I didn't find any large ones but I'm sure rod action can be exercised on an accumulated mass of beautiful fish.

67. UNNAMED (fishless)

68-70. UNNAMED (2) AND PIPIT LAKES

Location: T6S, R13E, S. 34 B
Elevation: 9,475 feet
Area: 2.6 acres; 2.3 acres; 2.0 acres, respectively
Maximum depth: 5 feet; 6 feet; 25 feet, respectively

This little stranger of wide waters is west of Wounded Man Lake right between the fork of trails #23 and #43. Pipit Lake tops the chain at 9,580 feet, and the toe lake (#68) is at

Wade Marcuson, 9, hoists two cutthroats taken from Martes Lake, where stocking cycles have produced the biggest cutts in the country. Pat Marcuson photo.

9,475 feet. Access is easy on Lake Plateau with lots of alpine grass, rolling terrain, and scattered timbered pockets.

Lots of rainbow and cutthroat hybrids frequent this appendage of the North Fork of Wounded Man Creek. The larger inhabitants were 15 inches.

71. OWL LAKE

Location: T6S, R13E, S. 27 C
Elevation: 9,541 feet
Area: 14.4 acres
Maximum depth: 30 feet

For those who have picked another name, I'm sorry. I arbitrarily related the owl shape of the hydrographic map to a pair of owls observed in 1969. It's not an official name, so have at it. I'm referring to the 14-acre lake northwest of Wounded Man Lake near the trail the Forest Service calls #121. The lake has lots of foot-long rainbow trout.

72. WOUNDED MAN LAKE

Location: T6S, R13E, S. 35 B
Elevation: 9,248 feet
Area: 50.2 acres
Maximum depth: 55 feet

One of the most popular lakes on Lake Plateau, this lake is located on the northernmost tributary of North Fork of Wounded Man Creek. Several trails serve the area. Hikers often ask the best route to Lake Plateau, but it's difficult to generalize. For those departing from the Boulder River side, which is shorter than the Stillwater route, your choice is the steep, get-it-over-with trail along Upsidedown Creek, or the longer, mellower Rainbow Creek trail. The Upsidedown route gets the hiker to the Plateau lakes and to the better fishing waters faster. Stillwater Trail #23 parallels Wounded Man on the west side. This area serves as a base camp for numerous outfitters who then have a choice of several nearby lakes to fish for colorful trout. Another route takes one up the West Fork of the Stillwater River. Wounded Man Lake contains a combination of rainbow, cutthroat, and mixtures of the two.

73. DIAPHANOUS LAKE

Location: T6S, R13E, S. 26, 27
Elevation: 9,631 feet
Area: 9.2 acres
Maximum depth: 25 feet

Diaphanous Lake sits at the intersection of trails #23 and #90 on Lake Plateau. Reduce speed and be sure to signal at the corner. It's the first lake viewed by those visiting Lake Plateau from the West Fork of the Stillwater trail #90.

Wounded Man Lake, one of the most popular Lake Plateau lakes, is used as a base camp by numerous outfitters. U.S. Forest Service photo.

No fish existed prior to an introduction of rainbow trout in 1980. Fresh water shrimp inhabit Diaphanous Lake and should provide excellent dining for the new residents.

74. ROOSEVELT LAKE (fishless)

75. SIENNA LAKE (fishless)

76-95. FLOOD CREEK LAKES
The gang of six lakes from the Pinchot Fork, two from Rabbit Gulch, one isolated lake, and seven from the Two Sisters Fork, collectively with four more lakes constitute the bulk of the Flood Creek Lake system. Confused? Read on. Flood Creek makes a quick exit down-valley over a waterfalls and into the Stillwater River upstream from Sioux Charley Lake. I rate the drainage an *A* as a fishery based on quantity, quality, and vivid color. There is not much pureness in species except for the newly introduced golden trout in the Two Sisters group of lakes. The mixture of golden, rainbow, and cutthroat and the degree to which each of these fish has mixed has developed in them a touch of hybrid vigor. By vigor, I mean the added degree fish grow as a result of varied blood lines.

Lake Pinchot, named after Gifford Pinchot, a former National Forest Service chief, was the site of a 1938 introduction of 12,000 golden trout. Not long after the golden introductions, the first aerial plants of rainbow trout in Montana were made in the 1930s in several "undesignated lakes" on Lake Plateau. But where did the cutthroat trout stock get introduced, and when and by whom? Jordan Lake has a long history of cutts. Were they transported to Pinchot by sheepherders or outfitters?

Access to Flood Creek is best from Lake Plateau. However, the route up Flood Creek is possible; in fact, remnants of an old trail along the edge of Cathedral Peak can provide a route that dodges the waterfalls. Beware—mosquitoes in vast quantities have been known to blanket one's entire surface area during the peak of their emergence. The meadows and standing water along the upper Flood Creek contribute to the pests' success.

76. BILL LAKE
Location: T6S, R14E, S. 20 AD
Elevation: 8,380 feet
Area: 10.4 acres
Maximum depth: 28 feet
This is the first lake encountered while traveling upstream from the mouth of Flood Creek. The shoreline is mostly timbered and at one time was rarely visited. Campsites and trash were not present, so please keep it that way.

A sample of 37 fish ranging from rainbow, cutthroat, and golden trout to hybrid combinations of the lot were examined. The average length and weight of the fish were 11 inches and .40 pounds. Fish ranged from 6.5 to 15.2 inches and were in excellent shape. Try the log jam in the outlet for excellent evening casting.

77. MINI LAKE
Location: T6S, R14E, S. 20 DB
Elevation: 8,430 feet
Area: 1.4 acres
Maximum depth: 8 feet
The second lake encountered up Flood Creek is a widewater in a meadow a few hundred feet upstream from Bill Lake. Hybrid fish of cutthroat, rainbow, and golden trout conglomerations are numerous. This area provides excellent stream, meadow, and lake fishing for some of the most colorful trout in the world.

78, 79, 80, & 83. NEEDLE, COMET, ASTEROID, AND PIECES LAKES
Location: T6S, R14E, S. 29, 30, 32
Elevation: 9,130-9,630 feet
Area: 2.3 acres; 6.3 acres; 3.2 acres; 9.9 acres, respectively
Maximum depth: 4 feet; 47 feet; 40 feet; 80 feet, respectively

This is the group of lakes in the Two Sisters fork of Flood Creek that were stocked with golden trout in 1982. Don't expect development very fast because the plant was a small introductory one. We should know if reproduction has occurred by 1987. It takes a female golden four years to become sexually mature, and then, the progeny take two years to reach a size large enough to sample. The fish were nearly one year old when planted in 1982.

The best way to get to this group of lakes is to follow the stream. Access is best by foot and camping is best along the main branch of Flood Creek.

81. LAKE VENGEANCE (fishless)

82. HERMIT LAKES (fishless)

84. DRYAD LAKE (fishless)

85. CIMMERIAN LAKE
Location: T6S, R14E, S. 19, 20
Elevation: 8,580 feet
Area: 18.8 acres
Maximum depth: 30 feet

A super fishery for color and real dandies. Cimmerian is a long, 19-acre beauty on the main branch of Flood Creek. Best access is from Lake Plateau. A fisherman's path and increased horse travel have entrenched a trail to the lake shore. Take your mosquito repellent.

86. LAKE SURRENDER
Location: T6S, R14E, S. 19 B
Elevation: 8,625 feet
Area: 9.1 acres
Maximum depth: 40 feet

Ever gone crazy from pesky mosquitos? I thought I was close here at this meadow-type area surrounding Lake Surrender. When finishing the job of sounding the lake's depths, my summer helper, Joe Ferguson, literally took off on a dead run through the brush. I could hear brush snapping and a few silence-breaking utterances from this normally quiet, mellow individual. From year to year the situation changes, and—who knows—maybe you will arrive during low skeeter density. I hope so, because Lake Surrender has some bragging sized trout. Flip a coin for ID: some trout are recognizable as rainbow and/or goldens, and others look mostly like cutts; but the majority are somewhere inbetwixt. Big fish swim the confines of this Flood Creek Lake.

87. RAVEN LAKE
Location: T6S, R13E, S. 24, 25
Elevation: 8,750 feet
Area: 10 acres
Maximum depth: 46 feet

The second lake below Lake Pinchot is good old Raven Lake, full of colorful golden trout hybrids. There are super inlets and outlets in this beauty. Access is by foot or horse from Lake Plateau or by a tough foot trip up Flood Creek.

The fish don't range as big as is typical in the lower Flood Creek Lakes. Reproductive conditions are probably a bit too good for the amount of fishing pressure. Nonetheless, Raven puts out lots of recreation with fish to 16 inches.

88. DREARY LAKE
Location: T6S, R13E, S. 25C
Elevation: 9,040 feet
Area: 15.5 acres
Maximum depth: 12 feet

The first lake below Lake Pinchot on upper Flood Creek. Access is easy by a fisherman's trail. It's a great lake for lots of colorful fish, mostly golden trout. Hybrids show more golden trout characteristics than common elsewhere in the Flood Creek chain of lakes. I have caught some fish to 18 inches in Dreary; however, most will average 9 inches.

89. TROUBLE LAKE (fishless)

90. CLAM LAKE (fishless)

91. LAKE PINCHOT
Location: T6S, R13E, S. 26
Elevation: 9,260 feet
Area: 53.9 acres
Maximum depth: 30 feet

Pinchot Lake, at 54 acres, is the largest in the Flood Creek Lake system. It is also the most popular camping spot on Lake Plateau. There is plenty of fuel for campfires and access routes are through open, easily hikeable country. Trails exist throughout the area.

Pinchot was stocked in 1938 with golden trout secured from Cottonwood Lakes in California's Sierra-Nevada Mountain Range. Rainbow and cutthroat were stocked later. Fishing is good for lots of colorful hybrid trout.

92. UNNAMED (fishless)

93. JAY LAKE
Location: T6S, R13E, S. 14 D
Elevation: 9,600 feet
Area: 23.7 acres
Maximum depth: 48 feet

Jay lake is a spectacular site from the heights of Chalice Peak. Camping is best away from the shore, especially if you like sunshine. The only tree cover is near the outlet, and it is sparse. The route up Rabbit Gul requires a 1,000-foot climb from Flood Creek. One can, however, pick a route around Chalice Peak from the Plateau.

Jay Lake was stocked August 17, 1977, with 2,300 cutthroat trout of the McBride variety. The lake received so little angling pressure that it was dropped from the stocking program.

94. CHALICE LAKE (fishless)

95. LONE RANGER LAKE (fishless)

96. MOUNTAIN VIEW (MOUAT) LAKE
Location: T5S, R15E, S. 20
Elevation: 6,750 feet
Area: 4.0 acres
Maximum depth: 13 feet

This lake has a few fish, but it is of little significance as a trout fishery. The lake is partly man-made with water piped in from the south. The old mining town of Mouat borders the lake. A road leads to Mountain View Lake but it is closed by a locked gate. It would be nice if some angling opportunity could be established if access was ever opened; however, the lake would need some modifications to be a trout fishery. Maybe largemouth bass would take.

97a. NO KETCHUM (HORSEMAN FLATS) LAKE
Location: T5S, R15E, S. 9
Elevation: 5,466 feet
Area: 1.9 acres
Maximum depth: 47 feet

I believe most maps label the lake Horseman Flats Lake. It is not really on Horseman Flats but on the route to it. The Mikelson Land Company owns the easiest access: the Cathedral Mountain Subdivision on the east. The lake is on Custer National Forest Land and can be approached on the road from Mouat mill to Horseman Flats. It is a poor fishery for rainbow trout.

97b. ZOETEMAN LAKE (fishless)

98. SADERBALM LAKE

Location: T6S, R14E, S. 5B
Elevation: 8,980 feet
Area: 7.4 acres
Maximum depth: 29 feet

Up Saderbalm Creek from the West Fork Stillwater River is this seven-acre lake. No trail exists from #90 on the West Fork. By trail from Initial Creek it is about 3.5 miles and then the work begins with a 2,200 foot elevation increase for the next three or four miles. I find access easier from Horseman Flats.

The lake does not have fish yet, but is scheduled for grayling; even at that, it is not a high priority plant.

98a & 99. SADERBALM PONDS (5) (fishless)

100. TUMBLE AND LITTLE TUMBLE (JASPER) LAKES

Location: T6S, R14E, S. 6B
Elevation: 9,080 feet; 9,180 feet, respectively
Area: 53.2 acres; 8.9 acres, respectively
Maximum depth: 77 feet; 8 feet, respectively

After a six-mile hike up trail #90 along the West Fork Stillwater River, a non-trail climb for 2.25 very steep miles awaits you. Once there, the opportunity for superb angling for large cutts is in store for you. Camping is ideal near the inlet and along the east shoreline. Once in the area, a side trip to Lightning Lake is recommended.

Tumble has been producing some exceptional fishing since first stocked in 1968. I've spent some enjoyable time here because of high quality, large-bodied fish. As time progresses, the lake's cutthroat population supports itself because of the excellent gravels in the inlet stream needed for egg incubation. If reproductive success gets too good, the trout population will increase to a point exceeding the food production needed to grow large fish. Let's hope the stream spawning site is not that good.

101. UNNAMED (fishless)

102. LIGHTNING LAKE

Location: T6S, R13E, S. 2
Elevation: 9,340 feet
Area: 61.3 acres
Maximum depth: 122 feet

From Lake Plateau, Lightning Lake is an easy jaunt around Chalice Peak. From the West Fork of the Stillwater, it's easy going from Initial Creek trailhead to Lightning Creek via trail. From Lightning Creek's confluence with the West Fork of the Stillwater, it's a tough pull and can be a nightmare if you choose the wrong route.

The easiest climbing is on the west side of Lightning Creek. Stay out of the creek drainage. This route takes you to the plateau country above Lightning Lake. Nobody likes climbing higher than necessary, but it is better than the downfall jungle encountered between Lightning and Tumble Creeks.

Lightning provides special memories for me because of numerous trips to study its extraordinary fish, the golden trout. Lightning Lake is by far the best golden trout fishery for several reasons. The goldens are pure-strain, achieve large size, are located in unspoiled country, and are self-sustaining but not overpopulated. To top it off, between Little Lightning and Lightning one can catch a dozen. The large lake can be hot or cold: when it's hot, look for a state record, and when it's cold, Little Lightning will produce lots of smaller but colorful trout.

Goldens are notorious for their stubborn resistance to a hook. In fact, many a golden trout lake was ruined because of complaints of no fish, followed by the stocking of another species, and a resulting crop of hybrids. The larger fish disappear after the spawning season when they seek the depths of the lake to feed on larger bottom organisms. If that doesn't suggest fishing deep, we're not communicating.

102a. LITTLE LIGHTNING

Location: T6S, R13E, S. 2 DA
Elevation: 9,280 feet
Area: 6.9 acres
Maximum depth: 12 feet

Just downstream from Lightning we find Little Lightning, an essential part of the Lightning Lake system because of the role it plays in the golden trout's survival. Because golden trout spawn in warmer outlet waters and the juveniles tend to move helplessly down current after birth, Little Lightning provides a catchment basin for these helpless little fellows. The lake is essentially a nursery and rearing area. When the fish become adolescents they move back up Lightning Creek to the big lake to visit their parents. Golden trout dwelling in lakes without the likes of a Little Lightning are usually short-termers.

102b. OKEEPANOKEE (fishless)

102c. UNNAMED (fishless)

102d. UNNAMED (fishless)

103. DIVIDE CREEK (fishless)

104. SOUTH PICKET PIN LAKE

Location: T5S, R14E, S. 6 CA
Elevation: 9,025 feet
Area: 5.0 acres
Maximum depth: 19 feet

There are two lakes on upper Picket Pin Creek, this one is on the South Fork. Look for it outside the A-B Wilderness Area near the Picket Pin road. It can be reached by 4x4 vehicle. The lake is marginal because of its shallowness and abundance of aquatic vegetation, thus subject to winter kill.

On the plus side, it has an abundant fresh water shrimp population and should provide good growth for the cutthroat trout. It is also close and can provide a semi-mountain fishing experience for those anglers limited on time. Picket Pin Lake is stocked on frequent occasion and should provide angling most anytime.

105. NORTH PICKET PIN LAKE

Location: T5S, R14E, S. 6 AC
Elevation: 8,825 feet
Area: 5.3 acres
Maximum depth: 24 feet

This Picket Pin Lake is somewhat larger, deeper, and more stable than the shallower South Picket Pin Lake. Look for it outside of the wilderness area on the north branch of Picket Pin Creek. The lake was planted with cutthroat trout that were taken from Big Timber Trout Hatchery in 1968 but were winter killed in 1970. It was stocked again in 1972, '79, and '82.

106. CASTLE CREEK (fishless)

107. UNNAMED (fishless)

Boulder River Drainage

'Over the mountains we were flying at altitudes of eleven to thirteen thousand feet, with nothing but rock-walled canyons, lakes, and snow-capped peaks for emergency landing had our motor failed. Tarrant finished his last trip with the Stearman at dusk, having traveled about 480 air miles, most at over 10,000 feet above sea level, planted 15,000 fish from two to five inches in length in approximately four hours flying time, and into one of the toughest places in the mountains.'' Thus Herman Hendrickson described the first fish stocked in Montana by airplane in 1939 in a report to the Billings Rod and Gun Club. The report bore the title, ''Stocking Isolated Virgin Mountain Lake with Young Fish for the Future Sportsman When Civilization Shall Have Pushed Trails into the Now Inaccessible Primitive Areas.''

Some of the recipients of these first fish dropped from an aircraft were lakes on Lake Plateau. Rainbow trout were supplied by the Fish and Game Department with the approval of Superintendent of Montana State Fisheries John W. Schofield. Once these initial plants were established, it became a common practice by private citizens to transplant fish to nearby lakes. That activity is now forbidden by state law.

The mountain lakes of the Boulder country number 103, but like the West Rosebud area, the lakes with fish are not plentiful. New introductions in recent years have pushed the total with trout up from 13 percent to 36 percent. There are three areas where most of the fishable lakes are found: Lake Plateau, Elk and Bridge Lakes, and the headwaters of Fourmile, Spectacular and Falls Creeks. These are not the only areas, but they surpass all other Boulder locales for alpine fishing opportunities.

The Boulder River drains 425 square miles of the Gallatin National Forest and another 131 square miles of lands in private ownership. The forest area is administered by the Big Timber Ranger District. Towns of McLeod and Big Timber are included in the Boulder River Valley. A large majority of the drainage within the Forest is in the Absaroka-Beartooth Wilderness Area. Fifty-seven lakes are in Park County while 46 are in Sweet Grass County.

The Boulder River separates two geologic areas, the granitic Beartooths to the east and the combination volcanic and granitic Absaroka range to the west. The Absaroka becomes considerably more unique towards its southern end, where volcanic intrusions, conglomerates, petrified trees, and the like replace the granite configuration to the north.

The 103 lakes cover 586 acres ranging from .2 to 39.7 acres in size. Kaufman (Falls Creek) Lake is the largest, Mirror Lake the deepest. Sixty-five percent of the lakes are located in the 9,000-10,000 foot elevation zone. An unnamed lake (#13) near Mirror Lake is the highest lake in the Boulder River drainage at 10,070 feet.

Some 23 lakes located near the Boulder River are accessible by vehicle. Another 54 are accessible by horse travel and 26 are restricted to foot traffic. Trails exist on Upsidedown Creek, Rainbow Creek, Bridge Creek, Meatrack, Fourmile, Great Falls Creek, Falls Creek, Davis Creek, and along the West Fork Boulder River. Access is also possible from the Yellowstone River on the west, Buffalo Fork to the south, and the Stillwater River on the east.

Probably the most unique characteristic in the Boulder is the lack of brook trout, one shared only with its neighboring drainages to the south—Slough, Buffalo Park, and Hell Roaring Creeks. Brookies were widely dispersed in the Beartooths in the 1920s. The Boulder River country was one of the last drainages in the A-B Mountains to receive significant numbers of fish. Long distances, steep climbs, and tough terrain left the area untrammeled and unstocked until recent times.

1. UNNAMED (fishless)

2. MOCCASIN LAKE (fishless)

3. CAMP LAKE

Location: T4S, R13E, S. 21, 22
Elevation: 8,995 feet
Area: 7.8 acres
Maximum depth: 58 feet

Camp Lake, very scenic and reasonably accessible, is located at the head of Canyon Creek, a tributary of the East Boulder River, four miles northeast of Chrome Mountain. Considerable mineral exploration in the Brownlee Creek area will be encountered enroute, but the lake itself is calm and, except for occasional blasting next door, still an exceptional recreational opportunity.

It has a population of cutthroat trout of the Yellowstone variety. A sample produced evidence of self-sustaining (naturally reproducing) fishery with fish averaging 10 inches. No hatchery records or historic records were located to explain the origin of these fish.

4. NARROW ESCAPE LAKE

Location: T6S, R13E, S. 19
Elevation: 9,340 feet
Area: 11.6 acres
Maximum depth: 20 feet

Narrow Escape Lake is long and slender and jammed between two ridges in the headwaters of Hawley Creek, a tributary of the Boulder River. Look for it on the west side of Mt. Douglas. The lake is accessible without trail from Rainbow and/or Mirror Lakes.

Cutthroat were stocked in the 1970s and produced fish from one-half to three pounds. The lake has enough inlet to allow a reproducing population. It also has a terrific food base which should allow continued good growth.

5. SQUEEZE LAKE

Location: T6S, R13E, S. 19, 20
Elevation: 9,535 feet
Area: 7.0 acres
Maximum depth: 45 feet

If you look at the code map you will see Squeeze Lake at the head of Hawley Creek, just upstream from Narrow Escape Lake. Again, I recommend walking in from Mirror Lake on Lake Plateau. No trail exists, but overland travel is not difficult.

After a survey in 1969 the lake was placed on the stocking program. The fish were not delivered and the lake remained fishless until 1979. It should be red hot in the mid-1980s and is proposed for restocking every eight years. My bet is that it will be the talk of the town—lots of lies about the location of this lake will be generated in the local barbershop.

6. HELICOPTER LAKE (fishless)

7. HAWLEY LAKE (fishless)

8. EMERALD LAKE (fishless)

9. LOWER HICKS LAKE (fishless)

10. UPPER HICKS LAKE (fishless)

11. HORSESHOE LAKE

Location: T6S, R12E, S. 36
Elevation: 9,490 feet
Area: 15.9 acres
Maximum depth: 10 feet

Just as you breach the top of the Upsidedown Creek Trail and start traveling plateau grasslands, you will come to Horseshoe Lake, a horseshoe shaped wide spot in Upsidedown Creek that is surrounded by alpine grass and scattered conifers.

It is shallow with little water over five feet deep. Prior to August 1970 it was fishless. Eight years later I rechecked the new fishery and found fish that averaged 13 inches and .75 pounds. The larger cutts were 14 inches and juvenile fish were visible. If this lake doesn't winterkill, it will remain a naturally producing fishery.

Boulder River Drainage

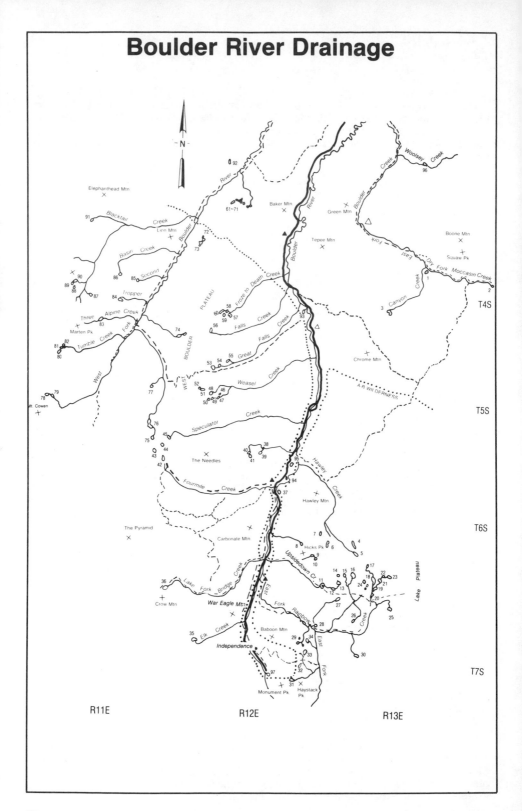

1. Unnamed Lakes
2. Moccasin Lake
3. Camp Lake
4. Narrow Escape Lake
5. Squeeze Lake
6. Helicopter Lake
7. Hawley Lake
8. Emerald Lake
9. Lower Hicks Lakes
10. Upper Hicks Lakes
11. Horseshoe Lake
12. Diamond Lake
13. Unnamed Lake
14. Unnamed Lake
15. Chickadee Lake
16. Mirror Lake
17-23. Rainbow Lakes
24. Unnamed Lakes
25. Fish Lake
26. Burnt Gulch Lake
27. Lake Raymond
28. Lake Kathleen
29a-b. Unnamed Lake
30. Lake Columbine
31. Blue Lake
32. Lamb Lake
33. Wool Lake
34. Mutton Lake
35. Elk Lake
36. Bridge Lake
37. Trout Lake
38-41. Bramble Creek Lakes
42. Silver Lake
43. Prospect Lake
44. Patient Lake
45. Speculator Lake
46-52. Weasel Lakes
53-55. Great Falls Creek Lakes
56. Falls Creek Lake
57-60. Froze to Death Lakes
61-71. Nurses Lakes
72-73. Lost Lakes
74. Icicle Lake
75. West Boulder Lake
76. Kaufman Lake
77. Pocket Lake
78. Yodel Lake
79. Unnamed Lake
80-82. Tumble Creek Lakes
83. Alpine Lake
84. Trapper Lake
85. Second Creek Lake
86. Basin Creek Lake
87. Davis Lake
88. Scout Lake
89-90. McKnight Lakes
91. Blacktail Lake
92. Horseshoe Lake
93. Ball Noah Lake
94. Jarrets Pond (private)
95. Unnamed Beaver Pond
96. Woolsey (private) Pond
97. Unnamed Beaver Pond

PRIMARY ROAD — — — — —
SECONDARY ROAD— — — —
TRAIL — — — — — — — —
PAVED ROAD ——————
CAMPGROUND △
RANGER STATION ▲
MOUNTAIN +
ABSAROKA — BEARTOOTH ·····
WILDERNESS BOUNDARY

½ 1   2   3
MILES

BOULDER RIVER
DRAINAGE AREA

12. DIAMOND LAKE *(fishless)*

13. UNNAMED *(fishless)*

14. UNNAMED *(fishless)*

15. CHICKADEE LAKE
Location: T6S, R13E, S. 30 CA
Elevation: 9,690 feet
Area: 4 acres
Maximum depth: 8 feet

An experimental plant of cutthroat trout was introduced into Chickadee in 1978. The main objective was to evaluate the carrying capacity of a spring-type environment. I really don't know if they survived. The lake is just west of Mirror Lake and in easily traveled country.

16. MIRROR LAKE
Location: T6S, R13E, S. 30
Elevation: 9,740 feet
Area: 16.4 acres
Maximum depth: 80 feet

Mirror Lake is on Lake Plateau, a mile and a half north of trail #26 (Upsidedown Creek Trail) and about seven miles from the jump-off spot on the Boulder River. Cross country access is nice, with alpine fauna, scattered trees, and excellent camping.

There is a nice population of fat rainbow, mostly 11 inches, good fighters and lots of fun.

17. RAINBOW LAKE *(fishless)*

18-23. RAINBOW LAKES (6)
Location: T6S, R13E, S. 28, 29, 32, 33
Elevation: 9,395-9,658 feet
Area: 17.5 acres; 6.8 acres; 7.9 acres; 5.1 acres; 2.4 acres; 9.5 acres, respectively.
Maximum depth: 30 feet; 25 feet; 34 feet; 12 feet; 10 feet; 24 feet, respectively.

Rainbow Lakes are a composite of seven lakes in the headwaters of Rainbow Creek. Six of the seven have rainbow trout. The northernmost headwater lake contains no fish. The lakes (see code map) are at the junction of several trails, many not shown on Forest Service or U.S. Geological Survey maps. The entire area has plenty of campsites and fuel for campfires.

The largest of the Rainbow Lakes (18 acres) has a nice population of rainbow and cutthroat trout hybrids. A mess of fourteen fish averaged 11 inches and .5 pounds, and were in excellent condition. The biggest fish were rainbow trout in Lake #21. Several 13-inch 'bows, many nearly a pound, were produced. The fish in lakes #21, 22, and 23 had little cutthroat influence. Don't pass up these lakes for more primitive locations without giving them a fair chance.

24. UNNAMED *(fishless)*

25. FISH LAKE
Location: T6S, R13E, S. 4
Elevation: 9,472 feet
Area: 18 acres
Maximum depth: 45 feet

An 18-acre beauty located in alpine grandeur on a bench at the headwaters of the South Fork of Rainbow Creek. No lawn has ever been landscaped like this distribution of alpine grasses, flowers, and scattered conifers. Access is via trails from numerous directions in the Lake Plateau area. The final assault is without trail and will hopefully remain so.

The cutts in Fish Lake take care of themselves; no help is needed from the Montana Department of Fish, Wildlife and Parks. I saw fish from babies to 12 inches—probably a few too many fish for their own welfare, but who cares with aesthetics like this?

26. BURNT GULCH LAKE

Location: T7S, R13E, S. 5, 6, 7, 8
Elevation: 9,040 feet
Area: 9.1 acres
Maximum depth: 43 feet

Burnt Gulch lies in a small basin between two forks of Rainbow Creek. The area burned long ago; the old fire-scarred snags are beautifully carved and time has given them a color all their own.

Burnt Gulch Lake is reached by hiking cross-country from Rainbow or Upsidedown creeks, the latter route being considerably easier. Cutthroat trout were stocked for the first time in 1970. No follow-up was made and the present status of the fish is unknown. Let me know.

27. LAKE RAYMOND *(fishless)*

28. LAKE KATHLEEN *(fishless)*

29a. UNNAMED *(fishless)*

29b. UNNAMED *(fishless)*

30. LAKE COLUMBINE

Location: T7S, R13E, S. 17
Elevation: 9,132 feet
Area: 5.3 acres
Maximum depth: 10 feet

Reached by Columbine Pass trail #30, Lake Columbine and its setting are stunning: a big meadow environment with alpine floral arrangements. The one thing lacking is a fishery, but I include Columbine with the fishy lakes because it is scheduled for a plant of grayling. It is a fitting beauty for the scene.

31. BLUE LAKE

Location: T7S, R12E, S. 27
Elevation: 9,460 feet
Area: 10.2 acres
Maximum depth: 27 feet

Blue Lake is at the northeast foot of Haystack Peak, near the old mining town of Independence. Access is possible by 4x4 vehicle from the Boulder River Canyon.

Blue Lake is stocked at intervals with McBride variety cutthroat trout from the Big Timber Trout Hatchery. At one time too many fish were stocked and growth was poor; but recent years have produced nice fat, pink-meated fish. It was last stocked in 1981 and is scheduled every four years.

32. LAMB LAKE *(fishless)*

33. WOOL LAKE *(fishless)*

34. MUTTON LAKE *(fishless)*

35. ELK LAKE

Location: T7S, R11E, S. 14A
Elevation: 9,480 feet
Area: 9.2 acres
Maximum depth: 22 feet

Approximately eight trail miles, if you can find it, from the trailhead, if you can find it, from the Boulder River road, this is a hot dog lake in country that has a greenish summer shade and very autumnal late summer coloration, very spectacular and placed in a grand setting.

I'm sorry, Mr. Kozniewski, but it never had cutthroat until 1977 when I had it stocked. The lake has considerable glacial silt which will not allow spawning. This is a super lake to fish for large, heavy-bodied, pink-meated cutts, and also a nice place to sit back and enjoy the mountain goats which frequent the shoreline.

You had better watch the stocking schedule for best fishing luck. The plan called for another plant in 1984 and one every six years thereafter. Growth is rapid and two-year-olds will be nice fish, but watch out for the three-year and older guys.

36. BRIDGE LAKE

Location: T6S, R11E, S. 34
Elevation: 9,585 feet
Area: 13.9 acres
Maximum depth: 42 feet

The splendor of this place can't be described. Like Elk Lake, it has volcanic, conglomerated rock, petrified wood, and contrasting colors, and the fishing matches the scene. Bridge Lake, where some of the best cutthroat trout in Montana grew up, has a reputation of producing large ones. I personally caught a cutt 21.5 inches long, 4.8 pounds on a number 12 gray-hackle peacock with a red tail. I suggest fishing the shallow shorelines and casting from a camouflaged locale.

Bridge Lake is located at the northeast base of Crow Mountain on trail #25. The trailhead is eight miles away on the west side of the Boulder River. Be prepared for a steep ascent at both ends of the journey.

37. TROUT (BRAY'S) LAKE

Location: T6S, R12E, S. 4
Elevation: 6,140 feet
Area: 0.9 acres
Maximum depth: 5 feet

This small lake is in the valley bottom near the Boulder River road. It's mostly 2-5 feet in depth with rooted aquatic plants around the shoreline. Find it north of the Hillary Bridge across the Boulder River. The surrounding land is both public and private. The lake has an abundant supply of freshwater shrimp which provide feed to the stocked trout, usually rainbow but sometimes cutthroat.

38, 39 & 41. BRAMBLE CREEK LAKES (4)

Location: T5S, R12E, S. 28, 29
Elevation: 8,350-8,775 feet
Area: 1.2 acres; 3.3 acres; 4.1 acres, respectively
Maximum depth: 3 feet; 26 feet; 70 feet, respectively

Bramble Creek has a group of four lakes, three of which provide homes for cutthroat trout (see code map). Lake #38 is a very shallow, boulder-strewn collection of water from two forks of Bramble Creek. An occasional fish from Lake #39 finds a home in this pool. The lake with cutthroat since 1965 is 425 feet upstream from lake #38. Both lakes are in the pines with a good portion of boulders. Bramble Creek Lake (#39) has fish that are typically 10-12 inches long. A small plant of 615 cutthroat trout was delivered to lake #41 in 1979, and it will be stocked every eight years.

40. BRAMBLE CREEK (fishless)

42. SILVER LAKE

Location: T5S, R11E, S. 34
Elevation: 9,046 feet
Area: 10 acres
Maximum depth: 30 feet

At the head of Fourmile Creek and reached by trail #22 from the Forest Guard station on the Boulder River, this lake, very scenic, is in the timber and camp spots are plentiful.

Silver has good-sized rainbow. In fact, the largest I ever sampled in a mountain lake were recorded right here. I have no idea how or when the 'bows were stocked. I do know they grow well. One sample of six averaged 13 inches and one pound. It takes a 15-incher in the mid-Yellowstone River to make a pound of flesh.

43. PROSPECT LAKE (fishless)

44. PATIENT LAKE (fishless)

Mountain goats frequent the shoreline of Elk Lake, below Crow Mountain, and heavy-bodied cutthroats swim there. Pat Marcuson photo.

Prospect Lake, above, and Patient Lake, below, are among 66 lakes in the Boulder River drainage with no fish. Pat Marcuson photos.

45. SPECULATOR LAKE

Location: T5S, R11E, S. 27 AC
Elevation: 9,449 feet
Area: 9.7 acres
Maximum depth: 35 feet

This 10-acre lake is located east of Boulder Mountain in the headwaters of Speculator Creek. The old trail, unless recently improved, is a mess. Access is easier from the Fourmile or Great Falls Creek trails. Fuel and camp spots are available.

The lake was stocked with cutthroat trout of the McBride variety on August 10, 1976, at a rate of 250 per acre. No natural reproduction was expected due to low flows in and out of the lake. I never went back for a second look, and the friend I sent hasn't come back yet.

46. WEASEL LAKE (fishless)

47. WEASEL LAKE (fishless)

48. & 51. WEASEL (CHIPPY) LAKES

Location: T5S, R11E, S. 12
Elevation: 9,440 feet; 9,890 feet, respectively
Area: 8.6 acres; 5.4 acres, respectively
Maximum depth: 75 feet; 35 feet, respectively

Only two of the seven lakes (see code map) that head up Weasel Creek, more commonly called West Chippy Creek, have fish. The best route is up trail #18 along Great Falls Creek, then south cross-country to Weasel Creek. Camping is best at lake #48 where there is firewood.

Weasel Lake (#48) has had a cutthroat trout fishery for some time. No records were found to pinpoint their origin or who put them in the lake, or when. They reproduce successfully, producing fish from little tykes to 16-inchers. Analysis of fish scales indicated the older cutts were six years old.

Weasel Lake (#51) was stocked in 1979 to produce large fish. Small numbers were introduced and the lake is to receive a plant of cutthroat trout every eight years.

49. WEASEL LAKE (fishless)

50. WEASEL LAKE (fishless)

52. WEASEL LAKE (fishless)

54. GREAT FALLS CREEK (fishless)

53. & 55. GREAT FALLS CREEK LAKES

Location: T5S, R12 E, S. 6
Elevation: 9,051 feet; 9,452 feet, respectively
Area: 12.8 acres; 6.6 acres, respectively
Maximum depth: 6 feet; 23 feet, respectively

The uppermost lake, (#53), of three Great Falls Creek lakes is a shallow meadow-type lake. It does, however, have extensive spring areas and, for this reason, a plant of rainbow trout was made in 1981. If they survived, it ought to be great fishing. The middle lake, (#54), is too shallow to support fish; but movement of fish in the stream could produce an occasional visitor here.

The lowermost lake, (#55), also has rainbow. A sample of 22 fish in 1972 produced a 9-inch average with little ones at 5 inches, big ones at 15 inches. When the upper lake was scheduled for stocking in 1980, the cargo was dumped in lake #55 instead of lake #53. The plant could do two things: 1) stunt the population, or 2) add new blood to the gene pool and make a better fishery. Let the FW&P biologist know what you catch.

A maintained trail (#18) parallels the lakes and Great Falls Creek. The lakes are six to seven miles from the trailhead on the Boulder River. Fuel and camping spots are plentiful.

56. FALLS CREEK LAKE (fishless)

57, 58, 59, & 60. FROZE TO DEATH LAKES (fishless)

61, 62, 63, 64, 65, 66, 67, 68, 69, 70, & 71. NURSES LAKES *(fishless)*

72 & 73. LOST LAKES *(fishless)*

74a. ICICLE LAKE *(fishless)*

74b. ICICLE LAKE *(fishless)*

75. WEST BOULDER LAKE
Location: T5S, R11D, S. 27B
Elevation: 9,628 feet
Area: 13 acres
Maximum depth: 55 feet

Head up Falls Creek and look up the steep rock slope at waters that eventually flow into Kaufman (Falls Creek) Lake. It is a haul from the West Boulder trailhead, a minimum of 17 miles. A horse trail is available to Kaufman Lake, but it's a foot trip to West Boulder Lake, which curls up to the base of Boulder Mountain in very scenic real estate.

For 14 years West Boulder Lake was home for golden trout. They tried for years to have little ones but finally died of old age without offspring.

Goldens are very difficult to get, difficult enough that they should only be stocked where they have a chance of perpetuating. West Boulder didn't qualify and was stocked with cutthroat trout in 1979 and placed on an eight-year stocking frequency.

76. KAUFMAN (FALLS CREEK) LAKE
Location: T5S, R11E, S. 21
Elevation: 8,942 feet
Area: 39.7 acres
Maximum depth: 70 feet

Travel up Falls Creek or sneak in from the Speculator Creek area. This is a popular lake with outfitters and a long walk without horses. Figure on 16 miles from West Boulder Ranger Station.

I believe Kaufman was a Forest Ranger in the 1930s. He was involved with some historical fish stocking in the backcountry. Kaufman Lake, like West Boulder, was stocked in the mid 1950s with golden trout. They failed to reproduce and died out due to their outlet spawning habit. Those escaping out Falls Creek were never seen again.

Kaufman Lake now houses cutthroat trout which are reproducing in the inlet stream. It is also scheduled for grayling when they become available.

77. POCKET LAKE *(fishless)*

78. YODEL LAKE *(fishless)*

79. UNNAMED *(fishless)*

80, 81, & 82. TUMBLE CREEK LAKES (3) *(fishless)*

83. ALPINE LAKE
Location: T4S, R11E, S. 30
Elevation: 8,680 feet
Area: 10.5 acres
Maximum depth: 20 feet

On Three Creek in the West Boulder River drainage approximately nine miles from the trailhead, with a shoreline that is 80 percent conifers, this lake should have become self-sustaining since its original planting in 1972, but it didn't. It was restocked with a better race of cutthroat trout in 1981 and should generate good fishing for all time.

84. TRAPPER LAKE *(fishless)*

85. SECOND CREEK LAKE *(fishless)*

86. BASIN CREEK LAKE *(fishless)*

87. DAVIS LAKE

Location: T4S, R10E, S. 24A
Elevation: 8,790 feet
Area: 5.1 acres
Maximum depth: 15 feet

Near the headwaters of Davis Creek, find an unnamed lake now christened Davis Lake for reference. One can reach the lakeshore by foot only. Traveling conditions are a little messy with scrub pine, talus rock, snowfields, and incline. The lake is in the trees and campsites can be selected along the north shoreline.

I was surprised to find 12- to 18.5-inch cutts here in 1972 with no indications of their source. In 1978 only two were caught, averaging 18.5 inches and 3.75 pounds. The lake was restocked in 1979, probably for the last time. I believe this new stock of McBride variety cutthroat will reproduce in the inlet stream.

88. SCOUT LAKE (fishless)

89. & 90. McKNIGHT LAKES (2)

Location: T4S, R10E, S. 13, 14
Elevation: 9,120 feet; 9,134 feet, respectively
Area: 3.4 acres; 10.8 acres, respectively
Maximum depth: 20 feet; 60 feet, respectively

McKnight Lakes are separated by a stone's toss of a few yards. Access is possible by trail #38 up Davis Creek, then up and cross-country to the lakes. Believe me, it is a scenic spot.

The McKnights received a plant of golden trout in 1982, in the hopes of making this a home forever. If the goldens take, these lakes will be the only golden trout water in the Boulder River System.

91. BLACKTAIL LAKE

Location: T3S, R10E, S. 36
Elevation: 8,700 feet
Area: 4.2 acres
Maximum depth: 20 feet

Nice cutthroat fishing hole. However, watch the stocking frequency for best timing. It was be stocked in 1984, and will be replanted in 1992, 2000, 2008, etc. When the fish were two years old, they were spunky 9-10 inchers, so I would imagine one should expect good fishing from two to four years after each plant, with large turkeys in the older age group.

Blacktail Lake is accessible by foot or horse trail from the West Boulder Ranger Station or from the Yellowstone River side of the mountain via the Mission Creek trail. Outflows take Blacktail Creek-Davis Creek-West Boulder, etc., to the Gulf of Mexico. Plenty of good camping areas and lots of fuel.

92. HORSESHOE LAKE (fishless)

93. BALL NOAH LAKE (fishless)

94. JARRETS POND (private)

95. & 97. UNNAMED BEAVER PONDS (2)

Location: T5S, R12E, S. 35B; T7S, R12E, S. 21
Elevation: 6,080 feet; 8,000 feet, respectively
Area: 0.5 acre; 0.2 acre, respectively
Maximum depth: 3 feet; 3 feet, respectively

Both of these ponds have been stocked with cutthroat trout. Don't expect anything great, but they could produce a fish. Both are accessible by vehicles, the one near Fourmile by car, the one near Independence by 4x4.

96. WOOLSEY (private)

Yellowstone, Hell Roaring, and Buffalo Fork Drainages

On either a float along or a drive on Highway 89 between Gardiner and Livingston, one is constantly treated to the grandeur of the snow-capped Absaroka Range. Tucked away in this mountainous grandeur are 26 lakes whose outflows end up in the Yellowstone River. Mill Creek, Emigrant Creek, and a series of streams flow westward from the Absarokas into the main stem of the river. In one way or another, all Absaroka-Beartooth waters described in this guide follow routes into this mighty river. This section describes those lakes connected directly to the Yellowstone, as well as Charley White and Carpenter lakes in the Hell Roaring Creek watershed and Hidden Lake in the neighboring Buffalo Creek Fork drainage.

The lowest and most accessible of this group of lakes is Dailey Lake at 5,241 feet. Dailey is, in part, a man-made reservoir. All others are truly alpine lakes ranging as high as 10,240 feet above sea level.

Access is somewhat more restricted than to lakes in the Absaroka-Beartooth interior. Routes to many of the Gallatin National Forest lakes described in this section begin on private land and permission must be obtained to enter. Forest trails with Highway 89 access are restricted to five locations.

Gravel roads wind up Mill, Emigrant, Sixmile and Bear creeks to public trailheads. Some travelers find it advantageous to approach some of these lakes from Davis Creek trail #46 on the West Boulder. Buffalo and Hell Roaring lakes are approachable from Independence on the Upper Boulder, or from Yellowstone National Park to the south.

With the exception of Hidden, Knox, Carpenter and Charley White lakes—steady fish producers—the remaining fishable lakes range from poor to good depending on their stocking schedules. Look for good times, fishing cutthroat trout at the peak growth stage following stocking.

Many of the following lake descriptions lack the precision of depth and area detail found elsewhere in the guide. My visits to Yellowstone country lakes were strictly for pleasure. Soundings and area calculations required work that was beyond my objectives. Thanks go to Montana State Department of Fish, Wildlife and Parks for the stats when available. Area figures not available were roughly computed from U.S. Geological maps.

1 & 2. PINE & JEWEL CREEK LAKES

Location: T4S, R10E, S. 14,15
Elevation: 9030 feet, 9035 feet, respectively
Area: 32 acres, 2 acres respectively
Maximum depth: 170 feet, respectively

About four miles from Pine Creek Recreational Area, a 3,400- feet elevation change, and a couple of sets of switchbacks along trail #47, you will find this pair of lakes. First encountered is Jewel, followed by Pine just upstream. The lakes are nestled in a grand setting at the feet of McKnight and Black mountains. Expect to see a couple of fantastic falls.

Who cares how good fishing is in a scene like this? Pine Lake was stocked in 1976 with 3,000 cutthroat trout. Latest reports are of fish 12-15 inches. Jewel Lake is a small wide spot which harbors a few cutts from stocks venturing out of Pine Lake.

3. GEORGE LAKE

Location: T4S, R10E, S30
Elevation: 7,760 feet
Area: 5.5 acres
Maximum depth: 8 feet

This is a rather shallow, 7-8 foot deep lake that has a habit of occasionally winter killing. A trail was partially completed in 1982 by the efforts of the sportsmen in the Livingston area. Thank them for their hard work. The lake is 2.5 miles up George Creek. Access is, in part, on private land; so get permission. The lake has a seepage problem, losing its water through the rocks.

The lake has had occasional populations of stocked cutthroat trout. Once the trail is completed, it will get a steady stocking.

4. FIRE LAKE

Location: T5S, R10E, S.20
Elevation: 9,590 feet
Area: 7.5 acres
Maximum depth: 90 feet

This lake is hard to get to because of the lack of a trail and the private lands in the foothills along Elbow Creek. When you get there, you will have hiked to 9,600 feet in elevation. The best route, with trail access partway, is from Elbow Creek.

In 1968 Fire Lake had no fish, but the Fish, Wildlife and Parks Department made up for lost time by stocking it in 1969, '71, '75 & '79. The stocking schedule apparently brought growth of trout to a standstill for a period of time; however, recent stocking has moderated and growth rates have improved. Look for cutts between 7 and 13 inches.

5. ELBOW LAKE

Location: T5S, R10E, S.27B
Elevation: 8,630 feet
Area: 9.0 acres
Maximum depth:

The trail head is on the East Fork of Mill Creek. After about one mile on trail #51, take trail #48, which climbs Upper Sage Creek and crosses the divide to Elbow Creek. You're looking at approximately 7 miles of trail from 5,800-9,000 feet and then down 1,000 feet into Elbow Creek, and finally to Elbow Lake at 8,630 feet.

Elbow Lake has a population of 10- to 13-inch cutthroat trout, apparently first stocked in 1968.

6, 7, & 8. UNNAMED (fishless)

9. CRYSTAL LAKE

Location: T5S, R11E, S.29
Elevation: 9,390 feet
Area: 2.6 acres
Maximum depth: 33 feet

Travel seven miles up the East Fork Mill Creek via trail #15, then two hard miles cross country to this jewel. One could ridge-hop from Mill Creek Pass, but this would be tough going.

In 1969, '71, '76, and '81, Crystal Lake was stocked with cutthroat trout. In 1972 an investigation of the fishery found yearlings 6-7 inches and a group of three-year-olds 13-14 inches. This lake depends on stocking to maintain a fishable population.

10. UNNAMED (fishless)

11. COLLEY LAKE (fishless)

12. THOMPSON LAKE

Location: T8S, R9E, S. 1
Elevation: 7,910 feet
Area: 8.0 acres
Maximum depth: 11 feet

The trailhead's on the West Fork Mill Creek road. Trail #61 parallels the West Fork. After 5.5 miles of maintained trail, travel along Thompson Creek trail another 3 miles to the lake shore. Good campsites and plenty of fuel for fires are nearby.

Interestingly, this lake's getting deeper. You heard right—deeper by the year. Apparently the mountain is sliding into the outlet stream. The lake is shallow and occasional winter kills reduce trout densities. Added depths would be beneficial. Cutthroat trout to 14 inches are reported in Thompson Lake.

Yellowstone, Hell Roaring and Buffalo Fork Drainages

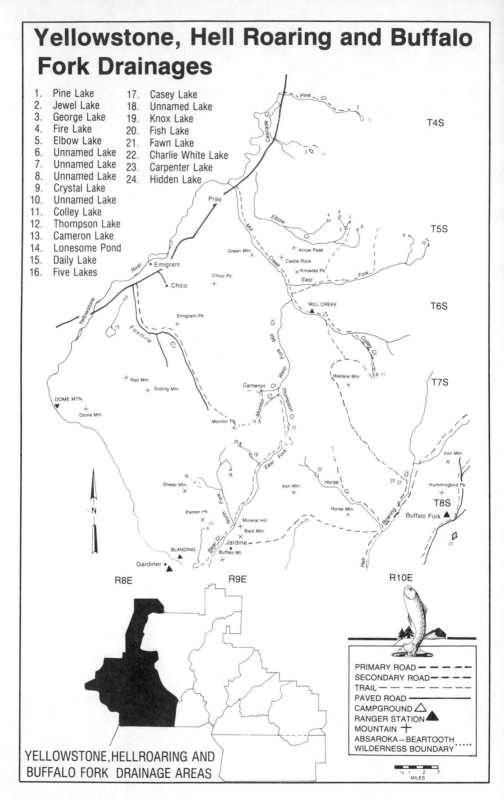

1. Pine Lake
2. Jewel Lake
3. George Lake
4. Fire Lake
5. Elbow Lake
6. Unnamed Lake
7. Unnamed Lake
8. Unnamed Lake
9. Crystal Lake
10. Unnamed Lake
11. Colley Lake
12. Thompson Lake
13. Cameron Lake
14. Lonesome Pond
15. Daily Lake
16. Five Lakes
17. Casey Lake
18. Unnamed Lake
19. Knox Lake
20. Fish Lake
21. Fawn Lake
22. Charlie White Lake
23. Carpenter Lake
24. Hidden Lake

T4S
T5S
T6S
T7S
T8S

R8E R9E R10E

YELLOWSTONE, HELLROARING AND
BUFFALO FORK DRAINAGE AREAS

PRIMARY ROAD
SECONDARY ROAD
TRAIL
PAVED ROAD
CAMPGROUND △
RANGER STATION ▲
MOUNTAIN +
ABSAROKA—BEARTOOTH
WILDERNESS BOUNDARY ·····

½ 1 2 3
MILES

13. CAMERON LAKE (fishless)

14. LONESOME POND

Location: T7S, R9E, S. 34
Elevation: 8,000 feet
Area: 1.7 acres
Maximum depth: 4 feet

We got us a little old shallow 1.7-acre pond 8,000 feet in the sky. The FW&P biologist flew over it and said "too shallow for fish." The boys down on main street, Gardiner, say different. It has fish, probably brookies or cutts. Take a 9-mile pack trail up Mill Creek to get there. It's hard to fish because of its shallowness and shoreline cover.

15. DAILEY LAKE

Location: T7S, R7E, S. 1B
Elevation: 5,241 feet
Area: 204 acres
Maximum depth: 24 feet

A prairie-foothill, semi-natural lake-reservoir on the east side of the Yellowstone River, 25 miles south of Livingston. Take a good dirt road 5.5 miles from U.S. 89 to get to Dailey Lake and campground. The lake is formed by a combination of spring water and diversion canal from Sixmile Creek.

The area is a reasonably popular fishing area for yellow perch, rainbow, and walleye.

16. FIVE (NORTH BEAR CREEK) LAKES (2)

Location: T8S, R8E, S. 25
Elevation: 9,510-9,680 feet
Area: 3 and .5 acres, respectively
Maximum depth: 16 and 8 feet respectively

These little lakes are just east of Sheep Mountain, approximately 4 air miles northwest of Jardine, Montana. A cross country hike from the end of the Bear Creek road is required. The country is a mix of scrub pine, rock, and open sage-grasslands. The southernmost lake has some cutthroat trout 6-13 inches. The other four are fishless.

16a. FIVE LAKES (3) (fishless)

17. CASEY LAKE (fishless)

18. UNNAMED (fishless)

19. KNOX (CASTLE) LAKE

Location: T8S, R9E, S. 15
Elevation: 8,450 feet
Area: 9.5 acres
Maximum depth: 14 feet

This is your basic widewater lake on a tributary of the East Fork of Bear Creek. It is accessible by pack trail #82 along Bear Creek to the Monitor Divide. Knox and the lake upstream (Fish Lake) are on the south side of Monitor, an area where a number of trail intersections open options to a number of locations.

Knox Lake, noted for good fishing, is in a timber-meadow environment approximately 7 miles from the trailhead. A good inlet stream keeps this shallow lake from freezing severely. Expect lots of pan-sized brookies and plenty of fishing action.

20. FISH LAKE

Location: T8S, R9E, S.9
Elevation: 8,950 feet
Area: 7.0 acres
Maximum depth: 12 feet

Another Bear Creek drainage lake, just upstream from Knox Lake, Fish Lake is about 7.5 trail miles from the trail head near Jardine. Like Knox Lake, it was stocked with brook trout in the 1940s. Rumor has it that cutthroat now occupy the lake.

A net always comes in handy—even when, as here, it scoops up a played-out fish from the wrong end. Michael Sample photo.

21. FAWN LAKE

Location: T9S, R10E, S.6
Elevation: 8,920 feet
Area: 3 acres
Maximum depth: 20 feet

Your basic brook trout lake has lots of 8- to 12-inch fish ready to bite. To get to Fawn Lake, take Crevase Creek drainage.

22. CHARLEY WHITE LAKE

Location: T8S, R10E, S. 19A
Elevation: 8,479 feet
Area: 12 acres
Maximum depth: Unknown

The lake is on the West Fork of Horse Creek in the Hell Roaring Creek drainage, a long distance from any access whether it be by Boulder River, Yellowstone National Park, or Jardine. Once in the country, however, travel is relatively easy. Numerous horse trails exist. The area is used mostly in the early fall elk and moose seasons. The lake has a self-sustaining population of cutthroat trout and produces numerous 8- to 10-inch fish.

23. CARPENTER (HELL ROARING) LAKE

Location: T8S, R11E, S. 19
Elevation: 7,491 feet
Area: 11 acres
Maximum depth: Unknown

Find it up Hell Roaring Creek approximately 3.5 miles from the old Hell Roaring Guard Station. Carpenter Lake is in the timber near the confluence of Grizzly and Hell Roaring creeks. Used mostly by outfitters during the early elk season, it has lots of medium-sized cutts.

24. HIDDEN LAKE

Location: T9S, R12E, S.7
Elevation: 7,720 feet.
Area: 9 acres
Maximum depth: Unknown

Between the Buffalo Fork Guard Station and the Montana Yellowstone National Park line, Hidden Lake is easily accessible with lots of fuel for camping near the shorelines. A fair fishery for rainbow trout 12-14 inches, it is just east of the south end of the big meadow on Buffalo Creek. Most of the fishing occurs during the early fall elk hunting periods. Access is from numerous directions: Slough Creek, Boulder Creek, Hell Roaring Creek, or the national park, the latter being the shortest and easiest route. If you plan on hunting, be aware that it is not permissible to carry a rifle in Yellowstone Park.

Slough Creek Drainage

From the heights of Wolverine Peak, Pinnacle Mountain, Roundhead Butte, and Lookout Mountain, the waters of Lost, Abundance, Wolverine, Rock, Wounded Man, Bull, and Tucker creeks are corraled into Slough Creek as it flows into Yellowstone National Park to join the Lamar River.

The Yellowstone cutthroat trout found its roots in Slough Creek before the influence of modern man. With the exception of a few isolated pockets of these native fish, very few streams in the A-B Mountains had resident fish that were not introduced through man's efforts. Most of the alpine country with its vertical nature was just too steep for fish invasion. Slough Creek, with its connection to the Lamar and eventually the Yellowstone River, provided a gradient and streamflow mellow enough to allow homesteading by wayward cutthroat trout.

In all probability, the only lakes in the A-B Mountains with native cutts are Heather and Peace lakes at the head of Wounded Man Creek. These lakes, at 8,725 and 9,275 feet above sea level, had the proper step-pool roadway leading to their doorways. If this was not the actual scenario, then it was man who intervened and assisted the extension of cutthroat up the creek. Regardless of the fishes' origin, their purity was attested to by two fish scientists specializing in identification. These professionals verified the cutts in the Slough Creek system as originals. The very presence of these fish adds special value to this Absaroka Mountain drainage.

The Montana portion of Slough Creek has a watershed of 104.8 square miles with 14 alpine lakes, all in the Gardiner Ranger District of the Gallatin National Forest. Nine of the lakes in the drainage are in Park County, five are in Sweet Grass County. The 14 lakes cover 57.5 surface acres, the largest being 17.2 acres. Besides being the largest, Lake Abundance is 37 feet deep while most of the others are less than 15 feet.

The overall elevation of the lakes in the Slough Creek system is lower than those in other A-B Mountain drainages. Pinnacle Lake is the highest at 9,725 feet. Eleven lakes are located in the 9,000-foot range and three are between 8,000 and 9,000 feet.

Lake Abundance is nearly accessible by all-wheel drive vehicle travel through Daisy Pass. Trails serve ten lakes and three others are within easy walking distance from trails. Horses can be taken to the shores of all but two lakes.

Four lakes have populations of cutthroat trout. Lake Abundance was chemically treated on September 5, 1969, with rotenone to rid the lake of chubs, then was restocked in 1970 with cutthroat trout from McBride Lake in Yellowstone Park. Heather and Peace Lakes have the indigenous stocks, and Horseshoe Lake was stocked. The remaining ten lakes are fishless. Only one of these lakes has the adequate depth and physical features capable of supporting a fishery.

1. LAKE ABUNDANCE

Location: T8S, R14E, S. 32
Elevation: 8,400 feet
Area: 17.2 acres
Maximum depth: 37 feet

Lake Abundance is located about 8 jeep miles northwest of Cooke City, Montana, just inside the Absaroka-Beartooth Wilderness Area. The outlet, Abundance Creek, flows 6 miles downvalley to Slough Creek. Plenty of camping opportunity exists near the road's end and near the lake.

Due to large numbers of lake chubs and small stunted cutthroat trout in Lake Abundance prior to 1969, the lake was chemically treated to eliminate the fish population. After restocking in 1970, growth was phenomenal, providing fish to 3.5 pounds. Since that initial good growth response, the number of very large fish has stabilized, but don't think that Lake Abundance is a poor fish producer. Fact is, the fish population produces catches of nice healthy, pink-meated cutts. Don't expect total isolation from other backcountry users. It's too accessible for that.

Slough Creek Drainage

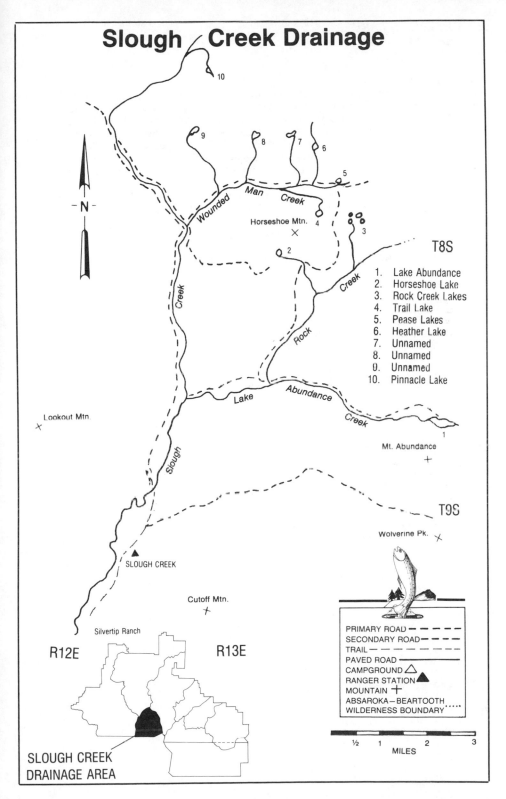

10

9

8 7 6

5

Wounded Man Creek

Horseshoe Mtn.
×

4

3

2

Rock Creek

T8S

1. Lake Abundance
2. Horseshoe Lake
3. Rock Creek Lakes
4. Trail Lake
5. Pease Lakes
6. Heather Lake
7. Unnamed
8. Unnamed
9. Unnamed
10. Pinnacle Lake

- N -

Lookout Mtn.
×

Lake Abundance Creek

1

Mt. Abundance
+

Slough Creek

T9S

Wolverine Pk. ×

SLOUGH CREEK ▲

Cutoff Mtn.
+

Silvertip Ranch

R12E

R13E

SLOUGH CREEK
DRAINAGE AREA

PRIMARY ROAD — — —
SECONDARY ROAD— — —
TRAIL — — —
PAVED ROAD ——
CAMPGROUND △
RANGER STATION ▲
MOUNTAIN +
ABSAROKA—BEARTOOTH
WILDERNESS BOUNDARY ·····

½   1   2   3
MILES

2. HORSESHOE LAKE

Location: T8S, R13E, S. 10, 15
Elevation: 9,180 feet
Area: 5.0 acres
Maximum depth: 13 feet

In Horseshoe Basin, an area of early mineral exploration in 1916 and from 1926-30, the area was accessible by four-wheel-drive vehicles from Independence on the Boulder prior to Wilderness status. Access is still possible via this old roadway route or by trail from Wounded Man Creek of Slough Creek. The lake has an old deteriorating earthen dam approximately 30 feet long and 10 feet high that impounds four feet of water. The dam was created by miners who operated a hydraulic sluiceway for exposing gold. Remnants of old mining activities such as roads, garbage, machinery, oil cans, shovels, old stoves, and other unattractive relics are common to the immediate area.

No fish were known to live in Horseshoe Lake prior to August 10, 1976. A small number of McBride Lake cutthroat were introduced and grew like wildfire. Three-year-old fish averaged 15 inches and 1.25 pounds in 1979. Horseshoe Lake receives little fishing except by elk hunters in the early fall. It was scheduled for more fish in 1984.

3a, 3b, 3c, & 3d. ROCK CREEK LAKES (4) (fishless)

4. TRAIL LAKE (fishless)

5. PEACE LAKES (2)

Location: T8S, R13E, S. 1,2
Elevation: 8,725 feet, 8,730 feet, respectively
Area: 4.8 acres, 0.9 acres, respectively
Maximum depth: 4 feet, 3 feet, respectively

This pair of small, shallow lakes head up Wounded Man Creek along the Wounded Man of Slough Creek-Lake of the Wood trail. An old prospector's or sheepherder's camp is located on the south shore. The area is intermittent timber-alpine grass with excellent camping.

Cutthroat trout have a long history of residence in these little lakes. Their numbers and sizes are not great enough to make Peace Lakes a must on anyone's summer recreational schedule. A ten-incher would be a whopper.

6. HEATHER LAKE

Location: T7S, R13E, S. 35D
Elevation: 9,275 feet
Area: 4.4 acres
Maximum depth: 4 feet

Heather Lake is perched in an isolated little valley of alpine flowers, grasses, and scattered conifers on the most northeastern tributary of Wounded Man Creek, near Timberline Mountain. Faint traces of an old trail from Wounded Man Creek parallel the east shoreline. Heather Lake is a shallow little lake with an obvious stream channel meandering across the lake floor.

Native cutthroat trout are found in small numbers. The only reason they do not perish during the long winter periods is the life-giving presence of several small underwater springs. It is a special little lake for numerous reasons, but of little importance as a recreational fishery.

7. UNNAMED (fishless)

8. UNNAMED (fishless)

9. UNNAMED (fishless)

10. PINNACLE LAKE (fishless)

Clarks Fork of the Yellowstone River Drainage—Wyoming

The Clarks Fork of the Yellowstone River finds its roots in the high country of Montana. From a maze of small Montana feeder streams, the river gathers into one beautiful channel in Wyoming. The river flows into the Cowboy State a couple of miles southeast of Colter Pass, then some 60 miles later it returns to Montana.

The 101 lakes described in this section include those found from north of the Clarks Fork River to the Montana-Wyoming state line (excluding those Wyoming lakes in the Rock Creek drainage which are described in Chapter 1).

Lakes are numbered from Deep Lake (#1) at the southeast corner, up and around each of eight stream drainages, to Bugle Lake (#101) in the northwest. You can refer to the code map to locate the numbers of lakes of interest, and proceed to the text for a short description of each lake.

The lakes are all outside the Absaroka-Beartooth Wilderness in the Shoshone National Forest. Access from the Beartooth Highway #212 is possible via numerous four-wheel-drive trails and four maintained roadways. Winter travel by snowmobile is allowed, making a speedy, convenient way to enjoy some winter angling. The biggest hassle is transporting the ice auger: it can be dangerous. If you take advantage of a nice March or April day, be sure to go with a buddy. The weather changes hastily, and many potential problems can be licked with an extra snow machine equipped with emergency provisions and gear.

I seldom had the luxury of company while working this area. Copious amounts of snow cover grow weak in late spring, which can cause you and your snowbuggy to drop out of sight into the wet depths or, worse yet, to be trapped in a creek channel because a snow bridge failed. I have found myself buried on occasion. On two occasions, I waited through the night until rotten snow solidified enough to remove the machine and the gear-laden sled to higher, firmer conditions. A supply of emergency provisions can make a long, unintended night's stay bearable.

My experience with these Wyoming lakes was a matter of personal curiosity. I never collected any hard data on fish populations unless in the company of a Wyoming Game and Fish employee. On my many trips, I passed each Wyoming lake so often that the scene became as familiar as my driveway. To make the trip less routine, I took different cross-country routes as often as possible to change the scene. My recreational angling, discussions with anglers, and use of Wyoming Game and Fish records provide the information on the lakes in this segment of the Beartooths. Ron Kent, Wyoming Game and Fish, is the official authority.

The 101 lakes in this region cover an estimated 2,251.8 acres of land surface. Exact depths of many of the lakes are unknown. Those that have been measured range from one to 125 feet deep. The lowest lake is Lily, at 7,670 feet above sea level. The lake situated at the highest elevation is unnamed at 10,550 feet.

Nowhere in the Absaroka-Beartooths will you find greater density of brook trout. Only 25 of the 101 lakes are fishless; most of these are small, pothole puddles isolated from major creek drainages. Many of the lakes were first stocked by Montanans living across the state line in nearby Red Lodge. These folks had access to brook trout and plenty of Wyoming waters to make homes for the brookies. They had no idea every inter-connected watercourse would eventually become a brook trout household. In addition, the Wyoming Game and Fish, in order to make sure the lakes in this region were well supplied, emphasized stocking brook trout.

These were infant days of fish management; today's fish managers wish they could push a button and automatically have more diverse stocking in these lakes. Brook trout will occupy these lakes well after the paper in this book has decomposed. The only variation from the brookie populations is a scattering of lakes containing a few other miscellaneous trout and salmon species.

The greatest regulator of brook trout in these lakes is nature itself—winterkill. Shallow lakes subject to periodic winterkill allow surviving fish opportunities to consume greater quantities of food and thus to outgrow their neighbors from deeper lakes.

Don't expect Wyoming Game and Fish to come up with a grand scheme for altering fisheries for greater species diversity. Too few anglers fish here; cost benefits are out of balance. So it's up to us to catch a greater share. Forget catch and release in these waters, no matter how popular the philosophy. In these lakes, it's catch and fry all the way.

1. DEEP LAKE

Location: T57N, R104N, S. 26, 27
Elevation: 7,993 feet
Area: 320 acres
Maximum depth: unknown

A rock slide across Littlerock Creek forms this 320-acre lake, the largest body of water described in this geographic area. Deep Lake is accessible by two packtrails, preceded by several miles of rough, four-wheel-drive travel from U.S. Highway 212 or Wyoming State Highway 120. This is big plateau country except for the sculptured canyon that houses Deep Lake. The shorelines are steep, banks rocky, and coulees filled with pines. Deep Lake's outlet seeps through the rock slide and emerges as springs in the canyon below. Brook trout make up the bulk of the fish population; however, both cutthroat trout and silver salmon have been introduced in the past. The silvers were approaching 13 inches at the last report.

2 & 3. SOLAR AND HAUSER LAKES

Location: T57N, R105W, S. 12
Elevation: 9,630 feet; 9,650 feet, respectively
Area: 10 acres; 12 acres, respectively
Maximum depth: 14 feet; 12 feet, respectively

On the west fork of Littlerock Creek are a couple of similar lakes—Solar and Hauser. Ray Guy, punter for the Los Angeles Raiders, could kick a football from lake to lake. Both lakes can be visited by four-wheel-drive vehicles and a short hike south of Highway 212. To get there, leave the Beartooth Highway about one-half mile from Long Lake.

Solar and Hauser were stocked with brook trout by members of the Red Lodge, Montana, Rod and Gun Club during the days when a holding area was established in Red Lodge. During the mid 1960s, Wyoming Game and Fish poisoned the stunted brookies and replaced them with cutthroat trout. Brook trout have since re-established themselves.

This is high plateau country with heavy and prolonged snow cover and little significant tree cover. However, fuel for camping is available on the west side of both lakes.

4. STOCKADE LAKE

Location: T57N, R104W, S. 7, 8
Elevation: 9,420 feet
Area: 30 acres
Maximum depth: 20 feet

Stockade has a maintained trail to the shoreline that meanders on down to Camp Sawtooth and Deep Lake. It doesn't take long to hike this trail (#614) from where it departs Highway 212 at Long lake. Should you elect to drive it (it's actually a four-wheel track), hang on—it is a rough one. Better yet, don't drive it and you'll spare this fragile country some erosion.

Expect lots of brookies when you get there.

5. LOSEKAMP LAKE

Location: T57N, R104W, S. 5
Elevation: 9,500 feet
Area: 20 acres
Maximum depth: 30 feet

Losekamp is 1.25 miles east of and 500 feet lower than the big switchback as you drive up Highway 212 from Long Lake. The lake is on Littlerock Creek .75 miles upstream from Stockade Lake. Fuel for camping is available here. You can get here either cross-country or via packtrail #614. Take the family and have a mess of good-eating brook trout—nutritious, too.

6 & 7. DAPHNIA AND BLACKSTONE LAKES

Location: T57N, R104W, S.6A & S 31
Elevation: 10,000 feet; 10,110 feet, respectively
Area: 2 acres; 2.5 acres, respectively
Maximum depth: Both lakes, unknown

These are two pretty nifty little lakes perched on a granite ledge with a backdrop of mountain cliffs. Although they are visible from Highway 212, you can expect a rough hike. Choose your route carefully and figure on exerting a fair amount of physical effort. You will be fishing by yourself, even though tourists traveling the Beartooth Highway (212) can see you. Both lakes have a few brook trout up to 12 inches long. Once both lakes supported a population of golden trout. Their occupancy in Daphnia and Blackstone was short-lived.

8. GARDNER LAKE

Location: T58N R104W, S. 32
Elevation: 9,950 feet
Area: 24 acres
Maximum depth: 25 feet

Gardner is a pretty lake at the foot of the Gardner Headwall, a popular summer ski slope. The lake is visible from the Beartooth Highway 212 at a location just west of the highway's summit at 10,936 feet. A trail snakes off the highway just east of Gardner Lake and intermittently meanders to the lake shores. High winds frequent the area, so take a jacket. You'll find brook trout here in numbers beyond the capacity of your hand calculator. Their size is about the size of the calculator.

9. CHRISTMAS LAKE

Location: T58N, R104W, S. 31
Elevation: 10,050 feet
Area: 22 acres
Maximum depth. 75 feet

One mile east of Gardner Lake on Littlerock Creek is 75-foot-deep Christmas Lake. This one isn't visible from Highway 212, but it lies only 400 yards from the pavement southeast of the 10,936-foot summit.

Christmas Lake was first stocked in 1933 with brook trout from Red Lodge, Montana. They are in good shape and make for good fishing when they are in the mood. Christmas Lake has been stocked at least twice with cutthroat trout, most recently in 1982.

10. PARADISE LAKE

Location: T57N, R105W, S. 23D
Elevation: 9,820 feet
Area: 12 acres
Maximum depth: Shallow

Paradise looks like a dying lake, gradually filling with organic ooze. The surrounding environs are swampy. It doesn't take much effort to hike the one mile to Paradise from the road at Fantan Lake. Water flowing out of Paradise Lake follows an unnamed tributary to Canyon Creek. This lake is rarely fished—probably because of its small brookies.

11. SPARHAWK LAKE

Location: T57N, R105W, S. 25AS
Elevation: 9,250 feet
Area: 9.5 acres
Maximum depth: 42 feet

Sparhawk sits on boggy country. It's a close neighbor of Sawtooth Lake (described below) and a small pond to the east. Like the rest of the lakes in Canyon Creek, it is loaded with brook trout that rarely attract visiting anglers.

12. SAWTOOTH LAKE

Location: T57N, R104W, S. 19, 30
Elevation: 9,230 feet
Area: 128 acres
Maximum depth: 73 feet

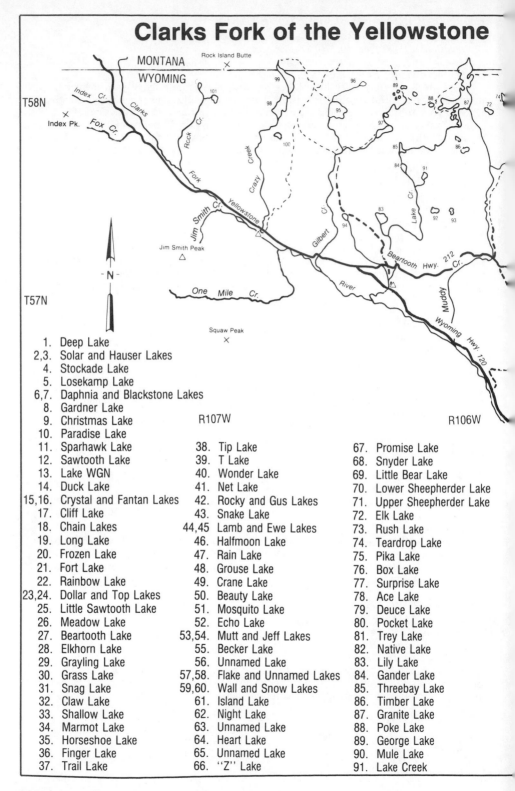

Clarks Fork of the Yellowstone

MONTANA
WYOMING

Rock Island Butte
×

Index Cr.

Clarks

T58N

Index Pk.
×

Fox Cr.

Rock Cr.

Creek

Crazy

Fork

Jim Smith Cr.

Yellowstone

Jim Smith Peak
△

- N -

One Mile Cr.

T57N

Squaw Peak
×

Gilbert Cr.

River

Beartooth Hwy. 212 Cr.

Muddy

Wyoming Hwy. 120

1. Deep Lake
2,3. Solar and Hauser Lakes
4. Stockade Lake
5. Losekamp Lake
6,7. Daphnia and Blackstone Lakes
8. Gardner Lake
9. Christmas Lake
10. Paradise Lake
11. Sparhawk Lake
12. Sawtooth Lake
13. Lake WGN
14. Duck Lake
15,16. Crystal and Fantan Lakes
17. Cliff Lake
18. Chain Lakes
19. Long Lake
20. Frozen Lake
21. Fort Lake
22. Rainbow Lake
23,24. Dollar and Top Lakes
25. Little Sawtooth Lake
26. Meadow Lake
27. Beartooth Lake
28. Elkhorn Lake
29. Grayling Lake
30. Grass Lake
31. Snag Lake
32. Claw Lake
33. Shallow Lake
34. Marmot Lake
35. Horseshoe Lake
36. Finger Lake
37. Trail Lake

R107W

38. Tip Lake
39. T Lake
40. Wonder Lake
41. Net Lake
42. Rocky and Gus Lakes
43. Snake Lake
44,45 Lamb and Ewe Lakes
46. Halfmoon Lake
47. Rain Lake
48. Grouse Lake
49. Crane Lake
50. Beauty Lake
51. Mosquito Lake
52. Echo Lake
53,54. Mutt and Jeff Lakes
55. Becker Lake
56. Unnamed Lake
57,58. Flake and Unnamed Lakes
59,60. Wall and Snow Lakes
61. Island Lake
62. Night Lake
63. Unnamed Lake
64. Heart Lake
65. Unnamed Lake
66. "Z" Lake

R106W

67. Promise Lake
68. Snyder Lake
69. Little Bear Lake
70. Lower Sheepherder Lake
71. Upper Sheepherder Lake
72. Elk Lake
73. Rush Lake
74. Teardrop Lake
75. Pika Lake
76. Box Lake
77. Surprise Lake
78. Ace Lake
79. Deuce Lake
80. Pocket Lake
81. Trey Lake
82. Native Lake
83. Lily Lake
84. Gander Lake
85. Threebay Lake
86. Timber Lake
87. Granite Lake
88. Poke Lake
89. George Lake
90. Mule Lake
91. Lake Creek

River Drainage—Wyoming

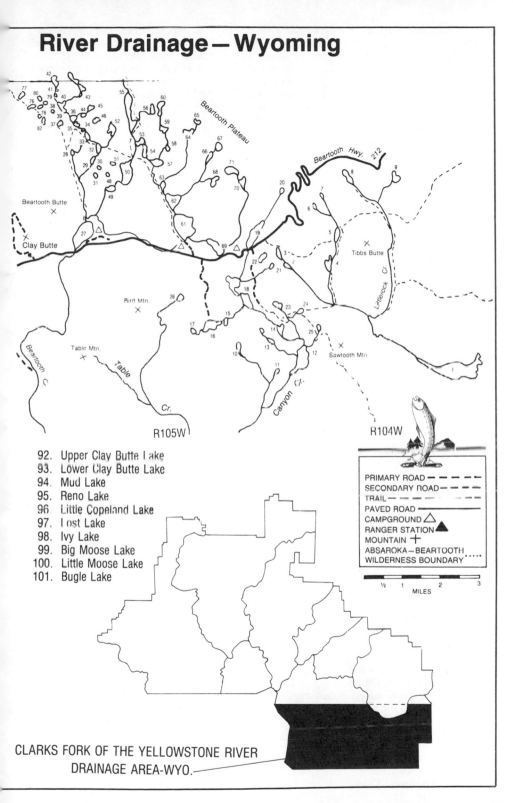

92. Upper Clay Butte Lake
93. Lower Clay Butte Lake
94. Mud Lake
95. Reno Lake
96. Little Copeland Lake
97. Lost Lake
98. Ivy Lake
99. Big Moose Lake
100. Little Moose Lake
101. Bugle Lake

PRIMARY ROAD
SECONDARY ROAD
TRAIL
PAVED ROAD
CAMPGROUND △
RANGER STATION ▲
MOUNTAIN +
ABSAROKA—BEARTOOTH
WILDERNESS BOUNDARY ·····

½   1   2   3
MILES

CLARKS FORK OF THE YELLOWSTONE RIVER
DRAINAGE AREA-WYO.

A big alpine-type lake, Sawtooth has a variety of fish. Brook trout make up the lion's share of the population; rainbow and cutthroat split the leftovers. Rainbow were stocked in 1933, cutts in 1957. Fishing pressure here is only moderate for a lake accessible by four-wheel-drive. Horseback and over-the-snow travel both make for a nice trip to Sawtooth. Three access routes will get you there—two are located five miles and one 18 miles from the oiled highway. Don't be surprised to see a few suckers and lake chub here; they're unusual, but some people do nasty things, such as dump minnows into lakes.

13. LAKE WGN

Location: T57N, R105W, S. 24C
Elevation: 9,500 feet
Area: 4 acres
Maximum depth: 12 feet

About .75 miles up the northwest tributary of Sawtooth Lake (#12), still in the Canyon Creek drainage, lies Lake WGN. This lake is neither very big nor very deep, but it has plenty of nice brookies. Most of the lake is about three feet deep with a small, 12-foot-deep hole near the center. Because it is shallow, brook trout population is regulated naturally by periodic die-offs. Survivors benefit and garner growth from ample feed—something to keep in mind while walking by any unlikely-looking fishing hole. WGN is not an easy lake in which to throw a line, but it produces well when anglers use small flies.

14. DUCK LAKE

Location: T57N, R205W, S. 24A
Elevation: 9,415 feet
Area: 25 acres
Maximum depth: 10-plus feet

Lots of people drive right by this one. Duck Lake is similar to Lake WGN in that its water spreads out over a large shallow area, mostly 10 feet deep or less, and aquatic vegetation covers the shoreline. Duck Lake is accessible by a rough, dry-weather, four-wheel driveway from the Beartooth Highway.

Duck is open year-round for all you can catch of any size. Do your freezer a favor and load up. The lake was stocked in 1933 by Montanans.

15 & 16. CRYSTAL AND FANTAN LAKES

Location: T57N, R105W, S. 22, 23
Elevation: 9,500 feet; 9,505 feet, respectively
Area: 9 acres; 50.8 acres, respectively
Maximum depth: 80 feet; unknown, respectively

Both lakes are located a short distance south of the Beartooth Highway along a reasonably good gravel road. The area is moderately popular as a fishing area because of good populations of brook trout. It takes about five fish to make a pound. Fish were first introduced to Fantan Lake in 1939, followed by another plant in 1950, and a rather large plant (10,380 fish) in 1952. The surrounding country is alpine plateau with grass cover and scattered conifer thickets. Fantan Lake water flows into little Crystal Lake before departing toward Chain Lakes and on out to the Clarks Fork River via Canyon Creek.

17. CLIFF LAKE

Location: T57N, R105W, S. 22
Elevation: 9,590 feet
Area: 4 acres
Maximum depth: Unknown

Cliff is a brookie fishery that has few visitors. Look for it about 400 yards upstream from Fantan Lake. Access is easy via gravel roadway from Highway 212 to Fantan. The hike is a short jaunt along the shoreline of Fantan Lake and up the inlet stream.

18. CHAIN LAKES

Location: T57N, R105W, S. 14
Elevation: 9,435 feet
Area: 80 acres
Maximum depth: 5 feet

Visible on the south side of the Beartooth Highway in the vicinity of Little Bear Lake, Chain Lakes are really one large lake constricted in the middle to appear as two. The lake sprawls over a large alpine meadow to a depth of five feet.

Although Chain is easily accessible via roads, fishing along the shoreline is difficult due to extremely soggy meadow and aquatic plant growth. The lake does, however, support some of the better brook trout in the vicinity. Ten-inch trout are quite common. For easiest fishing, try a boat. The Wyoming Game and Fish once introduced cutthroat in Chain Lakes, hoping to generate some variety from the overwhelming preponderance of brook trout in the area. Unfortunately, the cutts didn't find the habitat to their liking. The inlet streams lacked the necessary streambed gravels essential for successful spawning activity.

19. LONG LAKE

Location: T57N, R105W, S. 1, 2, 11
Elevation: 9,650 feet
Area: 80 acres
Maximum depth: 44 feet

Long Lake is adjacent to the Beartooth Highway midway between Red Lodge and Cooke City. Located in a scenic alpine setting next to a National Forest campground, the lake attracts fishermen during the nicer summer days. Occasionally a boat decorates the lake, its occupants enjoying the alpine splendor while trying to lure a brook trout for dinner.

Brook trout were first stocked here in 1935; stocking continued almost constantly at two- or three-year intervals until 1952. This policy has since been recognized as unnecessary and even detrimental to fisheries with little harvest. Long Lake is fortunate that anglers work it; this allows greater opportunity to creel bigger trout.

Long Lake was the scene for a drama involving two Minnesota Viking football stars, Dickson and Marshall; a snowmobile mechanic and his son; Vern and Marilyn Waples; and several others. The group had departed by snowmobile from the Red Lodge side of the Beartooth Mountains in the early afternoon, destined for Cooke City. After a difficult afternoon of manipulating snowmachines, they ran afoul of the alpine weather. The group, overheated from exercise and the bulk of warm clothes, witnessed their hot snowmobile engines stall out. One after another, the machines came to a halt as carburetors iced up—not an uncommon event when just the right atmospheric temperatures contact warm carburetors. Eventually, Vern Waples and the mechanic advised the group of the hopelessness of trying to start the engines and recommended the shelter of trees on down the highway at Long Lake.

Vern Waples, the best conditioned and most experienced of the group, headed south on foot toward the B4 Ranch where he could borrow a double track snowmobile and some experienced assistance. The football players, Marilyn, and the mechanic and son started their walk down the highway toward Long Lake. Three disbelievers stayed behind on the windy heights above Twin Lakes, futilely struggling with their snowmobiles. When they finally realized that Vern and the mechanic were right, they, too, started the hike to Long Lake, well behind the others.

At darkness, Vern took temporary shelter under the highway bridge at Long Lake. The second group wearily came in sometime later and found shelter in a timber patch a few hundred yards from Vern's protected spot under the bridge. Each party was unaware of the other's presence until morning. The tragedy occurred on up the switchback, where the last tired threesome took shelter in a natural snowcave adjacent to the highway. One of the three, Hugh Galusha, failed to exit the cave the following morning. His two companions, including a sportswriter for the Minneapolis *Tribune* who had instigated the trip, departed the cave and headed down the mountain toward Long Lake.

The surviving adventurers eventually rendezvoused at the Top of the World Store and were transported the following day to Cooke City. I saw the scene the following day. A rescue snowmobile from Yellowstone National Park came up later that day to retrieve Hugh's body. A series of unfortunate events had conspired to create this tragedy—a party too large and inexperienced, failure to take experienced advice, and a man in poor health.

20. FROZEN LAKE

Location: T58N, R105W, S.36
Elevation: 10,100 feet
Area: 3 acres

Upstream from Long Lake, east of the Beartooth Highway, south of the Wyoming switchbacks on Highway 212, lies Frozen Lake, located within a half mile of the highway in the treeless alpine zone. As the name implies, Frozen Lake is usually ice- and snow-covered. But when the ice breaks up, the brookies start jumping.

21. FORT LAKE

Location: T57N, R105W, S.12
Elevation: 9,650 feet
Area: 12 acres
Maximum depth: 15 feet

Directly south of the Beartooth Highway and upper Long Lake lies lonely little Fort Lake. This secluded lake is only a mile from the pavement of Highway 212. Scattered trees at Fort Lake provide fuel and shelter from alpine breezes that frequent the plateau country. Despite numerous attempts at establishing cutthroat trout here, brook trout prevail.

22. RAINBOW LAKE

Location: T57N, R105W, S. 12
Elevation: 9,510 feet
Area: 18 acres
Maximum depth: 40 feet

One-half mile south of the Beartooth Highway at Long Lake, you'll find pretty little Rainbow Lake. The surrounding country is basically comprised of alpine grass with scattered granite rock outcrops and small pine thickets.

Rainbow Lake has a variety of paper fish; that is, those fish that show up on record sheets but not necessarily in the lake. Records show brook trout, which probably retired to a neighboring lake; cutthroat trout, which were captured in experimental gill netting by Wyoming Game and Fish; and golden trout, which were planted erroneously. The goldens were scheduled to have been planted in upper Sheepherder, 2.5 miles to the north; but due to an error on the part of the pilot, they were released in Rainbow Lake instead.

My experiences at Rainbow Lake in the 1970s were all with golden trout—an extremely beautiful trophy. Rainbow Lake provides easy access to this rare fish. Take advantage—the golden ones may still be available.

Eat all the small fry you can, or fish populations too large for their environments will produce stunted trout like this brookie. Michael Sample photo.

23 & 24. DOLLAR AND TOP LAKES

Location: Dollar, T57N, R105W, S. 13D; Top, T57N, R104W, S. 18
Elevation: 9,405 feet; 9,475 feet, respectively
Area: 11 acres; 4 acres, respectively
Maximum depth: 12 feet; 15 feet, respectively

These two are not particularly attractive compared to the larger, deeper, clearer lakes nearby, but they distinguish themselves from the others by rearing *fat* brook trout. Don't expect one every cast, but when one hits, it is likely to measure 12 inches or better.

The lakes lie in an alpine grassland environment north of Sawtooth Lake. Both lakes are accessible from Highway 212, by a poor-quality four-wheel-drive trail that passes south of the lake. No large elevation gains are encountered along the three-mile distance from Highway 212, so walking to both shorelines is quite easy.

25. LITTLE SAWTOOTH LAKE

Location: T57N, R104W, S. 19
Elevation: 9,430 feet
Area: 8 acres
Maximum depth: 12 feet

Little Sawtooth lies in the dead center of Sawtooth Meadow, ringed by wet shorelines composed of swamp peatbog. Fishing is difficult here—you never know whether your floating shore will stay afloat. In some places 10 feet of water undercuts the shore as much as 10 to 15 feet. Brook trout of 12-inch size with well-formed bodies make up the catch. Food organisms thrive in the pond-like lake. To get here, either take a rather rough four-wheel-drive trail that departs Highway 212 near Long Lake, or walk cross-country about as quickly. Little Sawtooth makes a great winter fishing spot; then the lake is free of the poor bank conditions common in the summer. It does, however, help to have a good idea which snowbank to look under for the lake.

26. MEADOW LAKE (fishless)

27. BEARTOOTH LAKE

Location: T57N, R105W, S. 6, 7
Elevation: 8,901 feet
Area: 110 acres
Maximum depth: 86 feet

Nestled at the toe of picturesque Beartooth Butte is one of the highlight lakes in the Beartooth Mountains—Beartooth Lake. It features highway access, scenic grandeur, flowered meadows, Beartooth Falls, and the raw beauty of a geological timepiece—Beartooth Butte. Clear and productive, Beartooth Lake is the terminal end of over 40 alpine lakes, all of which flow into Beartooth Lake via three major inflow streams. Furthermore, it is the largest and most diversified fishery of the Beartooth Mountain lakes. It also offers public camping, picnicking, and boat launch facilities. Dense conifer forest, composed of large fir and pine, covers a portion of the shoreline. The mix of physical features, fishing opportunities, accessibility, and options for recreation at Beartooth Lake are hard to beat.

Fishing pressure at Beartooth Lake is moderate to heavy during the summer. This, along with the presence of carnivorous lake trout, helps keep the brook trout at an optimum density to allow good growth. Besides brook trout and Mackinaw or lake trout, Beartooth has rainbow, cutthroat, and grayling.

Mackinaw up to 22 pounds are not unheard of: their average size is 15 inches. Grayling average 13 inches, rainbow and cutts 12 inches, and brook trout 11 inches. It's not hard to understand why the lake has a certain amount of popularity. It also has a recent reputation for its appeal as a quality diving location for scuba enthusiasts.

28. ELKHORN LAKE (fishless)

29. GRAYLING LAKE

Location: T58N, R105W, S. 30, 31
Elevation: 9,670 feet
Area: 12 acres
Maximum depth: 10 feet

Beartooth Creek has three forks which join at Beartooth Lake. The easternmost of these forks drains 23 lakes, the largest and most significant of which is Grayling Lake, a very irregularly shaped lake with 8-10 islands of varying sizes.

Access to Grayling by foot or horseback requires a 1.5-mile hike from the north end of Beartooth Lake. The climb is gradual, changing 1,274 feet in elevation from start to finish.

Mr. James R. Simon, a Wyoming Game and Fish biologist, reported grayling in this lake in 1941; this report undoubtedly generated the lake's name. Grayling have since disappeared, and brook trout now are the sole inhabitants. Look for an average 9-inch fish.

30. GRASS LAKE

Location: T58N, R105 W., S. 29, 30
Elevation: 9,675 feet
Area: 1 acre
Maximum depth: 5 feet

About 100 yards east of the upper end of Grayling Lake lies Grass Lake. During spring runoff, brook trout move between the two lakes. Look for 10-inchers.

31. SNAG LAKE *(fishless)*

32-36. CLAW, SHALLOW, MARMOT, HORSESHOE, AND FINGER LAKES

Location: T58N, R105W, S. 19, 30
Elevation: 9,350-9,820 feet
Area: 10 acres; 8 acres; 5 acres; 12 acres; 10 acres, respectively
Maximum depth: 30 feet; 5 feet; 27 feet; 30 feet; 26 feet, respectively

A series of five broadwater lakes, all on a mile-long portion of the northwest fork of Beartooth Creek, these lakes are linked in a nearly continuous chain between Grayling (#29) and "T" (#39) lakes. The entire reach is loaded with small brook trout begging for a spot in your creel. Take plenty; the number limit is wide open.

The combined total of 45 acres of lake water is within easy hiking distances of Beartooth Lake. The trail (#614) is good for either foot or horse travel. Plenty of fuel is available for camping.

37. TRAIL LAKE *(fishless)*

38. TIP LAKE *(fishless)*

39. T LAKE

Location: T58N, R105W, S. 19CB
Elevation: 9,910 feet
Area: 15 acres
Maximum depth: 33 feet

T Lake is the confluence of two splits in the northeast fork of Beartooth Creek. The inlet on the westernmost branch of the T receives water from Lonesome Lake on the Montana-Wyoming state line. The other fork drains a series of little lakes originating near the state line.

T Lake is readily accessible by a number of good packsaddle trails from several directions. You'll find numerous small brook trout here.

40, 41, & 42. WONDER, NET, ROCKY (AND GUS) LAKES

Location: T58N, R106 W, S. 24 A
Elevation: 9,940-10,080 feet
Area: .5 acres; 1 acres; 2 acres; 16.7 acres respectively
Maximum depth: 8 feet; 12 feet; 6 feet; 21 feet, respectively

The west inlet of T Lake originates near the Wyoming-Montana state line. The headwaters lake, Gus, is actually in Montana so it isn't numbered as part of this series. Ron Kent, a biologist for Wyoming Game and Fish, tagged the Montana lake with the handle of "Gus." Ron found a three-pound brookie in Gus; I found nothing—typical of a lake with large, big-type brookies. Usually they contain very few fish—but those they do contain find plenty of food.

This series—Wonder, Net, Rocky, and, if you like, Gus—are all accessible from the trail systems in and around T Lake. Hike up the rocky drainage to visit these little widewaters. It might be worth it. This country becomes more hostile for fish than the T Lake area. It has less ideal spawning conditions, shorter open water periods, and more winterkill. All this helps keep brook trout from over-reproducing. The survivors benefit by having a large amount on which to feed.

43. SNAKE LAKE

Location: T58N, R105W, S. 19 AC
Elevation: 10,040 feet
Area: 4 acres
Maximum depth: 6 feet

Snake is really a little outlet lake of Lonesome Lake, which was described in the section dealing with Clarks Fork lakes in Montana. Snake Lake and the lower tip of Lonesome Lake are south of the state line. These interstate waters are visited by both backpackers and horsepackers. Commonly used trailheads are located at Beartooth and Island lakes, but you aren't restricted to those two. Either approach contains a 4.5- to 5-mile trip.

Snake Lake contains brook trout like most of the other lakes in this section of the Beartooths. Hope you are not into catch and release. These lakes require catch and fry fishermen to keep the brookie population manageable.

44 & 45. LAMB AND EWE LAKES

Location: T58N, R105W, S. 19 D
Elevation: 9,915 feet; 9,930 feet, respectively
Area: 4 acres; 10 acres, respectively
Maximum depth: 8 feet; 21 feet respectively

A couple of brook trout lakes, both northeast of Finger Lake (#36), Lamb and Ewe contain some fish of fair to respectable size. Ewe Lake is one of those low-density lakes that occasionally sports large fish. Don't expect a fish every cast; just work all day and maybe you'll catch a trophy.

46. HALFMOON LAKE

Location: T58N, R105W, S. 20 CC
Elevation: 9,990 feet
Area: 4 acres
Maximum depth: 5 feet

Halfmoon lies a half-mile northeast of, and on a tributary to, Shallow Lake (#33). Brook trout live here—big ones. Enough said.

47 & 48. RAIN AND GROUSE LAKES (fishless)

49. CRANE LAKE

Location: T58N, R105W, S. 32 C
Elevation: 9,350 feet
Area: 10 acres
Maximum depth: 28 feet

If you proceed upstream on the middle inlet of Beartooth Lake (#27), you'll have your work cut out just keeping track of the trail. One can lose contact with the trail when climbing the rock benches, scattered through the forest. The trail from Island Lake (#61) approaches the north end of Beauty Lake (#50). From Beauty, it is just a ways downstream to Crane Lake. And, of course, brook trout await you.

50. BEAUTY LAKE

Location: T58N, R105W, S. 32 A
Elevation: 9,429 feet
Area: 90 acres
Maximum depth: 115 feet

Beauty is one fine looker, with the scenic qualities befitting its name. It lies in timber country that is interspersed with alpine grass meadows. Take the trail from Island Lake (#61) and walk about four flatland-type miles. I wish I didn't have to say this, but, once again, expect to find brook trout.

51. MOSQUITO LAKE

Location: T58N, R105W, S. 32 BA
Elevation: 9,500 feet
Area: 4 acres
Maximum depth: 15 feet

Mosquito lies next to Beauty Lake (#50) on the northeast tributary of Beartooth Creek. This one looks to be another brook trout lake with lots of 8- to 9-inch fish—fat little fish, but that changes over time. I doubt the name refers to the prevalent resident inhabiting this neck of the woods.

52. ECHO LAKE (fishless)

53 & 54. MUTT AND JEFF LAKES

Location: T58N, R105W, S. 28
Elevation: 9,675 feet
Area: 4 acres; 8 acres, respectively
Maximum depth: 15 feet; 25 feet, respectively

The most common route to Mutt and Jeff is via the well-traveled trail starting at Island Lake (#61). The hike or ride is about 4.5 miles from the trailhead. A good part of the trail traverses Island and Night (#62) lakes. It's easy going, with only a 157-foot elevation gain from start to finish. Expect loads of easy-to-catch brook trout. Nice camping country surrounds the lake, featuring alpine grass and stands of big conifers.

55. BECKER LAKE

Location: T58N, R105W, S. 20, 29
Elevation: 9,693 feet
Area: 80 acres
Maximum depth: 85 feet

If you are heading for Albino Lake in Montana, you'll walk by Becker Lake—for what'll seem like forever. Becker is a pretty lake, but it sure takes time to go from end to end. Better take a break and have a granola bar. Trails in this area are good and camp spots are excellent.

You'll find lots of vertical shoreline here, some of it leading to the deep 85-foot hole. Becker is one of those lakes that make you wish you had a wet suit and scuba gear.

The lake is home for brook trout originating from a single plant back in 1939. Angling is good, fishing pressure is light, and an occasional cutthroat trout can be found. The cutts slid down the drainage from Albino Lake in Montana.

56. UNNAMED (fishless)

57 & 58. FLAKE LAKE AND UNNAMED LAKE

Location: T58N, R105W, S. 28, 33 & 28, DA
Elevation: 9,624 feet; 10,060 feet, respectively
Area: 20 acres; 30 acres, respectively.
Maximum depth: 20 feet; 6 feet, respectively

This pair is centrally located in the midst of a group of 43 lakes in the Beartooth Creek watershed north of Beartooth Lake. This is brook trout country: every drop of water deep enough to harbor a fishy body holds a brookie. And there is absolutely no limit to the number you can take home to feed the neighborhood.

59 & 60. WALL AND SNOW LAKES

Location: T58N, R105W, S. 28A & 21
Elevation: 10,220 feet; 10,390 feet, respectively
Area: 30 acres; 32 acres, respectively
Maximum depth: 82 feet; 50 feet, respectively

A couple of high country gems, Wall and Snow both lie above timberline in rocky alpine country not too far from the divide breaking over the mountain to Rock Creek in Montana. These lakes are spectacular in all seasons, of which, in this country, there are two—winter and winter with a touch of summer.

Wall Lake is named for its vertical shoreline which leads to deep, clear water averaging 70 feet in depth. It has a short growing season and holds medium-bodied (8-inch average) brook trout. You'll also find brook trout in Snow Lake, which is up the hill from Wall Lake. Snow's brookies aren't too big, around 10 inches—but it's a privilege to be able to catch any fish at 10,390 feet in elevation.

61. ISLAND LAKE

Location: T58N, R105W, S. 3
Elevation: 9,518 feet
Area: 146 acres
Maximum depth: 100 feet

Big Island Lake features 146 acres of brook trout pasture. And yes, it does have an island—in fact, a pair of them. To get to Island Lake, take the well-marked gravel road from the Beartooth Highway. It even has a campground and boat launch. If you plan to fish around the lake, you had better take a lunch and a fanny pack with your rain gear. A sunny summer day at this elevation can give way to a violent storm in short order.

It would be nice if the Wyoming Game and Fish would take a look at the multiple species occupying Beartooth Lake (#27) and adapt the same philosophy to the many niches in Island. A few predator trout in the brook trout patch would do the area a big favor. The greatest problem with this management option is getting the predators large enough to consume the brookies. I have seen some brookies close to a dozen inches in length in Island Lake.

This is a nice spot just to kick back, do a little camping and fishing, and watch the marmots play in the alpine splendor.

62. NIGHT LAKE

Location: T58N, R105, S3, 4
Elevation: 9,538 feet
Area: 51 acres
Maximum depth: 43 feet

Night Lake lies 100 yards upstream from Island Lake and is 20 feet higher. Walk about one mile plus a hop, skip, and jump from the trailhead at the Island Lake campground to get to Night. Fishing is similar to the fishing in Island—lots of brookies, some approaching a foot in length. Night Lake can be loads of fun with a floating flyline and a small number 8-10 hook. A gray hackle peacock should prove a winner.

63. UNNAMED LAKE

Location: T58N, R105W, S. 33
Elevation: 10,375 feet
Area: 5 acres
Maximum depth: 18 foot

Just past Night Lake (#62) is a small, shallow widewater lake without a name. It's on the trail from Island to wherever the trail goes. You'll find brook trout heaven here.

64. HEART LAKE

Location: T58N, R105W, S. 27
Elevation: 10,375 feet
Area: 40 acres
Maximum depth: Unknown

Heart Lake nestles right below the Beartooth Plateau, above tree line, and next to a snow bank—no matter which season you visit it. This is tough, majestic, beautiful alpine country. You can follow the creek from Night Lake (#62) or, if you feel tough, you can cut cross-country from the Beartooth Highway switchbacks along Long Lake. Despite the numerous elevation changes, the trip is worth it. Pick a nice day; it's not so fun in 45-degree hail, hard rain, or blowing snow. Catch five brook trout per pound and have a good time.

65. UNNAMED (fishless)

66. Z LAKE (fishless)

67. PROMISE LAKE (fishless)

68. SNYDER LAKE (fishless)

69. LITTLE BEAR LAKE

Location: T58N, R105W, S11B
Elevation: 9,549 feet
Area: 30 acres
Maximum depth: 18 feet

Along the Beartooth Highway between Long (#19) and Island (#61) lakes, you'll encounter Little Bear Lake. You'll rarely see many anglers here even though there is a parking area next to the lake. I understand why tourists pass it by; they have most likely already pulled over at Long or Island lakes and caught their fill.

Fishing is pretty good at Little Bear Lake with lots of 10-inch brookies. These are colorful and, in general, in pretty good condition. Attempts were made to establish a cutthroat trout population here in the late 1930s and early 1940s, without success. The ponds occupying the main inlet are fun to fish for larger brookies.

70. LOWER SHEEPHERDER LAKE

Location: T58N, R105W, S. 35D
Elevation: 9,800 feet
Area: 20 acres
Maximum depth: Unknown

Lower Sheepherder lies on the easternmost fork of Beartooth Creek, 1.25 miles west of the Beartooth Highway. The surrounding country is alpine, with small, scattered clumps of krummholtz pine. Lower Sheepherder makes an excellent winter fishing hole. Brook trout are abundant—not large, but very tasty.

71. UPPER SHEEPHERDER LAKE

Location: T58N, R105W, S. 35
Elevation: 9,880 feet
Area: 40 acres
Maximum depth: Unknown

I've heard that golden trout and Upper Sheepherder go together like milk and cereal. Unfortunately, the milk's missing—so are the golden trout. I've always had a thing about chasing golden trout, and in checking out Upper Sheepherder I was shocked to find a lake full of brookies. At least they were nice, stocky, fat ones.

The lake sits in the subarctic zone, above timberline, about 300 yards upstream from Lower Sheepherder Lake. Lower Sheepherder was stocked with brook trout in 1935. No impassable barriers in the interconnecting stream prevent upstream trout migration to Upper Sheepherder Lake; therefore, the upper lake still benefits from the stocking. If you don't like the cross-country route from the Beartooth Highway switchbacks, try the horse trail departing at Long Lake.

72 & 73. ELK AND RUSH LAKES *(fishless)*

74. TEARDROP LAKE *(fishless)*

75. PIKA LAKE *(fishless)*

76, 77, 78, & 79. BOX, SURPRISE, ACE, AND DEUCE LAKES

Location: T58N, R105W, S. 24
Elevation: 9,830-9,910 feet
Area: 15 acres; 8 acres; 2 acres; 5 acres, respectively
Maximum depth: 40 feet; unknown; 5 feet; 20 feet, respectively

This group of lakes lies directly north of Beartooth Butte, east of Granite Lake and within one-half mile of the Wyoming-Montana state line. Take the Muddy Creek road from Highway 212 to the trailhead, then proceed along the pack trail for three miles before cutting northeast up the tributary that issues from this series of lakes. Alternatively, you can take the Beartooth Creek trail from Beartooth Lake (#27).

You are going to find lots of brook trout in the interconnected lakes of Box, Ace and Deuce. Some reach significant sizes, especially in those shallow waters where fish are subjected to periodic winterkill. Actually, these little lakes will produce better sized fish than neighboring Granite Lake. You'll also find fuel here for comfort camping.

Supper's in the icebox for some hungry angler, who found this rainbow trout a spirited if reluctant dinner guest. Pat Marcuson photo.

Surprise Lake sits on a bench northwest of the chain that runs from Box to Deuce Lakes. It, too, offers plenty of excellent camping areas. It also holds a nice array of brook trout, ranging up to 18 inches, thick bodied and playful on the end of a light-weight rod.

80. POCKET LAKE (fishless)

81. TREY LAKE (fishless)

82. NATIVE LAKE

Location: T58N, R105W, S. 24DC
Elevation: 9,835 feet
Area: 7 acres
Maximum depth: 40 feet

Native Lake lies north of Beartooth Butte along the Beartooth Creek trail. It sits in a small, seven-acre depression of rock and scattered trees, where you'll find adequate shelter and plenty of room for camping.

Native is one of those lakes capable of producing large fish; in fact, brook trout up to four pounds have been caught here. Limited reproduction in Native limits the number of fish, thus, the food levels are more than adequate for the existing population.

83. LILY LAKE

Location: T57N, R105W, S. 6D
Elevation: 7,670 feet
Area: 40 acres
Maximum depth: 53 feet

If you cruise the Beartooth Highway from the southeast, you will intersect the Lily Lake road just after the spectacular falls and rapids on Lake Creek. From the west, look for the signed road right after the Sunlight Basin road intersection. You can launch a boat at Lily, but don't expect an easy time of it.

Lily Lake has a reputation for producing some fair-sized brook and rainbow trout. Besides these two critters, an occasional cutthroat and golden trout can be taken: these are particularly common to the outlet stream. The goldens were apparently planted by a confused pilot; they were planned for Upper Sheepherder. Upper Sheepherder's management plans seem to have gotten spread all over the mountains.

However, it's not impossible (and probably likely) that the goldens worked their way down Lake Creek from Hidden Lake in Montana.

The shoreline around Lily Lake is pondlike with lilies growing abundantly during the warmer summer days. Camping is possible here, but you'll probably fare better at one of the maintained campgrounds along the Beartooth Highway or the Sunlight-Crandall road.

84 & 85. GANDER AND THREEBAY LAKES

Location: T58N, R106W, S. 29, 32
Elevation: 8,305 feet; 8,320 feet, respectively
Area: 8 acres; 20 acres, respectively
Maximum depth: 7 feet; unknown, respectively

These two are located on the main fork of Lake Creek between Granite Lake (#87) and the Clarks Fork of the Yellowstone River. Both are basically widewater-type lakes with the same fish species as Granite: brookies and rainbow. Consider fishing the stream environment, which could produce some nice fish. Once upon a time some rainbow up to five pounds were hauled out of these waters. Forest surrounds both lakes, so you'll find plenty of fuel and shelter. Don't expect lots of company unless you go during elk season. A hike up the east side of Lake Creek will get you here. Take a look at area maps and notice numerous other trail options into the general area.

86. TIMBER LAKE (fishless)

87. GRANITE LAKE

Location: T58N, R106 W, S. 21, 22
Elevation: 8,620 feet
Area: 228 acres
Maximum depth: 125 feet

Montana and Wyoming share the privilege of holding Granite Lake. Granite is also described as lake #147 in the Clarks Fork-Montana section. This is a very aesthetic forest lake, dominated by an irregular shoreline surrounding 228 acres of water, 179 of which are in Wyoming. Granite reaches depths of 125 feet in Montana and 70 feet in Wyoming. Access is possible by a number of routes resulting from horseback and pack outfits that find the area to their liking during elk season. The most direct route involves five miles of trail from the Muddy Creek launch site. Other trails include the one from Copeland Lake in Montana; the Parks Rapid trail along the state line; a trail from Theil Lake in Montana; and one from Lost Lake (#97) in Wyoming—take your pick. Check with the Forest Service on horse use regulations; they may not want you pasturing your steed for long periods. If you do travel by horse, you probably ought to take a bag of feed; wet alpine grass, besides being fragile and aesthetic, fails to provide much nutrition.

The fishing varies from day to day. Most of the lake's area is full of brookies, with a mix of rainbow thrown in for the talented fisherperson. The fish here are reputed to reach 12 inches, but I haven't seen any that large.

88. POKE LAKE (fishless)

89. GEORGE LAKE (fishless)

90. MULE LAKE

Location: T58N, R106W, S. 23
Elevation: 9,360 feet
Area: 10 acres
Maximum depth: 22 feet

Mule Lake resides along the Beartooth Creek trail next to the Montana-Wyoming state line just south of Theil Lake in Montana. This is mostly a brook trout haven with a possible golden trout still hanging around. The golden ones ventured downstream from Hidden Lake in Montana. The little devils don't recognize state lines; they probably don't even have the proper permits or vaccinations. You'll find a pretty lake here with a nice setting, and lots of good camping opportunities. You might even see a bear.

91. LAKE CREEK (fishless)

92. UPPER CLAY BUTTE LAKE

Location: T57N, R106W, S. 4BD
Elevation: 8,315 feet
Area: 18 acres
Maximum depth: 25 feet

Look for the Clay Butte lakes about 1.5 miles east of Lily Lake, west of Clay Butte, north of the Beartooth Highway. You could strike out from Muddy Creek or from Lake Creek to get to where they lie hidden in the forest. I won't promise a fish will await you (neither will the Wyoming Game and Fish folks); however, the lake once held grayling. It was stocked to the hilt in 1962, 1964, and 1965. Nobody to my knowledge ever went back to check it out. You might want to check with the fish managers at the Wyoming Game and Fish's Cody office, or go explore the situation for yourself. If you do, let me know what you find.

The Lower Clay Butte Lake once was stocked with cutthroat trout, but failed to become self-sustaining.

93. LOWER CLAY BUTTE LAKE (fishless)

94. MUD LAKE (fishless)

95. RENO LAKE

Location: T58N, R107W, S. 24, 25
Elevation: 8,244 feet
Area: 140 acres
Maximum depth: 30 feet

You can depart from the Lily Lake road and drive a four-by-four to this one. If you're operating a two-wheel drive, go as far as you feel comfortable and hike the remaining distance. Reno is a woods lake—very picturesque. This is a good area to pitch a tent and stay awhile. Reno hosts rainbow and brook trout averaging over 9 inches.

96. LITTLE COPELAND LAKE

Location: T58N, R107W, S. 19
Elevation: 9,690 feet
Area: 12 acres
Maximum depth: 20 feet

On the Wyoming border, downstream from Copeland Lake in Montana, is Little Copeland Lake. Outflows from this lake meet the Clarks Fork via Gilbert Creek. Access is possible by trail to the north end of the lake. Little Copeland likes brook trout, lots of them.

Pat Marcuson, seated on his snowshoes, proves that neither ice, nor snow, nor dead of winter can keep an angler from his appointed rounds. Stoneberg photo.

97. LOST LAKE

Location: T58N, R107W, S. 29, 30
Elevation: 8,237 feet
Area: 30 acres
Maximum depth: 45 feet

Lost Lake is on the easternmost fork of Gilbert Creek. The watershed draining into Lost is a maze of small wet meadows and ponds. A trail meanders along the creek flowing out of Lost Lake. Again, the lake is another favorite spot for lots and lots of brook trout. Take your mosquito dope.

98. IVY LAKE

Location: T58N, R107W, S. 23
Elevation: 7,998 feet
Area: 75 acres
Maximum depth: 30 feet

Ivy is the down-valley lake of the Crazy Lake chain, which includes Big Moose, Widewater, and Fox lakes upstream. If you're up for a walk, start at Crazy Creek campground on the Beartooth Highway and walk four miles to the outlet of Ivy Lake. If you want a shorter walk, take the Lily Lake road as far as you like and expect a 2.5 mile walk to the inlet end of Ivy.

Expect a big, flat-bottomed, widewater lake with lots of shallow area, scattered boulders, and surrounded by forest. Rainbow trout were stocked here in 1955 and have remained the dominant fish. You might possibly take a 20-incher. Brook trout have increased their numbers in the upper lakes, so don't be surprised if a brookie ends up in your creel.

99. BIG MOOSE LAKE

Location: T58N, R107W, S. 23
Elevation: 8,000 feet
Area: 83.8 acres
Maximum depth: 46 feet

Just upstream from Ivy Lake is Big Moose Lake (described as #71 in the Clarks Fork—Montana section of this *Guide*.) This is another wide spot in Crazy Creel. I dove into it once and found nothing but a flat underwater carpet of aquatic grass covered with three to six feet of water, plus one little 46-foot-deep hole.

Big Moose (formerly called Crazy Lake) harbors mostly rainbow trout, lots in the 12-inch bracket with an occasional two-pounder. Take either a Montana or Wyoming fishing license, as the lake occupies both states.

100. LITTLE MOOSE LAKE

Location: T58N, R107W, S. 26
Elevation: 8,040 feet
Area: 9 acres
Maximum depth: 50 feet

Little Moose produces some big rainbow trout. This is a very pondish, but productive, lake that is stocked periodically. If you catch it toward the end of the stocking schedule, you may be rewarded with a fish up to 10 pounds. Watch your footing on the shore as it's not too stable: peat mats overhang the lake—very spongy, wet, bouncy stuff. The north and west shorelines are a little stiffer. Pond weeds are common here, so are mosquitos.

101. BUGLE LAKE

Location: T58N, R107W, S. 21
Elevation: 7,820 feet
Area: 8 acres
Maximum depth: 14 feet

Out in the middle of no man's land, halfway between Ivy Lake and Index Creek lies Bugle Lake. I've never been to this one. I assume you can get to it by walking cross-country from Crazy Creek. Look for 9-inch brookies for your efforts.

Clarks Fork of the Yellowstone River Drainage—Montana

My neck stiffened. My heart pounded in my chest. My head fumbled for a quick solution, waiting for the moment my tent would unzip where no zipper existed. The heavy rummaging outside had to be a griz: I'd seen two that early evening foraging on fish that were dying from rotenone applied to the lake where I was camping.

They say you should take a position protective of your vital areas and stay still in your bedroll. Not me—I wasn't going to die in the sack. It was going to be straight up, one on one. My feet hit the turf, jello legs apparently disagreeing with that plan. Suddenly the darkness in the timbered hollow was pierced with glowing eyes—as a pine martin jumped off my backpack and disappeared into the darkness.

The sight of grizzly bears near camp can make the mind rerun the vision of their magnificent forms all through a sleepless night. I have encountered numerous black bears in the high country and have never given them a thought. Grizzlies are another story. They play havoc with the nervous system. One night I slept under the stars less than 500 feet from a photo station that had been established, unknown to me, by the Grizzly Bear Study Team. After hearing unusual noises that night, I scouted the area at daylight. I found time-lapse cameras carefully aimed at the deer carcass that lay up the hill from my temporary bedroom. It was my error; the area was signed, but the street lights were out when I turned in.

Grizzlies are rare in most of the Absaroka-Beartooth Area, but they can be encountered in the Clarks Fork and further west in Slough Creek country. Watch your camp habits; don't invite a visitor to a meal you might enjoy more by yourself. Keep a clean camp and hang your food. Remember—the chances of getting hurt while driving to the trailhead are many times greater than the chances of getting hurt by a grizzly.

The Clarks Fork was like a home away from home for me while I was surveying the 424 lakes there. The country is pleasant, not as steep as the U-shaped glacial canyons to the north. The Clarks Fork slopes more gently from the northern boundary peaks to the Wyoming state line. There are basically three elevation zones as you move along the north-south axis. The lowest lake in the Montana portion is 7,880 feet high; the highest, at 11,200 feet, tops any other lake in Montana.

This area may very well have the highest density of alpine lakes anywhere. The drainage is only 117.2 square miles, but lakes cover 4,274 acres: 5.7 percent of the whole area is under lake water. The largest (292 acres) and deepest (195 feet) is Upper Aero Lake. Nine lakes exceed 100 acres; 15 lakes exceed 100 feet in depth. Ninety percent of the lakes are 9-10,000 feet in elevation.

The Beartooth Pass (Highway 212) between Red Lodge and Cooke City provides access to four jeep trails—to Goose Lake, Lulu Pass, Daisy Lake, and Crazy Lake. The hiking trails are typically good and numerous below timberline; above treeline, however, most of the travel is cross-country.

The lower elevation lakes near Cooke City are the first in the Absaroka-Beartooth Mountains to rid themselves of ice, which they do around late May to early June. Some of the cold valleys in the high country don't give up on winter until August.

The western area of the drainage is best approached from the notorious Goose Lake jeep trail. Further east, the Crazy Creek drainage provides access trails. Still further east, access trails leave from the Clay Butte-Beartooth Lake area. East of Clay Butte-Beartooth is the Island Lake jump-off point. The drainage's eastern boundary can be approached from the Beartooth Highway on the switchbacks above Long Lake.

Clarks Fork of the Yellowstone

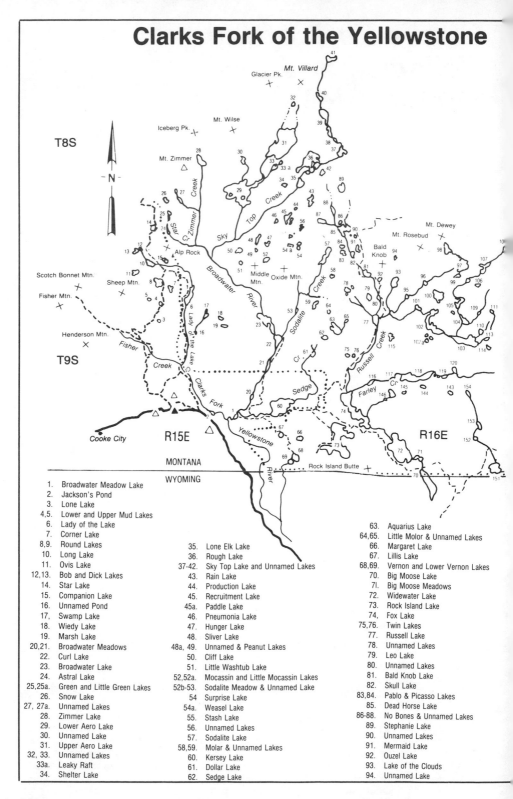

T8S

Mt. Villard
Glacier Pk.
Mt. Wilse
Iceberg Pk.
Mt. Zimmer

Zimmer Creek
Star Cr.
Sky Top Creek

Scotch Bonnet Mtn.
Sheep Mtn.
Alp Rock
Fisher Mtn.
Henderson Mtn.
Fisher

T9S

Lady of the Lake Creek
Broadwater River
Middle Mtn.
Oxide Mtn.
Sodalite Creek

Mt. Dewey
Mt. Rosebud
Bald Knob

Russell Creek

Clarks Fork
Sedge Cr.
Farley Cr.

R15E
Cooke City
Yellowstone
R16E

MONTANA
WYOMING
River
Rock Island Butte

1. Broadwater Meadow Lake
2. Jackson's Pond
3. Lone Lake
4,5. Lower and Upper Mud Lakes
6. Lady of the Lake
7. Corner Lake
8,9. Round Lakes
10. Long Lake
11. Ovis Lake
12,13. Bob and Dick Lakes
14. Star Lake
15. Companion Lake
16. Unnamed Pond
17. Swamp Lake
18. Wiedy Lake
19. Marsh Lake
20,21. Broadwater Meadows
22. Curl Lake
23. Broadwater Lake
24. Astral Lake
25,25a. Green and Little Green Lakes
26. Snow Lake
27, 27a. Unnamed Lakes
28. Zimmer Lake
29. Lower Aero Lake
30. Unnamed Lake
31. Upper Aero Lake
32, 33. Unnamed Lakes
33a. Leaky Raft
34. Shelter Lake

35. Lone Elk Lake
36. Rough Lake
37-42. Sky Top Lake and Unnamed Lakes
43. Rain Lake
44. Production Lake
45. Recruitment Lake
45a. Paddle Lake
46. Pneumonia Lake
47. Hunger Lake
48. Sliver Lake
48a, 49. Unnamed & Peanut Lakes
50. Cliff Lake
51. Little Washtub Lake
52,52a. Mocassin and Little Mocassin Lakes
52b-53. Sodalite Meadow & Unnamed Lake
54. Surprise Lake
54a. Weasel Lake
55. Stash Lake
56. Unnamed Lakes
57. Sodalite Lake
58,59. Molar & Unnamed Lakes
60. Kersey Lake
61. Dollar Lake
62. Sedge Lake

63. Aquarius Lake
64,65. Little Molor & Unnamed Lakes
66. Margaret Lake
67. Lillis Lake
68,69. Vernon and Lower Vernon Lakes
70. Big Moose Lake
71. Big Moose Meadows
72. Widewater Lake
73. Rock Island Lake
74. Fox Lake
75,76. Twin Lakes
77. Russell Lake
78. Unnamed Lakes
79. Leo Lake
80. Unnamed Lakes
81. Bald Knob Lake
82. Skull Lake
83,84. Pablo & Picasso Lakes
85. Dead Horse Lake
86-88. No Bones & Unnamed Lakes
89. Stephanie Lake
90. Unnamed Lakes
91. Mermaid Lake
92. Ouzel Lake
93. Lake of the Clouds
94. Unnamed Lake

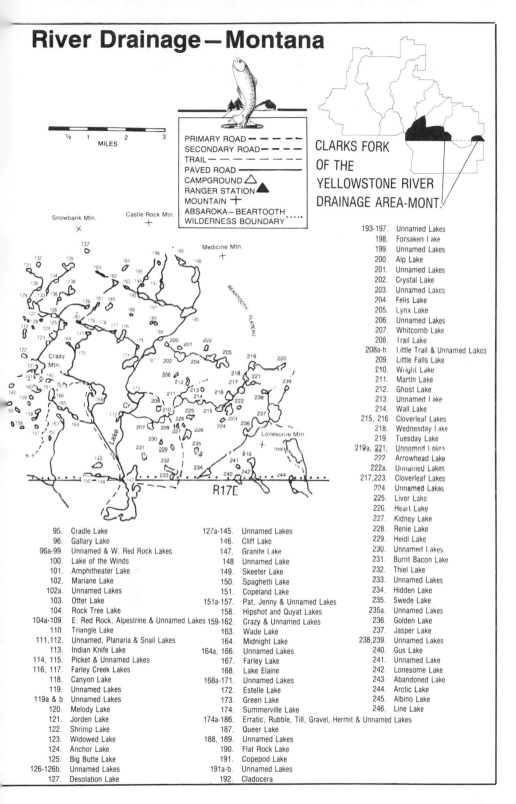

River Drainage — Montana

Legend:
- PRIMARY ROAD — — — —
- SECONDARY ROAD — — — —
- TRAIL — — — — — — —
- PAVED ROAD ————
- CAMPGROUND △
- RANGER STATION ▲
- MOUNTAIN +
- ABSAROKA — BEARTOOTH WILDERNESS BOUNDARY ·····

CLARKS FORK
OF THE
YELLOWSTONE RIVER
DRAINAGE AREA-MONT.

MILES ½ 1 2 3

Snowbank Mtn. ✕ Castle Rock Mtn. + Medicine Mtn. +

BEARTOOTH PLATEAU

Crazy Mtn.

Lonesome Mtn. +

R17E

193-197.	Unnamed Lakes
198.	Forsaken Lake
199.	Unnamed Lakes
200.	Alp Lake
201.	Unnamed Lakes
202.	Crystal Lake
203.	Unnamed Lakes
204	Felis Lake
205.	Lynx Lake
206.	Unnamed Lakes
207.	Whitcomb Lake
208.	Trail Lake
208a-b.	Little Trail & Unnamed Lakes
209.	Little Falls Lake
210.	Wright Lake
211.	Martin Lake
212.	Ghost Lake
213.	Unnamed Lake
214.	Wall Lake
215, 216	Cloverleaf Lakes
218.	Wednesday Lake
219.	Tuesday Lake
219a, 221.	Unnamed Lakes
222	Arrowhead Lake
222a.	Unnamed Lakes
217,223.	Cloverleaf Lakes
224.	Unnamed Lakes
225.	Liver Lake
226.	Heart Lake
227.	Kidney Lake
228.	Renie Lake
229.	Heidi Lake
230.	Unnamed Lakes
231.	Burnt Bacon Lake
232.	Thiel Lake
233.	Unnamed Lakes
234.	Hidden Lake
235.	Swede Lake
235a.	Unnamed Lakes
236.	Golden Lake
237.	Jasper Lake
238,239.	Unnamed Lakes
240.	Gus Lake
241.	Unnamed Lake
242.	Lonesome Lake
243.	Abandoned Lake
244.	Arctic Lake
245.	Albino Lake
246.	Line Lake

95.	Cradle Lake
96.	Gallary Lake
96a-99.	Unnamed & W. Red Rock Lakes
100.	Lake of the Winds
101.	Amphitheater Lake
102.	Mariane Lake
102a.	Unnamed Lakes
103.	Otter Lake
104.	Rock Tree Lake
104a-109.	E. Red Rock, Alpestrine & Unnamed Lakes
110.	Triangle Lake
111,112.	Unnamed, Planaria & Snail Lakes
113.	Indian Knife Lake
114, 115.	Picket & Unnamed Lakes
116, 117.	Farley Creek Lakes
118.	Canyon Lake
119.	Unnamed Lakes
119a & b	Unnamed Lakes
120.	Melody Lake
121.	Jorden Lake
122.	Shrimp Lake
123.	Widowed Lake
124.	Anchor Lake
125.	Big Butte Lake
126-126b.	Unnamed Lakes
127.	Desolation Lake

127a-145.	Unnamed Lakes
146.	Cliff Lake
147.	Granite Lake
148	Unnamed Lake
149.	Skeeter Lake
150.	Spaghetti Lake
151.	Copeland Lake
151a-157.	Pat, Jenny & Unnamed Lakes
158.	Hipshot and Quyat Lakes
159-162.	Crazy & Unnamed Lakes
163.	Wade Lake
164.	Midnight Lake
164a, 166.	Unnamed Lakes
167.	Farley Lake
168.	Lake Elaine
168a-171.	Unnamed Lakes
172.	Estelle Lake
173.	Green Lake
174.	Summerville Lake
174a-186.	Erratic, Rubble, Till, Gravel, Hermit & Unnamed Lakes
187.	Queer Lake
188, 189.	Unnamed Lakes
190.	Flat Rock Lake
191.	Copepod Lake
191a-b.	Unnamed Lakes
192.	Cladocera

111

This Guide's numbering system for these lakes starts in the west, following each of the tributaries of the Broadwater River up the west sides and back down the east sides, and continues up each tributary of the Clarks Fork River to the eastern boundary. Line Lake, which on first examination looks to be a part of Rock Creek but actually flows into the Clarks Fork of the Yellowstone, constitutes the last lake in the numbering system.

1. BROADWATER MEADOW

Location: T9S, R15E, S.28A
Elevation: 7,978 feet
Area: 1.4 acres
Maximum depth: 4 feet

Your basic wide spot in the Broadwater River, Broadwater Meadow is not really a lake but is a popular fishing hole. It's easily accessible by jeep or walking Forest trail #3 for a short distance from the trailhead near Cooke Pass. You can also wade the Broadwater River near Forage Creek for faster access. The meadow is outside the Absaroka-Beartooth Wilderness Area.

Brook trout at Broadwater are abundant but small in size. An occasional cutthroat or grayling might lurk here; however, they're considered rare. These species come from parent stock located elsewhere in the Broadwater drainage and have not become self-sustaining—probably due to intense competition from brook trout.

2, 3, & 4. JACKSONS POND, LONE LAKE, AND MUD LAKE (fishless)

5. SCHOOLMARM (UPPER MUD) LAKE

Location: T9S, R15E, S.7BA
Elevation: 9,520 feet
Area: 3 acres
Maximum depth: 25 feet

Schoolmarm, known to some as Upper Mud, is a pretty little lake west of Mud Lake. No trail leads to the lake, but you can easily get to it by walking from the Goose Lake jeep trail. I can't guarantee any fish are left here. It was stocked in 1977 and all the stock may have been winter-killed. Someday, FW&P will try again.

6. LADY OF THE LAKE

Location: T9S, R15E, S.5.8
Elevation: 8,800 feet
Area: 42.8 acres
Maximum depth: 29 feet

Lady lies in a meadow and forest area in the hole east of the Goose Lake jeep trail. To get there you can take trail #31, which departs the jeep trail on the corner before getting to Long and Companion lakes, or hike the creek trail (#563), or hike via the old Mill Site. The Lady is full of little brook trout: they're not leader snappers, but they make great eaters.

7. CORNER LAKE

Location: T9S, R15E, S.5, 6, 8
Elevation: 9,220 feet
Area: 11.1 acres
Maximum depth: 42 feet

Corner is a favorite of mine for a quick trip to some cutthroat trout action. I won't brag about their size, but I still enjoy the rascals on a small gray-hackle fly. It's near the Goose Lake jeep trail and is accessible by four-wheel drive vehicles. The stream that dumps into Corner flows out of Mud Lake. Fish 9-11 inches are about average. I tried several tricks to increase their size but still come up with 9—11-inch fish.

8 & 9. ROUND LAKES

Location: T9S, R15E, S. 6D
Elevation: 9,340 feet
Area: 31 acres
Maximum depth: 32 feet

Round Lake is one of the popular lakes along the Goose Lake jeep trail. One cabin occupies the shoreline, the road is close enough to the lake to allow trolling from the window. Excellently conditioned brook trout and a few cutthroat live in Round Lake. Brookies average 11.5 inches and are hard to persuade.

10. LONG LAKE

Location: T9S, R15E, S.6
Elevation: 9,471 feet
Area: 11.9 acres
Maximum depth: 21 feet

Long Lake, which incidentally is 1,874 feet long, drains into Lady of the Lake. You'll find it on the Goose Lake jeep trail about 4.5 miles from the Beartooth Highway 212. The jeep trail parallels the north shoreline before heading up the hill to Star Lake. Long Lake lies outside the Absaroka-Beartooth Area.

The lake has a prolific population of brook trout. A few tricks were attempted to increase fish size, and they worked—but only temporarily. A few cutthroat trout escapees from Ovis Lake reside in Long Lake. Fuel is available for camping and many other lakes are nearby.

11. OVIS (SHEEP) LAKE

Location: T9S, R15E, S.6
Elevation: 9,600 feet
Area: 8.6 acres
Maximum depth: 45 feet

Ovis Lake, sometimes called Sheep Lake, nests on the slope above Long Lake near Sheep Mountain. Accessible by jeep or by a short walk from the Goose Lake jeep trail, Ovis features a scenic camping area with plenty of fuel nearby. The lake holds a mixture of brook and cutts, which usually provide good action. Ovis Lake is outside the Absaroka-Beartooth Wilderness Area.

12 & 13. BOB AND DICK LAKES

Location: T8S, R15E, S. 31CC
Elevation: 9,480 feet, 9,475 feet, respectively
Area: 2.3 acres; 1.9 acres, respectively
Maximum depth: 15 feet; 15 feet, respectively

These little lakes are separated by a short channel that allows brookies to visit either lake. Both lakes lie one-half mile west of the Goose Lake jeep trail. The outlet flows from Bob to Dick and on down Lady of the Lake Creek to the Clarks Fork River. The residing brookies are too small to measure.

14. STAR LAKE

Location: T8S, R15E, S. 31 AC
Elevation: 9,646 feet
Area: 7.9 acres
Maximum depth: 36 feet

Star Lake has a history of various fisheries-related activity. It was once (in the 1940s) considered for artificial enrichment with nitrate and phosphate fertilizer. The job was never completed, but a load of aquatic food organisms were released here. Star hosted albino rainbow and brook trout for part of its history. Lately it has been an excellent cutthroat trout fishery. Located along the Goose Lake jeep trail, Star has numerous camp sites with plenty of fuel. The lake is stocked every four years, with the last plant in 1984.

15. COMPANION LAKE

Location: T9S, R15E, S. 6AA
Elevation: 9,415 feet
Area: 5.2 acres
Maximum depth: 24 feet

Companion Lake is a neighbor to Long Lake; the two lie within easy walking distance of one another. The Goose Lake jeep trail meanders through the real estate between the two lakes. Companion is about 4.5 miles from U.S. Highway 212. Fish here are numerous but not very big. Recently fish size was improved considerably by partially thinning the population. This practice should be repeated about every four years to keep the quality of recreation at an acceptable level. My thoughts for best management would be to completely rehabilitate Companion Lake to a grayling fishery, thereby providing some accessible and varied fishing in the area.

16. UNNAMED POND

Location: T9S, R15E, S. 17AB
Elevation: 7,810 feet
Area: 2.1 acres
Maximum depth: 4 feet

This small pond is on Swamp Creek downstream from Swamp Lake. This puddle is below timberline; therefore, fuel for camping fires is available. No trail leads to it, but it's not far from Lady of the Lake Creek trail. Numerous small brook trout were observed in this pond and in the creek between the pond and Lady of the Lake Creek.

17. SWAMP LAKE

Location: T9S, R15E, S. 8
Elevation: 8,940 feet
Area: 10.4 acres
Maximum depth: 21 feet

Swamp Lake is hidden in the trees between Lady of the Lake and Broadwater Lake. The lake produced excellent growth for an experimental plant of cutthroat trout; these fish have long since died out, however, and Swamp Lake is fallow, waiting patiently for a grayling plant. Check with the fishery manager to see if and when the fish were delivered. This is a perfect lake for the graceful grayling beauties, and ideal for their self-perpetuation.

18. WIEDY LAKE

Location: T9S, R15E. S. 9 CA
Elevation: 9,010 feet
Area: 7.1 acres
Maximum depth: 68 feet

WARNING: This is a high density mosquito area—take repellent and keep your mouth shut! The mosquitoes really aren't that bad by late summer but they can be bad early on. Wiedy Lake is somewhat like a pond, but it's amazingly deep for its mellow surroundings and marshy characteristics. Some rooted aquatic plants occupy the shoal areas, with a considerable number of conifers surrounding the immediate shoreline. Access is by foot, probably best from trails near Lady of the Lake Creek. This is another great grayling candidate. It's barren as this book goes to press, but a plant is scheduled. Check with the FW&P before expecting a lake full of grayling.

19. MARSH LAKE

Location: T9S, R15E, S. 9 CD
Elevation: 9,018 feet.
Area: 3.8 acres
Maximum depth: 25 feet

Here's a scenic little lake, somewhat like a pond located within a wet forest environment. It's located near Swamp and Wiedy lakes. Access is best by foot due to the thickness of trees and downfalls. There are no trails in the immediate vicinity; however, access is easy from trails in the Lady of the Lake area. Marsh Lake was stocked with an experimental plant of rainbow trout in 1980. Because of the rich food source, I expect leader snappers.

20 & 21. BROADWATER MEADOWS

Location: T9S, R15E, S. 22C
Elevation: 8,030 feet
Area: 3.6 acres; 7.8 acres, respectively
Maximum depth: 3 feet; 4 feet, respectively

The Broadwater has three large meadows, one near Cooke Pass (#1 in this section) where the Broadwater changes its name to the Clarks Fork of the Yellowstone River, and two upstream. Number 20 is the middle meadow and #21 is just below Curl Lake. Trail #564 leads by both of these meadow areas to Curl and Broadwater lakes. Good fishing for brook

114

trout, and a possible grayling or cutthroat could reside. Plenty of fuel exists in the valley for camping opportunities.

22. CURL LAKE

Location: T9S, R15E, S. 15A
Elevation: 8,398 feet
Area: 30.6 acres
Maximum depth: 45 feet

Look for Curl Lake about four miles from the trailhead #564 at Colter Pass. This well-maintained trail follows the Broadwater River. Curl Lake connects with Broadwater Lake immediately upstream. Try Curl for lots of good-eating, pan-sized brookies. Also, a rare grayling may be enticed to take a small fly but don't count on it.

23. BROADWATER LAKE

Location: T9S, R15E, S. 10
Elevation: 8,298 feet
Area: 93.6 acres
Maximum depth: 64 feet

Broadwater and Curl are essentially one large lake. Both wide spots in the Broadwater River, they cover 124.2 combined surface acres. A good pack trail (#564) leads to and past Broadwater Lake. The lake lies approximately five miles from the trailhead at Colter Pass. A timbered valley surrounds the lake.

A sample of 45 brook trout taken from the lake were found to average 8 inches and a quarter pound. One 14-inch grayling was also captured. The brookies ranged from 5.5 to 10.5 inches. The grayling most likely come from Rough Lake in the headwaters of the Broadwater.

Formed by a massive rock slide, Star Lake was recommended as a transplant site for aborigine grayling from southwest Montana. U.S. Forest Service photo.

24. ASTRAL LAKE

Location: T8S, R15E, S. 31 AD
Elevation: 9,320 feet
Area: 5.2 acres
Maximum depth: 4 feet

Brook trout went wild in this country. This little lake is the furthest downstream lake on Star Creek, a tributary of the Broadwater. Maximum depth is only four feet, but it contains numerous brook trout (of 5-9 inches). One thing about these little fish is that they are fat and in good shape. The lake is accessible from the Goose Lake jeep trail by hiking down Star Creek. It's also accessible from Broadwater country trails.

25 & 25a. GREEN AND LITTLE GREEN LAKES

Location: T8S, R15E, S. 30, 31
Elevation: 9,640 feet
Area: 4.8 acres; 1.8 acres, respectively
Maximum depth: 16 feet; 6 feet, respectively

A couple more of the small lakes found in the Star Creek drainage of the Broadwater, Green and Little Green are accessible by a short hike down Star Creek from Star Lake or by a long hike from the trails in the Broadwater. Both lakes harbor brook trout of 6-9 inches.

26, 27, & 27a. SNOW AND UNNAMED LAKES (3) *(fishless)*

28. ZIMMER LAKE

Location: T8S, R15E, S. 20 CA
Elevation: 10,140 feet
Area: 26 acres
Maximum depth: 55 feet

Zimmer Lake lies in a cold valley just east of Goose Lake. You can hike over Zimmer Mountain to get there, but that route is much slower than going up the trail to Grasshopper Glacier, across the glacier, and then back down to Zimmer Lake. You won't find a lot of fuel here—just short, stunted krummholtz conifers.

Zimmer has had a variable, up-and-down fishery for years, but finally the right numbers and frequency of stocking have been achieved to provide the best opportunity for fish growth. Look for some nice cutts, but schedule your visit based on the eight-year stocking interval.

29. LOWER AERO LAKE

Location: T8S, R15E, S. 27, 28
Elevation: 9,995 feet
Area: 189.9 acres
Maximum depth: 185 feet

Lower Aero is the second largest lake in the Clarks Fork of the Yellowstone River drainage. You can get there by a partly-unmaintained trail up "Cardiac Ridge," or by going up Sky Top Creek Trail to an area near Lone Elk Lake (#35) where you should take the grass valley to the north end of the Lower Aero. I have often come in to Lower Aero from Goose Lake, Grasshopper, Zimmer, and around the horn.

Lower Aero is one of the best, most consistent producers of heavy-bodied fish in the Clarks Fork. The lake has both cutts and brookies. Apparently, the brookies are in check due to limited spawning and thus don't overpopulate. Brookies range from six to 15 inches; many weigh in at or near a pound. The cutts provide some real excitement with a lightweight rod. You'll find good camping in the area.

30. UNNAMED *(fishless)*

31. UPPER AERO LAKE

Location: T8S, R15E, S. 14, 15, 22, 23
Elevation: 10,140 feet
Area: 291.8 acres
Maximum depth: 195 + feet

Upper Aero lake is the largest lake in the Clarks Fork drainage; in fact, it's the second largest (next to Mystic Lake) in the Absaroka-Beartooth Mountains. Also impressive is the 100-foot depth within five feet of the northern shoreline. See Lower Aero (#29) for commonly traveled routes to the Aero Lakes. Fuel is scarce here, not absent but not adequate for camping with fire. It's better to use your stove in the backcountry anyway.

Look for big cutts in Upper Aero. They get large, heavy, and mean here. A word of advice: don't bother fishing the lakeward length of your line. Fish the shoreline. The cutts in Upper Aero are grazers, moving in schools in the shoreline rocks, picking up food in the choicest parts of the lake. Casting down the shoreline in front of a herd usually prompts an aggressive attack. If they are choosey, I find a second fly on a dropper works well. Hang the tip-fly loosely on a rock and let the second dangle teasingly in and out of the water. The stocking schedule calls for stocking every six years; the last plant took place in 1982.

32 & 33. UNNAMED (6) (fishless)

33a. LEAKY RAFT LAKE

Location: T8S, R15E, S. 22 DA
Elevation: 10,170 feet
Area: 8.5 acres
Maximum depth: 30 feet

Leaky Raft is on the same geologic bench as the Aero lakes. It's the larger of the two little lakes east of the midway point between the two Aero Lakes. There are no trails here, just rock and snowbanks. The first batch of cutts planted here measured 11 inches and nearly one-half pound their second year of life; then growth slowed. To produce a nice fish in Leaky Raft will require a low stocking density and lots of time between plants. The program calls for stocking 100 fish per acre every eight years. The last plant was in 1984.

34. SHELTER LAKE

Location: T8S, R15E, S. 26 BB
Elevation: 10,040 feet
Area: 6.8 acres
Maximum depth: 45 feet

At this elevation, shelter is a scarce commodity. There are no trees to speak of, just big rocks under which to wait out a heavy cloudburst. Shelter Lake is a scenic little lake in the Sky Top Creek drainage about one-half mile west of Lone Elk Lake. No trail exists for that half mile; however, a nice trail leads up the west side of Sky Top Creek.

A sample of 24 brookies in Shelter averaged 8 inches. I assume the brook trout were transplanted from either Lower Aero Lake, Rough or Lone Elk lakes.

35. LONE ELK LAKE

Location: T8S, R15E, S. 26 BA
Elevation: 10,070 feet
Area: 18.1 acres
Maximum depth: 40 feet

Lone Elk is your basic greenish-colored, glacial-water lake. To get there, take the trail up Sky Top Creek. You have lots of options to get to Sky Top Creek, including the Broadwater, Lady of the Lake, or Companion Lake routes. Lone Elk is a part of Sky Top Creek.

Don't let the green color or the lack of fish jumping deter you from fishing or send you running up to Rough Lake. This lake is better than Rough—slower, but better. You stand a chance of catching the state record grayling or a 16-inch brook trout here. Both species are happy and fat as kings in Lone Elk Lake. The green color of the lake comes from glacial silts. These silts limit reproduction but not necessarily food organisms—a combination allowing for the growth of large fish.

36. ROUGH LAKE

Location: T8S, R1E, S. 23
Elevation: 10,150 feet
Area: 102.2 acres
Maximum depth: 110 feet

A large, irregular-shaped lake between Lone Elk and Sky Top Creek lakes, Rough is accessible by a new man-made trail. Fuel is sparse, however, so you should take your little gas stove if you like warm beans. The lake harbors good numbers of both brook trout and grayling. The brookies in my sample averaged 9 inches, .35 pounds. Grayling were 13.5 inches, .7 pounds. Both species spawn at the foot of an appealing waterfall that slides into Rough Lake.

It's a glorious spot, but at this elevation you need to be prepared for sudden changes in the weather.

37-43. SKY TOP, RAIN, AND UNNAMED LAKES (14) (fishless)

44. PRODUCTION LAKE

Location: T8S, R15E, S. 26AD
Elevation: 10,070 feet
Area: 3.1 acres
Maximum depth: 42 feet

If you head up Sky Top Creek trail and go cross-country to the east, leaving Sky Top Creek approximately .75 miles downstream from Lone Elk Lake, you will arrive at Production Lake. This is a brook trout factory, producing fish of 7-10 inches. The role it plays is important to a lake called Recruitment (#45) downstream. Recruitment receives some juvenile brookies from Production; in Recruitment, they grow and grow—and fail to reproduce.

45. RECRUITMENT LAKE

Location: T8S, R15E, S. 35 BB
Elevation: 10,038 feet
Area: 13.1 acres
Maximum depth: 53 feet

Recruitment Lake is a receiver lake, the one into which little brookies from Production Lake upstream escape and grow large on the abundant zooplankton. Don't expect lots of fish, but do take a good look from a high vantage point and watch for some big shadows lurking in the depths. I caught a 19.7-inch fish and a 19.6-inch fish here, weighing 3.75 and 3.25 pounds respectively. See the Production Lake description for access to Production and Recruitment lakes. Check the code map for the distinction between the two.

Fishing these alpine lakes by boat is not impossible if you're willing to carry an inflatable raft. Pat Marcuson photo.

118

45a, 46, & 46a. PADDLE, PNEUMONIA, AND UNNAMED LAKES (fishless)

47. HUNGER LAKE

Location: T8S, R15E, S. 34 DB
Elevation: 9,665 feet
Area: 5.1 acres
Maximum depth: 31 feet

Straight east of the floral meadow where Sky Top Creek emerges from Lower Aero Lake is a lake called Sliver (#48), followed by Hunger Lake. Hunger is not an official name, just a handle describing my state of affairs during one of my visits. No trail leads here from Sky Top Creek trail. Very few anglers have fished this lake for its many brook trout. Hunger Lake is to Sliver Lake as Production Lake is to Recruitment Lake (see #44 & 45 for details): it supplies Sliver with a few fish which grow very large. Those in Hunger Lake, however, grow only to about 6-9 inches.

48. SLIVER LAKE

Location: T8S, R15E, S. 34C
Elevation: 9,520 feet
Area: 6.9 acres
Maximum depth: 22 feet

Sliver Lake (unnamed on maps) is a long, slender lake with large, heavy brookies. It is easily accessible by foot from the Sky Top Creek trail. The distance through the trees from Sky Top is about .75 miles. Several little ponds occupy niches in the outlet stream from Sliver Lake.

Sliver receives brookies from Hunger Lake upstream when the flows are high enough to allow fish passage. I caught two fish in Sliver Lake weighing 4-5 pounds—very nice brook trout. So nice that I had planned to treat them with loving care and take them home to mount over the fireplace. I carefully wrapped the fish in a wet burlap bag, built a cave in a large snowbank, fortified the entrance with a large rock, placed logs over the top, and went on with my work. The following morning I approached my cache. Footprints and a bloody trail led me to believe things were not to be as I had planned. The large brook trout over the fireplace would have been replaced by a pine martin, had I found the little thief.

48a, 48b, 49, & 49a. PEANUT AND UNNAMED LAKES (6) (fishless)

50. CLIFF LAKE

Location: T8S, R15E, S. 33D
Elevation: 9,249 feet
Area: 6.6 acres
Maximum depth: 20 feet

If Cliff Lake is supposed to be a reflection of the area's geology, then it's poorly named. The shoreline has no cliffs—numerous islands, but no cliffs. Remnants of a poor trail lead from Sky Top Creek to Cliff Lake. This involves fording Sky Top Creek, which, during high flows, requires some effort. Timber is present at Cliff and several campsites are located on the west shore.

Brook trout occupy Cliff Lake. The population is periodically altered by winter mortality. Occasionally the lake abounds with fish: other times, the few winter survivors show the impact of hard times. On one expedition, I caught fish in the 13-inch, .81-pound range.

51. LITTLE WASHTUB LAKE

Location: T9S, R15E, S. 4A
Elevation: 9,190 feet
Area: 2.2 acres
Maximum depth: 30 feet

Little Washtub is a small lake pocketed in the trees one-quarter mile east of Cliff Lake. Access is easy from Broadwater Meadows and somewhat more difficult from Sky Top Creek. The lake is fishless at present, but it's looking for a future plant of grayling. Contact the state FW&P in Billings, Montana, for current stocking plans.

52 & 52a. MOCCASIN AND LITTLE MOCCASIN LAKES

Location: T9S, R15E, S. 3
Elevation: 9,400 feet
Area: 6.8 acres; .8 acres, respectively
Maximum depth: 30 feet; 11 feet, respectively

You'll find Moccasin and the little neighbor pond between Middle and Oxide mountains. The discharge of water from Moccasin Lake flows to the Broadwater River. Even without a maintained trail, horses can maneuver along intermittent game trails through the forest and meadows to the lake shore. The lake hosts lots of 7 to 10 inch brookies.

52b & 53. SODALITE MEADOW AND UNNAMED LAKES (2) (fishless)

54. SURPRISE LAKE

Location: T8S, R15E, S. 35 CA
Elevation: 9,860 feet
Area: 7.1 acres
Maximum depth: 33 feet

A skillful horse mounted with a talented rider could weave through the backcountry barriers to this scenic surprise, which lies in the Broadwater River watershed north of Oxide Mountain. Scattered trees provide adequate fuel and shelter for camping in comfort. The surprise is the fishing. When I first found the lake it had cutts at 17 inches, 2.25 pounds. This was a surprise since no planting records existed, and the fish had to be of hatchery origin—we biologists know such things. Repeated visits to Surprise Lake suggested that the cutts hadn't reproduced; thus, the lake went on the trophy management list. The stocking schedule looks like this: A small batch of cutthroat trout were delivered in 1977, with another scheduled in 1985, and another eight years after that. Fishing in 1987, '88 and '89 should be excellent.

54a. WEASEL LAKE

Location: T8S, R15E, S. 35 CB
Elevation: 9,940 feet
Area: 3.7 acres
Maximum depth: 20 feet

To make things interesting, once-barren little Weasel Lake right next door to Surprise Lake, is now a fishery. Like Surprise, it must be stocked, but the timing was altered so that either one or the other of the lakes will always be producing. That way no one will get skunked. Weasel Lake was last planted with cutthroat trout in 1981 and is on an eight-year schedule. So between the two lakes, you ought to be able to find the right combination of trophy fishing and just plain catching fun.

55. STASH LAKE

Location: T8S, R15E, S. 35 BC
Elevation: 9,985 feet
Area: 3.1 acres
Maximum depth: 24 feet

Fun times await. Let's add it up: we have Surprise Lake (#54), Weasel Lake (#54A) and Stash Lake (#55), all in a conveniently arranged little group and all with fish. Stash Lake is stocked every eight years, starting in 1983. Surprise Lake will have hot fishing in 1987-89; Weasel Lake should be great in 1983-87; and Stash Lake will be best in 1986-89. Then the whole cycle rotates. Camp right in the middle and go beserk.

56. UNNAMED (11) (fishless)

57. SODALITE LAKE

Location: T8S, R15E, S. 36 CC
Elevation: 9,840 feet
Area: 25.8 acres
Maximum depth: 90 feet

Sodalite Lake is a long, slender canyon lake at the head of Sodalite Creek, a tributary of the Broadwater River. Easiest access to Sodalite is across the rolling alpine rock knobs from Bald Knob-Fossil Lake along trail #567. Hikers can also maneuver up Sodalite Creek to get to Sodalite Lake. Granite rock, snowfields, and scattered clumps of trees are dominant features of the landscape. Sodalite Lake is loaded with brook trout 6-10 inches in length. It's a pretty spot and a fun lake to fish.

58 & 59. MOLAR AND UNNAMED LAKES (5) (fishless)

60. KERSEY LAKE

Location: T9S, R15E, S. 22 D
Elevation: 8,070 feet
Area: 118 acres
Maximum depth: 68 feet

Kersey Lake is easily accessible either by a jeep trail leading to the northwest corner of Kersey that is passable from July to September or by hiking well-used but usually muddy trail #13. The hike from the Cooke Pass trailhead involves about two miles of mild gradient. You'll find Kersey a great place to escape the crowds and fish a mountain lake environment. Sedge Creek meanders through the meadow at the upper end of the lake providing excellent stream fishing for brook trout. This large, private meadow has a couple of cabins. At one time it was partially drained and the grasses harvested for horses and mules that were used in early Cooke City area mining adventures. The grasses were harvested in late summer, then transported across the frozen lake by sled.

Timbered meadow surrounds Kersey and rocks cover its shores. The north shoreline has greater quantities of rock (bluff type) and is usually the most productive for good catches of brookies. The lake was chemically treated in 1969 and restocked with cutthroat trout. Since the rehabilitation, brook trout have reoccupied the lake. Some dandy colorful brookies can be yours during the entire year. A small batch of lake trout may also be cruising the depths of Kersey Lake. Beware, however, of early spring break-up when the ice is unsafe. A lot of folks walk right by this one.

61. DOLLAR LAKE

Location: T9S, R15E, S. 14 AD
Elevation: 8,920 feet
Area: 1.1 acres
Maximum depth: 12 feet

This little one-acre lake is actually just a wide spot on Sedge Creek. Dollar isn't easy to find because Sedge Creek splits before it enters Kersey Meadow. After hiking through Kersey's wet meadow, follow Sedge Creek, keeping to the left of any forks or small tributaries you encounter. Dollar Lake contains numerous grayling, which have occupied the lake since 1955 when grayling were planted in Aquarius Lake upstream. The grayling are not braggers, but they are usually easy to catch on a grey-hackle fly. Recent years have seen more cutthroat in the Dollar-to-Aquarius portion of Sedge Creek.

62. SEDGE LAKE

Location: T9S, R15E, S. 13 B
Elevation: 9,100 feet
Area: 4.7 acres
Maximum depth: 28 feet

Sedge Lake is the second of three lakes on Sedge Creek. Follow the drainage from Kersey Meadow; once you find Dollar Lake your uncertainty about your location will be dispelled. Aquarius and Sedge lakes can also be approached from Russell Lake. This route has a landscape that leads you in the right direction. Both grayling and cutts provide lots of action. You'll find plenty of fuel and isolation for a great backpacking experience.

63. AQUARIUS LAKE

Location: T9S, R15E, S. 1 C
Elevation: 9,180 feet
Area: 4.6 acres
Maximum depth: 65 feet

I hope the sun shines on you in your travels to beautiful Aquarius Lake. To get there, your choices are the route up Sedge Creek or the cross-country route along an old abandoned trail which departs trail #567 between Twin and Russell lakes. The lake once supported grayling (stocked in 1955). Now the only grayling are downstream in Sedge and Dollar lakes. The lake was stocked with cutthroat in 1967 and 1977. These rascals reproduced, and fishing looks good for years to come. Aquarius is a nice area with plenty of fuel and shelter.

64 & 65. LITTLE MOLAR AND UNNAMED (3) (fishless)

66. MARGARET LAKE
Location: T9S, R15E, S. 26
Elevation: 8,100 feet
Area: 3.9 acres
Maximum depth: 22 feet

Margaret Lake is a small, pond-like lake located halfway between Kersey and Rock Island lakes in the Gallatin National Forest. Since Margaret was stocked and has produced whoppers, a trail to the lake has been stomped into the turf from the Vernon Lake trail. Another path to it has been beaten from the east end of Kersey Lake.

The shoreline is somewhat difficult to fish. The banks are either very bushy or floating mats of wet sod. One little point of rocks provides a dry casting platform on the north shoreline. Margaret has potential for super fish, with cutts of the McBride Lake variety awaiting your skills. Don't expect a fish every cast; the lake abounds with excellent feed and the lunkers favor big food items.

67. LILLIS LAKE
Location: T9S, R15E, S. 27 D
Elevation: 9,200 feet
Area: 2.7 acres
Maximum depth: 30 feet

Lillis is a small, three-acre, pond-type lake along the trail from Kersey to Vernon Lake. The country is nice for a day hike. To get to Lillis, leave the Kersey Lake trail (#567) at the first appearance of Kersey Lake. Lillis is hard to fish with its aquatic vegetation, brushy banks, and wet, swampy borders blanketing the shoreline. Lillis does have some nice brook trout, though, with many up to 12 inches—thick, colorful, and tasty.

68 & 69. VERNON AND LOWER VERNON LAKES
Location: T9S, R15E, S. 35 BA
Elevation: 7,900 feet
Area: 8.2 acres
Maximum depth: 32 feet

Take the cut-off trail southeast of trail #567 just before the approach of Kersey Lake. Vernon is about 1.5 miles from this junction and 2.75 miles from the trailhead at Cooke Pass. Vernon, like its neighbor lakes, Margaret and Lillis, is pond-like, brownish in color, and has similar wet, brushy banks. Campsites are located near the lakeshore.

Both cutthroat and brook trout dwell in Vernon and Lower Vernon lakes. Both species grow well and can provide plenty of action when they're in the mood. I suggest fishing in early summer before the aquatic plants make shoreline fishing difficult. You might even give it a try in the winter; some days a properly located hole can be real productive.

70. BIG MOOSE LAKE
Location: T58N, R107W, S. 23
Elevation: 8,000 feet
Area: 83.8 acres
Maximum depth: 46 feet

The vast majority of Big Moose Lake lies in Wyoming, part of the Crazy Lake chain. Access is by a jeep trail (Lily Lake Road) from the Beartooth Highway or trail #3 along the Widewater-Fox-Rock Island Lake ridge. Check your steering before driving the snaky road. Big Moose contains mostly rainbow trout, with some dandies weighing two pounds. The lake also has some brookies and even a possible grayling. You'll find a nice campsite at the jeep trail's termination.

71. BIG MOOSE MEADOWS

Location: T9S, R16E, S. 28C
Elevation: 8,004 feet
Area: 7.5 acres
Maximum depth: 3 feet

Big Moose Meadows is a wide meadow in Crazy Creek between Widewater and Moose lakes. Fish can move between waters, so the meadow makes for a nifty stream-type fishing experience—a good break if action is slow in the lake. The dominant species is rainbow trout, with brook trout and grayling in lesser numbers.

72. WIDEWATER LAKE

Location: T9S, R16E, S. 29
Elevation: 8,008 feet
Area: 110.7 acres
Maximum depth: 110 feet

Widewater is the biggest of the four Crazy Lakes and typically has the best fishing. The lake is accessible by a good foot trail (#3), an easy hike up Crazy Creek, or the jeep trail. It is approximately six miles from the trailhead at Crazy Creek Camp. Don't forget the jeep trail as a possible route.

This big lake has rainbow, brookies, and grayling. I've seen each species have its turn at being dominant over the others. I'll lay odds the brook trout ultimately win the struggle.

73. ROCK ISLAND LAKE

Location: T9S, R15E, S. 25
Elevation: 8,166 feet
Area: 137 acres
Maximum depth: 110 feet

Mr. Steady, if you need large fish then Rock Island Lake is the place. It has its slow days, but if you like your catch to consist of a few big fish rather than a load of little ones, fish here. Both cutthroat and brook trout provide the angler with a challenge. Dedicated fishermen tempt Rock Island Lake fish during all seasons except spring break-up.

Rock Island Lake is close enough to allow day-trip fishing and far enough not to gather a crowd. The most commonly used route to get there is to take trail #567 from Cooke Pass for 2.5 miles, then go .75 miles via trail #565. All trails are well maintained. Camping is excellent in the forest environment around the lake. Beware of moose. A friend of retired game warden Vern Waples had a horse eviscerated by a bull moose while the horse was picketed for the night.

74. FOX LAKE

Location: T9S, R15E, S. 24, 25
Elevation: 8,055 feet
Area: 111.4 acres
Maximum depth: 75 feet

Fox is approachable from several directions: up Crazy Creek or from the Interstate 90-type trail #567, the Cooke Pass-Alpine Trail. The latter route is fastest and easiest. Fox Lake falls within the day trip category but approaches the limit for having time for relaxed fishing. The lake lies in the pines; you'll find plenty of camping spots. Expect to catch brook trout in the 8 to 10 inch category. Don't be surprised, however, to find a rainbow or grayling. Fox Lake was predominantly a rainbow trout fishery prior to 1970, but brook trout from Russell Creek and grayling from the Cliff Lake drainage invaded the lake and have suppressed the rainbow to poor growth and lower reproductive levels. Grayling became the most successful fish in the lake, reaching the 12-inch size, but their dominance was only momentary. Brook trout have the ability to dominate because they spawn in the fall and can use a wide variety of habitat to perpetuate their kind.

75 & 76. TWIN LAKES (2) (fishless)

77. RUSSELL LAKE

Location: T9S, R16E, S. 7A
Elevation: 8,780 feet

Area: 27.5 acres
Maximum depth: 95 feet

Russell is located 5.5 miles from Cooke Pass on the "highway trail" (#567). The country in and around Russell Lake provides a good overnight stay for travelers on the Cooke City-East Rosebud Lake hike. Plenty of fuel, shelter, and fresh water await the tired hiker.

Two major inlets add to Russell Lake's pristine nature. Its outlet presents a striking scene as it cascades over large granite rock on its way to Crazy Creek and eventually the Clarks Fork of the Yellowstone.

You have a choice of directions from Russell: you can head along a pack-trail to Marraine-Otter lakes; cross-country toward Aquarius-Sedge lakes; or north-south along the main trail. You'll find excellent fishing for camp fare at Russell, with lots of brook trout of 8-11 inches.

78. UNNAMED (5) (fishless)

79. LEO LAKE

Location: T9S, R16E, S. 6D
Elevation: 9,300 feet
Area: 8.5 acres
Maximum depth: 55 feet

An inconspicuous, pristine lake west of trail #567, Leo Lake lies midway between Russell and Bald Knob lakes (see code map). Even though Leo is not visible from the trail, you can feel its presence: the trail is mildly gradient, the creek has time to pool, and the contour of the land looks mellow enough for a lake basin. Leo was stocked in 1968; since then it has become self-sustaining and provides excellent fishing for dandy cutthroat trout. Let the FW&P folks know what you see—better, what you catch. This will help them know whether Leo needs another shot of fish.

80. UNNAMED (2) (fishless)

81. BALD KNOB LAKE

Location: T9S, R16E, S. 6A
Elevation: 9,420 feet
Area: 15.4 acres
Maximum depth: 38 feet

For the travelers from the south trailhead at Cooke Pass, Bald Knob provides a new scene: a sub-arctic setting with runty, sparse trees; permanent snowfields; exposed granites; and alpine grasses and floral arrangements. This invites unlimited cross-country tours.

Bald Knob Lake sits at the base of Bald Knob Mountain, along trail #567. The shoreline is open and mostly unrestricted for broadcasting a fly. The lake area provides a popular overnight spot along this well-used (Cooke Pass-East Rosebud) trail. The fishing is good for lots of little, but yummy, brook trout.

82. SKULL LAKE

Location: T8S, R15E, S. 36 DDC
Elevation: 9,640 feet
Area: 5.5 acres
Maximum depth: 16 feet

This lake is on trail #567 between Bald Knob and Fossil lakes. Bald Knob is one-half mile downstream. Skull holds loads of brookies.

83 & 84. PABLO AND PICASSO LAKES (fishless)

85. DEAD HORSE (FIZZLE) (WINDY) LAKE

Location: T8S, R15E, S. 36 AC
Elevation: 9,830 feet
Area: 36.7 acres
Maximum depth: 48 feet

Call it whatever you like; fish it for brook trout. This lake has an overpopulation problem—the typical rabbit-like explosion of brook trout. Dead Horse, located in an open sub-arctic area where trees stand in small krummholz thickets, makes a good camping spot with plenty of fresh fish for camp enjoyment.

86, 87, 88, & 90. NO BONES AND UNNAMED LAKES (12) (fishless)

89. STEPHANIE LAKE

Location: T8S, R15E, S. 25 B
Elevation: 10,260 feet
Area: 13.9 acres
Maximum depth: 65 feet

A mile and a half northwest of Fossil Lake near the head of the Clarks Fork drainage divide is a 14-acre beauty named Stephanie. She occupies the rugged high country, where the terrain is probably impassable except for those willing to walk. Stephanie was stocked with cutthroat in 1982 and is scheduled for a refill in 1990.

91. MERMAID LAKE

Location: T8S, R15E, S. 36 DDA
Elevation: 9,700 feet
Area: 6.8 acres
Maximum depth: 30 feet

Mermaid lies southeast of Fossil Lake about .75 miles east of the Fossil-Bald Knob trail #567. Just above Bald Knob Lake, you'll find three lakes along an east-west axis. The trail parallels the middle (Skull) lake. Mermaid is the easternmost lake. This emerald green lake on Russell Creek was stocked in 1982 and it contains, believe it or not, not brookies but cutthroat. Since the cutts have abundant food, this lake will be, I believe, a winner.

92. OUZEL LAKE

Location: T9S, R16E, S. 5BB
Elevation: 9,410 feet
Area: 3.5 acres
Maximum depth: 24 feet

Located on the Bald Knob-Russell segment of trail #567, Ouzel Lake lies about 300 yards east of Bald Knob Lake at just about the place where most normal folks must pause to catch their wind. This teardrop lake sits at the foot of Bald Knob Mountain.

Cutthroat trout were stocked in Ouzel in 1971, 1977, and 1981, to provide some needed change from the steady diet of brook trout common to the Clarks Fork side of the Cooke City-East Rosebud trail. Cutthroat are not entirely alone; an occasional brook trout might also be enticed to bite. If you camp at Bald Knob and want a treat, visit this little gem.

93. LAKE OF THE CLOUDS

Location: T9S, R16E, S. 5B
Elevation: 9,680 feet
Area: 23.6 acres
Maximum depth: 24 feet

If you're in the vicinity of the Cooke-East Rosebud trail country, I suggest a cross-country hike to Lake of the Clouds. One easy way is to head up and over the ridge west of Ouzel Lake. A trip from the Marraine-Lake of the Winds area is also nice. Take your camera; the Lake of the Clouds outlet breaks out of a narrow gap, providing a great photo.

Camping here is great—lots of alpine grass, trees near the outlet, and great fishing for beautiful cutts. Lake of the Clouds is on a six-year stocking frequency. The last load was air-dropped into Lake of the Clouds in 1982. Figure it out—fishing will be best when fish are three to five years old with trophies thereafter.

94. UNNAMED (2) (fishless)

95. CRADLE LAKE

Location: T9S, R16E, S. 5 DA
Elevation: 9,595 feet
Area: 2.9 acres
Maximum depth: 37 feet

Cradled in a small alpine valley, holding the waters from the Red Rock Lakes system, lie two picturesque lakes, Cradle and Gallary (#96). Cradle receives a few "donor" fish from Gallary Lake, which lies immediately upstream. Look for a few nice rainbow trout. No trail exists. Trees in the area are limited to krummholtz patches; the scenery is excellent.

96. GALLARY LAKE

Location: T9S, R16E, S. 4 BC
Elevation: 9,920 feet
Area: 7.4 acres
Maximum depth: 40 feet

Gallary Lake was stocked with rainbow trout about 1980. It's hard to judge whether the rainbow will reproduce and continue to exist in this scenic lake—let's hope so.

Gallary Lake is about two miles from Russell Lake and about halfway between Lake of the Clouds and Lake of the Winds. A beautiful little falls spills into Gallary Lake as it flows down the valley to Russell Lake. Don't expect trails, but do expect lots of rock-hopping.

96a, 97, 98, & 99. W. RED ROCK AND UNNAMED LAKES (7) (fishless)

100. LAKE OF THE WINDS

Location: T9S, R16E, S. 4D
Elevation: 9,910 feet
Area: 40.7 acres
Maximum depth: 186 feet

Lake of the Winds is at timberline; therefore you'll need to hike the short distance south toward Mariane Lake (#102) to get wood for camping. No trail leads to the lake; it is, however, only a short walk from the unmaintained trail at Mariane Lake.

Lake of the Winds was stocked with golden trout in 1956, fishermen pulled goldens out as late as 1970. These fish failed to reproduce, however, and in 1977, Lake of the Winds was stocked with cutthroat trout of the McBride variety. The first plant of cutts grew into fat, pink-meated fish. The lake is scheduled for more cutts in 1985 and should provide great fishing by 1987.

101. AMPHITHEATER LAKE

Location: T9S, R16E, S. 5 DD
Elevation: 9,320 feet
Area: 8.7 acres
Maximum depth: 16 feet

Take a beautiful meadow, an arrangement of alpine flowers, grasses and trees, carefully arrange this setting in an alpine box canyon and you've got Amphitheater Lake. Look for it between Mariane and Russell lakes along an unmaintained trail. Fuel and horse pasture is good. The only problem here is the monotony of small, all-the-same-sized brook trout.

102. MARIANE LAKE

Location: T9S, R16E, S. 9
Elevation: 9,542 feet
Area: 50.8 acres
Maximum depth: 70 feet

A 566-foot-long, 441-foot-wide, 70-foot-deep lake in the Russell Creek subdrainage of the Clarks Fork drainage, Mariane is accessible by foot or horse on an unmaintained trail from Russell Lake. You can also get to it from Otter Lake immediately to the east. The lake had a reputation for large rainbow trout; then some scalawag planted brookies, which eliminated the rainbow and took over the whole lake environment. Brook trout range from little devils to 10 inches.

102a. UNNAMED (2) (fishless)

103. OTTER LAKE

Location: T9S, R16E, S. 10C
Elevation: 9,620 feet
Area: 61.1 acres
Maximum depth: 177 feet

This is another lake that once had rainbow trout but now belongs to lots of 8 to 10 inch brookies. Otter is easily accessible from Jorden Lake, served by forest trail #568 or the unmaintained pack trail up the east fork of Russell Creek from Russell Lake. It's a big lake at 61 acres, near and almost connected to Mariane Lake. Good looking country with lots of alpine grass, scattered clumps of trees, and plenty of room to roam by horse or on foot.

104. ROCK TREE LAKE

Location: T9S, R16E, S. 10 B
Elevation: 9,820 feet
Area: 18.1 acres
Maximum depth: 130 feet

Rock Tree is a scenic 18-acre lake on one of the many forks of Russell Creek. It has an outlet that falls into Otter Lake. Take your camera. The main inlet flows from Z Lake, north of Rock Tree. Fuel for campfires is limited to a few small patches of krummholtz pine thickets. In 1982, Rock Tree Lake was stocked with golden trout with the idea that they would take up permanent residence. The parent stock of these golden reside in Sylvan Lake, in the East Rosebud Creek drainage.

104a-109. E. RED ROCK, ALPESTRINE, AND UNNAMED LAKES (10) (fishless)

110. TRIANGLE LAKE

Location: T9S, R16E, S. 10 DB
Elevation: 9,830 feet
Area: 6.3 acres
Maximum depth: 55 feet

No shortage of Triangle Lakes in the Beartooths. This one is northeast of Otter Lake in a spectacular alpine setting. No trail exists, nor is there any need for one. Access is easy from the Otter-Pickett-Jordan lake country. The area is excellent for camping, with several choices of fish in nearby waters.

Triangle was first stocked in 1979 because of the need to diversify fish species in a predominantly brook trout area. Cutthroat trout of the McBride variety were planted into a source of abundant trout food. Triangle is scheduled for restocking every eight years, so it will be replanted in 1987. Should be excellent fishing.

111 & 112. PLANARIA, SNAIL, AND UNNAMED LAKES (7) (fishless)

113. INDIAN KNIFE LAKE

Location: T9S, R17E, S. 10 DA
Elevation: 9,740 feet
Area: 5.3 acres
Maximum depth: 35 feet

Beartooth country offers a popular combination—wilderness hiking and wilderness fishing. Bill Schneider photo.

Just .25 miles northeast of Otter Lake near the Russell-Farley Creek divide. Access is easy with lots of open alpine grass underfoot. The plan is to stock grayling as soon as available. The little meadow inlet should provide just the right amount of spawning to keep the lake stocked and still keep the population density low enough not to stunt growth.

114 & 115. PICKET AND UNNAMED LAKES (5) (fishless)

116 & 117. FARLEY CREEK LAKES

Location: T9S, R16E, S. 17 & 18
Elevation: 8,500 feet; 8,680 feet, respectively
Area: 1.7; 4.2 acres, respectively
Maximum depth: 4 feet; 7 feet, respectively

Two wide-waters in Farley Creek, both downstream from Canyon Lake. Both of these so-called lakes are found in thick timber. Access from the low country is best from Forest trail #567 to Fox Lake, then by a jaunt up Farley Creek. Cutthroat-rainbow hybrids from 5-15 inches reside in both of these environments, lots of fun for the fly rod enthusiast.

118. CANYON LAKE

Location: T9S, R16E, S. 16, 17
Elevation: 8,780 feet
Area: 67.7 acres
Maximum depth: 87 feet

A popular lake for those in the know, with opportunities for landing large hybrid rainbow. The easiest route is up Farley Creek from Fox Lake, not all that bad a hike if one picks and chooses a route through the forest along the creek. A partial trail exists with plenty of fuel along the shorelines. A rocky cliff occupies the north shore. Most of the fish are rainbow with traces of cutthroat, many of them 13-16 inches long.

119. UNNAMED (2) (fishless)

119a & 119b. UNNAMED LAKES

Location: T9S, R16E, S. 16D
Elevation: 8,860 feet; 9,000 feet, respectively
Area: 2.8 acres total
Maximum depth: 4 feet; 8 feet, respectively

These lakes are a part of Farley Creek between Canyon Lake and the one upstream I call Melody Lake (#120). Access is without trail; however, a horse could be guided down Farley Creek from Crazy Mountain with careful route selection. Fuel for fires is abundant. The easiest alternative involves an approach from the west out of Canyon Lake. The lakes have a self-sustaining population of cutthroat trout.

120. MELODY LAKE

Location: T9S, R16E, S. 15, 16
Elevation: 8,940 feet
Area: 4.8 acres
Maximum depth: 12 feet

From a vantage point on Crazy Mountain near Jorden Lake, look down a long canyon to the east toward Canyon Lake, and see a small body of water glistening in the sun. The lake you see is Melody Lake. Access is fairly steep any way you approach it, but the rewards are great. This canyon setting provides solitude and fishing for colorful, red-meated, nice-sized cutthroat trout. The fish occupying Melody were migrants from Jorden Lake. Here they found ideal spawning conditions and set up housekeeping. Fuel is available and access is without the aid of trails.

121. JORDEN LAKE

Location: T9S, R16E, S. 14
Elevation: 9,625 feet
Area: 36 acres
Maximum depth: 120 feet

At just about the center of the east half of the Gallatin National Forest, you'll find Jorden Lake with 7,315 feet of shoreline. Located in a scattered timber-boulder-grass zone, it is commonly used by packers who follow the Crazy Creek trail #568 from Beartooth Highway 212. Numerous other routes are possible from other locations in the drainage.

Jorden was stocked with Yellowstone cutthroat trout in 1959 and 1967. They grew well and provide good fishing. They failed to reproduce in Jorden Lake, but did find a home in Melody Lake (#120) down Farley Creek. In 1981, cutts of the McBride variety were stocked, and should be beautiful fish.

Look for some goldens in Jorden in the future. The Desolation(#122)-Big Butte(#125)-Anchor(#124) chain of lakes were stocked in 1983 with golden trout which are expected to eventually find their way to Jorden Lake.

I established a base camp at Jorden during my survey days because of its proximity to numerous lakes. The camp was constructed of a large orange-white paneled parachute affectionately tagged "the circus tent." On one particular evening at camp a distinguished guest, the Lieutenant Governor of Montana, Mr. Christenson, occupied the adjacent outfitter's camp. Sharing the mountain experience with him were representatives of the Orvis Company, all excellent fly casters with impressive equipment. Coincidentally, a group of eager Boy Scouts from Gardiner, Montana, had also invaded Jorden Lake. Noticing an obvious lack of luck along the lake, I took out my old whip, donned it with a very simple beat-up gray-hackled peacock, and proceeded to the lake shore where numerous Scouts were enjoying themselves. I offered to show them how to persuade a cutthroat into a striking frenzy. Whaling the water with my line I created a little artificial surface disturbance, then pulled a fly away from some semi-interested fish a time or two, and then I let the fly settle down. I took a beaut right next to the shore. The Scouts had little trouble mastering my crude style and a few fish were soon headed for the frying pans.

While the Scouts were enjoying their success, the distinguished camp watched. Soon the fancy flies were bussing from the finest equipment in the country. I heard comments like, "Come on, guys, a hatch is on." The distinguished guests failed to draw a fish, but they did manage some of the most beautiful casts I had ever seen towards the center of the lake.

The Scouts pounded the shores and pulled in the fish, many up to two pounds. Get the picture? Cutts like the shoals, especially windward shores where their food windrows.

122. SHRIMP LAKE *(fishless)*

123. WIDOWED LAKE
Location: T9S, R16, S. 11 DD
Elevation: 10,010 feet
Area: 3.2 acres
Maximum depth: 15 feet
First lake up the Desolation-Jorden Lake chain, this is a small three-acre lake with two outlets, soon to be teeming with golden trout.

124. ANCHOR LAKE
Location: T9S, R16E, S. 11 & 12
Elevation: 10,045 feet
Area: 12 acres
Maximum depth: 90 feet
Anchor is one of my favorites. Once Anchor Lake had some whopper cutthroat that had drifted downstream from Big Butte Lake. Let those days rest. However, Anchor will shine again with golden trout, and may well be the future star attraction of the Desolation-to-Jorden chain of lakes. Golden trout were introduced to the chain in 1983.

125. BIG BUTTE LAKE
Location: T9S, R16E, S. 12
Elevation: 10,060 feet
Area: 22.1 acres
Maximum depth: 55 feet
I don't know why it's called Big Butte, but I do know that it is above treeline and that rock and alpine grasses prevail. Northeast of Jorden Lake, and Jorden's major inlet, you will find this 22-acre alpine lake. Take the Crazy Creek trail #568 past Crazy Mountain, then cross-country up the major tributary to Big Butte Lake which was stocked with goldens and should be one of the best golden trout fisheries in Montana.

126a & 126b. UNNAMED LAKES (2)

Location: T9S, R16E, S. 1 BB
Elevation: 10,130 feet
Area: 3.6 acres; 3.8 acres, respectively
Maximum depth: 20 feet; 20 feet, respectively

From Jorden Lake (#121), we have advanced up the Desolation chain of lakes to these two little lakes located 50 yards downstream from Desolation Lake (#127). And, yes, we left timberline near Jorden Lake, so don't expect a nice warm fire. These lakes, like the others in the chain, were stocked with golden trout in 1983.

127. DESOLATION LAKE

Location: T9S, R16E, S. 2 & 1!
Elevation: 10,155 feet
Area: 31.4 acres
Maximum depth: 75 feet

My visits to Desolation always featured rain that was more like ice blowing at an unavoidable 45 degree angle—really fun in an inflatable boat with nowhere to hide. The surrounding country is treeless. Look for golden trout, but I suspect the better fishing will be in the lakes downstream. Desolation has little potential because food is very limited.

127a-145. UNNAMED (41) (fishless)

146. CLIFF LAKE

Location: T9S, R16E, S. 20 BA
Elevation: 8,550 feet
Area: 18.4 acres
Maximum depth: 83 feet

The Beartooths have several cliff lakes, but this one is probably best suited for the title. Cliff Lake is a local handle and does not appear in print on the maps of the area. A highly photogenic granitic cliff borders the north shore.

The lake is found north and uphill of Fox Lake and has been a grayling producer since the mid-1950s. I suspect it will probably have grayling for years to come. Grayling found in the Crazy Lakes (Fox to Widewater) downstream came from strays from grayling in this cliff lake. Fish range from 7-11 inches, averaging 10 inches in Cliff Lake.

Don't expect lots of human company. A rested traveler won't find the hike to Cliff all that bad a jaunt from Fox Lake. The biggest hassle is getting across Russell Creek from the east or wading Crazy Creek from the southeast.

Cliff Lake is in the timber and camping spots are plentiful.

147. GRANITE LAKE

Location: T9S, R17E, S. 31, 32
Elevation: 8,625 feet
Area: 228 acres
Maximum depth: 125 feet in the Montana portion

Forty-nine acres of Granite Lake are found in Big Sky Country with 179 acres in the Cowboy State. Routes approach Granite from several directions. Riders of trusty steeds along Muddy Creek and hunters of the wily elk are its most common visitors. Expect these hunters from mid-September until significant snow accumulates. Granite Lake has numerous hunting camps in the protection of the timbered west and north shorelines.

Outlet waters flow to Lake Creek and eventually rumble under Highway 212 at a popular viewing point. Granite has gads of small 8-inch brook trout and a few rainbow trout that have a similar growth problem.

148. UNNAMED (fishless)

149. SKEETER LAKE

Location: T9S, R17E, S. 30 CC
Elevation: 9,310 feet
Area: 10.7 acres
Maximum depth: 25 feet

No trail serves the immediate area of this small, shallow pond-like lake on the Montana-Wyoming border. However, Skeeter is only a short cross-country hike from the Granite or Copeland lake trails. Grayling were planned for 1983 or 1984.

150. SPAGHETTI LAKE

Location: T9S, R16E, S. 36 AA
Elevation: 9,190 feet
Area: 6.3 acres
Maximum depth: 54 feet

A long, slender lake on the Montana-Wyoming border, Spaghetti is located in a heavily-timbered, wet area of Gilbert Creek. The outlet waters flow to Copeland Lake before taking the Gilbert Creek route to the Clarks Fork River.

The lake is accessible by cross-country travel, not very distant from trails at Granite or Copeland lakes. Grayling were in the offing, but this was not a high priority plant, so call the Fish, Wildlife and Parks office in Billings for the skinny.

151. COPELAND LAKE

Location: T9S, R16E, S. 34, 35
Elevation: 8,780 feet
Area: 36 acres
Maximum depth: 125 feet

To reach this round-shaped lake on the Montana-Wyoming border, you can drive to trail #568 by leaving Highway 212 at the Lily Lake turn-off. The road turns into a jeep trail at the point where you pick up the trail. Copeland is about a mile hike from this trail-jeep road intersection, or 4.5 miles from the Crazy Creek trailhead at Crazy Creek campground on Highway 212.

The lake is tucked in the trees, with numerous old campsites situated along the west and south shorelines. It is full of small brook trout with possiblities of a few wayward grayling.

151a-157. PAT, JENNY, AND UNNAMED LAKES (12) (fishless)

158. HIPSHOT AND QUYAT LAKES

Location: T9S, R16E, S. 23 CB
Elevation: 9,750 feet; 9,650 feet, respectively
Area: 9.6 acres; 2.5 acres, respectively
Maximum depth: 47 feet; 6 feet, respectively

This pair is similar to Vernon (#68) and Lower Vernon (#69). The larger lake, Hipshot, is 47 feet deep; the lower, Quyat, only six. The pair are just west of trail #568, two miles north of Copeland Lake. The management goal called for big cutts so Hipshot was given a shot of 1,000 fish in 1979 and was put on an eight-year stocking frequency to allow plenty of grits for all the finny occupants. If it's planted again in 1987, it should be a goodie.

159-162. CRAZY AND UNNAMED LAKES (10) (fishless)

163. WADE LAKES (2)

Location: T9S, R16E, S. 24 CB
Elevation: 9,620 feet
Area: 10.5 acres; 1.8 acres, respectively
Maximum depth: 15 feet; 8 feet, respectively

A favorite of mine, these lakes are secluded, scenic, and serene. Take trail #568 from where it crosses the Lily Lake road, and then it is about a 4.5 mile trail hike and a half mile jaunt through timbered meadows eastward. Wade Lake might be described as the southern point of an awkward triangle between Farley Lake on the west and Lake Elaine on the east. Fuel for camping and feed for horses are both available. Better check the Forest Service rules, however, for proper horse use regulations. Outlet waters flow south to Skeeter Creek, Copeland, and then out Gilbert Creek to the Clarks Fork River. Associated with Wade is a junior lake. Both support brook trout to 11 inches.

164. MIDNIGHT LAKE

Location: T9S, R16E, S. 24 DB
Elevation: 9,480 feet

Area: 5.1 acres
Maximum depth: 30 feet
Right down the outlet stream from Farley Lake are several lakes. The last one before dumping into Lake Creek is Midnight Lake. There is no trail to the lake but there is easy access from trail #568. Look for loads of brookies.

164a & 165. UNNAMED (2) (fishless)

166. UNNAMED LAKE
Location: T9S, R16E, S. 24 BC
Elevation: 9,740 feet
Area: 2.4 acres
Maximum depth: 12 feet
This little lake is the first lake downstream from Farley Lake, just 100 yards off trail #568. Brook trout again.

167. FARLEY LAKE
Location: T9S, R16E, S. 23 AA
Elevation: 9,740 feet
Area: 24 acres
Maximum depth: 35 feet
On the east slope of Crazy Mountain along trail #568, Farley Lake is a popular overnight stay for those heading on up to Lake Elaine. There's not a lot of fuel for camping but this is a pleasant spot about a five-mile hike from the intersection of trail #568 and the Lily Lake road. Lots of recreational fishing for 10 to 12 inch brook trout.

168. LAKE ELAINE
Location: T9S, R16E, S. 19 BB
Elevation: 9,250 feet
Area: 132.4 acres
Maximum depth: 156 feet
One of the bigger lakes in the Clarks Fork River drainage: Elaine is almost a mile long and three miles around. Both USFS trail #668 north of Granite Lake and trail #568 from Farley Lake contour the west shoreline. Lake Elaine is excellent for brook trout of 8-10 inches, the size fluctuating from year to year depending on the density (the higher the density the smaller the fish).

168a, 169, 170, & 171. UNNAMED (15) (fishless)

172. ESTELLE LAKE
Location: T9S, R17E, S. 19 DB
Elevation: 9,200 feet
Area: 18.7 acres
Maximum depth: 30 feet
Southwest of Green Lake (#173) or southeast of Lake Elaine (#168) find a long, slender lake and call it Estelle Lake, scenic, lonely, and loaded with brook trout. I once caught a cutthroat in Estelle and never could figure where it came from. Estelle Lake is basically a widewater portion of Lake Creek in a striking mountain setting worthy of a visit. It is in timber but has lots of elbow room.

173. GREEN LAKE
Location: T9S, R17E, S. 19, 20
Elevation: 9,150 feet
Area: 35.7 acres
Maximum depth: 129 feet
Hey! You talk about pretty! Green Lake qualifies as one of the best and it also qualifies as one of the more popular. One can ride a horse or hike to Green from several approaches with or without the use of a trail. Camping is good near Green Lake, a good location for a base camp from which to explore other lakes at higher altitudes beyond the timberline. Brookies, brookies, and more brookies.

The largest in a sample of 97 fish averaged 12 inches and .81 pounds, but 7-inch fish are typical. You may catch a 'bow but don't count on it.

174. SUMMERVILLE LAKE
Location: T9S, R17E, S. 17, 18
Elevation: 9,560 feet
Area: 43 acres
Maximum depth: 50 feet
This lake has good camp spots, fuel, and lots of fish, so don't carry too many beans. There are lots of brookies to fill your needs, so please, eat your share.

174a-186. ERRATIC, RUBBLE, TILL, GRAVEL, HERMIT, & UNNAMED LAKES (23) (fishless)

187. QUEER (CASTLE) LAKE
Location: T9S, R17E, S. 8 CD
Elevation: 9,600 feet
Area: 26.4 acres
Maximum depth: 49 feet
Just northeast of Summerville Lake is the Lake Creek watershed, which drains a large area of the northeast portion of the east half of the Gallatin National Forest. A faint horse trail follows the north shore. Some trees exist in the area. Queer Lake, slightly greenish in color due to the influence of glaciers in the headwaters, is one of several lakes in the Lake Creek drainage. Again, brook trout, 6-11 inches, loaded.

188 & 189. UNNAMED (5) (fishless)

190. FLAT ROCK LAKE
Location: T9S, R17E, S. 4, 9
Elevation: 9,990 feet
Area: 37 acres
Maximum depth: 85 feet
Lake Creek Valley (northeast of Summerville #174) and Queer Lake (#187) are a refreshing and nice approach to Flat Rock. The last climb could cause horses some grief. This is above timberline, so if comfort is essential to your body, camp at a lower elevation. It was stocked with cutthroat trout in 1968 and 1978. The FWP plans on stocking it again in '86 and every eight years thereafter to provide some high country recreation. Don't expect huge fish; it is a little too rough for them at this elevation.

191-197. COPEPOD, CLADOCERA, AND UNNAMED LAKES (12) (fishless)

198. FORSAKEN LAKE
Location: T9S, 17E, S.4A
Elevation: 10,450 feet
Area: 30.5 acres
Maximum depth: 66 feet
A lake in the clouds on the cutthroat stocking schedule, Forsaken might not stay on the stocking list long if it fails to provide recreation. In the headwaters of Lake Creek (near the Rock Creek-Clarks Fork divide), it is scheduled for cutts in 1985.

Forsaken Lake and Marker Lake (in the West Fork of the Rock Creek) are the highest lakes with fish in the State of Montana. Boulders, rock, and snow are the main components of the surrounding terrain. Don't expect any bushes to hide in during your basic mountain hail storm. A trail shouldn't be expected either.

198a & 199. UNNAMED (3) (fishless)

200. ALP LAKE
Location: T9S, R17E, S. 8 DA
Elevation: 9,760 feet
Area: 2.8 acres
Maximum depth: 25 feet

A little three-acre pool downstream from Crystal Lake (#202) near Lake Creek, this lake is on the south side of Lake Creek between Queer (#187) and Flat Rock (#190) lakes. It might be interesting, since both cutts and brookies are found in Alp Lake, and in the creek environment near the lake. There is no trail or fuel, but there is easy going in pleasant alpine country.

201. UNNAMED (5) (fishless)

202. CRYSTAL LAKE
Location: T9S, R17E, S. 16 DA
Elevation: 9,910 feet
Area: 27.5 acres
Maximum depth: 85 feet
I suggest a stop here if you're in the neighborhood. I usually visit Crystal Lake from the Jasper Lake (#137) area, relatively mild going for high country hiking. The terrain sort of guides you there. It could also be approached from the Lake Creek area—by following the outlet stream—with no trail. Some minor stunted pine live near the inlet, along with lots of rock interspersed with alpine grass. A beautiful little falls on the outlet makes a nice background for taking a picture of your hiking companion.

Crystal Lake was first stocked in 1968, then again in 1978, and is on the list for restocking in 1986 and every eight years thereafter. The first batch of cutthroat trout were 13-18 inches at six years of age. The stocking schedule should maintain this nice size.

203-206. FELIS, LYNX, AND UNNAMED LAKES (6) (fishless)

207. WHITCOMB (ROBIN) (HUNTER) LAKE
Location: T9S, R17E, S. 20 C
Elevation: 9,575 feet
Area: 8.3 acres
Maximum depth: 58 feet
This lake has been called Robin as well as Hunter Lake and is now named after the Whitcombs of Red Lodge. Whitcomb Lake is in one of the truly beautiful spots in the world. I'm always overwhelmed by the awesome scenery in the Martin (#221) to Estelle (#172) lake chain. No pack trail is shown on the maps but one exists from Theil Lake (#232) to Spogen (Little Falls Lake) #209 and on to Green Lake (#173). One way to pick up this trail system is to depart from the Clay Butte road in Wyoming, or from Granite Lake.

208. TRAIL LAKE
Location: T9S, R17E, S. 20 AC
Elevation: 9,800 feet
Area: 7.1 acres
Maximum depth: 55 feet
This lake lies a quarter mile west of Wright Lake on the trail to Green Lake. Forest trail #614 from Clay Butte or trail #619 from Beartooth Lake, Wyoming, will put you on line for Trail Lake. This portion of the trail will not be evident on most maps, but it is obvious once in the area. The terrain is easy, rolling, and piney from Wright Lake to Green Lake.

Trail Lake is split into two lakelets, one on each side of the trail. Cutthroat trout were introduced in 1979 and provide some excellent fishing opportunities. The plan calls for restocking at the end of eight years, thus in 1987, 1995, etc.

208a & 208b. LITTLE TRAIL AND UNNAMED LAKES (7) (fishless)

209. LITTLE FALLS (SPOGEN) LAKE
Location: T9S, R17E, S. 20 D
Elevation: 9,620 feet
Area: 11.4 acres
Maximum depth: 40 feet
A beautiful lake in a beautiful setting: this is probably one of the prettiest places in the world. Amen! Access is easy by foot or horse from the trail at Wright Lake. Fuel is plentiful for camping and plenty of trees provide shelter.

Little Falls would have been a great place for a spring spawner like cutthroat or rainbow trout, but such is not the case. The lake is full of brookies averaging 8 inches in length. A sample of 60 fish produced one rainbow trout 12 inches in size.

210. WRIGHT LAKE

Location: T9S, R17E, S. 21 CB
Elevation: 9,650 feet
Area: 7.9 acres
Maximum depth: 40 feet

The Beartooth trail from Beartooth Lake or Clay Butte puts you on the shores of Wright Lake—after approximately nine miles of travel. It is a pretty spot in scattered pine-rock surroundings, with plenty of open grassland. Camping (with fuel) is excellent on the north side of the lake. Brook trout prevail, commonly 8 inches with a few to 10 inches.

211. MARTIN LAKE

Location: T9S, R17E, S. 21 B
Elevation: 9,660 feet
Area: 31.4 acres
Maximum depth: 42 feet

Good lake for brookies of 6-10 inches and for camping: mostly alpine meadow with plenty of trees scattered on rocky knobs around the lake. It makes another good base camp location for exploring the treeless environment to the north and west. An island near the branched inlet adds to the scenic qualities of Martin Lake.

212 & 213. GHOST AND UNNAMED LAKES (2) (fishless)

214. WALL LAKE

Location: T9S, R17E, S. 21 AA
Elevation: 9,900 feet
Area: 14.4 acres
Maximum depth: 28 feet

The most recent Forest Service maps refer to this lake as Rachel Lake, named after Rachel Spogen of Red Lodge. Nice person. The lake is at treeline just a half mile and 300 feet higher than Martin Lake. The country here is subject to sudden changes in weather; be prepared. The hike from Martin Lake is mostly over granite boulders. Lots of good fishing for brook trout but nothing big.

215, 216, 217, & 223. CLOVERLEAF LAKES (4)

Location: T9S, R17E, S. 22
Elevation: 10,150 10,180 feet
Area: 18.4 acres; 23.9 acres; 2.9 acres; 31.0 acres respectively
Maximum depth: 66 feet; 30 feet; 12 feet; 65 feet, respectively

This group of four lakes is arranged as a three-leafed clover: #215 on the southwest, #216 on the north, #223 on the southeast, and #217 forming the stem on the northeast. The lakes nestle on barren, glaciated bedrock devoid of significant tree cover.

I find it easiest to travel to Jasper Lake by taking trail #620 from Island Lake, Wyoming, for seven miles. Once at Jasper or Golden lakes, head northeast over a couple of rock ridges for another mile as the crow flies. It can be done in a day's hike. If you're in the country, your options are nearly limitless. All lakes have medium-sized cutthroat.

218-222a. WEDNESDAY, TUESDAY, ARROWHEAD, AND UNNAMED LAKES (5) (fishless)

224, 225, & 226. LIVER, HEART, AND UNNAMED LAKES (5) (fishless)

227. KIDNEY (QUESTION MARK) LAKE

Location: T9S, R17E, S. 21 CC
Elevation: 9,910 feet
Area: 2.8 acres
Maximum depth: 15 feet

Shaped like a kidney, on the Beartooth trail, this lake is north of Thiel Lake (#232). Beware of new Custer National Forest maps which label Kidney Lake incorrectly as Liver

Lake (#225). Liver Lake has no fish and is not on the trail. Kidney Lake drains into Wright Lake via a rather steep incline. The species of fish in Kidney Lake and its connecting stream is brook trout, none of which are very large. I believe I saw an eight-incher once.

228. RENIE LAKE

Location: T9S, R17E, S. 28 BA
Elevation: 9,900 feet
Area: 15.3 acres
Maximum depth: 55 feet

About halfway between Thiel and Martin lakes is this pretty 15-acre lake, with a mile of shoreline following the curvature of the granite bedrock. A few small pines stubbornly cling to the southeast faces of protruding granite hills. The green grasses contrast with lichen rock and brilliant blues of lake water.

The new Custer National Forest maps which include the Gallatin National Forest recently gave new names to many of the lakes in this area. Renie was labeled North Hidden Lake. Find it east of the Beartooth trail not distant from the real Kidney Lake. I was impressed with the brookies in Renie Lake: up to 13 inches, healthier, and generally better looking.

229. HEIDI LAKE

Location: T9S, R17E, S. 28 BC
Elevation: 9,720 feet
Area: 8.2 acres
Maximum depth: 25 feet

This pretty little alpine meadow lake is between Thiel and Kidney lakes just east of the trail. Travel by horse or foot is pleasant, without any strenuous climbing. The lake specializes in brook trout 6-9 inches, not too big for the pan.

230. UNNAMED (4) (fishless)

231. BURNT BACON LAKE

Location: T9S, R17E, S. 29CA
Elevation: 8,950 feet
Area: 15 acres
Maximum depth: 46 feet

Burnt Bacon Lake is one of those well hidden beauties tucked in an isolated little canyon. Thick forest hides it even more. It can be visited from Granite or Thiel lakes, about one-quarter air mile from the north end of Granite Lake.

I don't know who burnt the bacon, but the handle stuck with the local people who hunt elk during Montana's early mountain season. No trail leads to the lake but it can be approached from a pack-trail between Granite and Thiel. The lake is scheduled for grayling and should be a prime home for this colorful lady.

232. THIEL (TIEL) LAKE

Location: T9S, R17E, S. 28, 29, 32, 33
Elevation: 9,260 feet
Area: 18.5 acres
Maximum depth: 35 feet

A meadow lake with rooted aquatics on three sides and talus rock on the other. This is a nice area for a camp, with plenty of fuel, fresh air, and shelter. Grizzly bears like to swim in the lake and sometimes like to raid camp supplies. Steve Sweedberg, Montana's FW&P biologist, has some well ventilated cans and a ripped pack sack to prove they're here.

Please catch all the brook trout you can because they need more room to swim. A party of three once ate 60 brookies in an attempt to set a record. The lake appears as Tiel Lake on most maps, but I believe it was named after Mr. Thiel of Clark, Wyoming.

233. UNNAMED PONDS (4)

Location: T9S, R17E, S. 32, 33
Elevation: 9,080-9,300 feet
Area: 2.9 acres; 4.1 acres, respectively
Maximum depth: 30 feet; 8 feet respectively

Here we have a series of small ponds along the Montana-Wyoming state line, located in heavy timber, south and west of Thiel Lake, along the Park Rapids-Thiel Lake trail. The pond next to Thiel Lake, just 200-300 yards south, doesn't look to be a fish haven but yes, Hershel, it has some winners. I managed to hook a 16-inch brookie, much to my surprise and delight, made a nice photo, and returned the fish for your pleasure. On down the trail is a maize of waters joining at another little pond. This one had both brookies and a few cutthroat trout. Where the cutthroat came from is a mystery to this dude.

234. HIDDEN LAKE

Location: T9S, R17E, S. 33 A
Elevation: 9,500 feet
Area: 18.0 acres
Maximum depth: 46 feet

Another state boundary lake, this one is part of the Jasper-Golden-Hidden-Mule lake chain. A semi-wooded, semi-distinct trail from Thiel Lake puts you at Hidden Lake in short order. Hidden has been a fishery for many years, beginning in the 1940s, when golden trout from a 1938 plant in Jasper found their way down drainage to Hidden. The whole string from Jasper to Mule Lake, Wyoming, was saturated with goldens by 1943. By 1965, the goldens no longer inhabited Jasper and Golden lakes upstream, but were present in the stream and in Hidden Lake. In 1968, Jasper lake was stocked with cutthroat trout and by 1972 they also invaded Hidden Lake. Now both species exist in Hidden Lake.

In 1974, no fish were found in Hidden Lake but redds (spawning beds) were noted in the outlet and inlet. Strange: spawning, but no adults. In 1976, I found cutthroat and goldens again, all the same size and all two years old. This evidence convinced me that both cutthroat and goldens had successfully spawned in 1974 but the parents aged out and died. It also suggested that successful spawning does not occur every year. Present species in Hidden? Maybe you ought to find out.

235. SWEDE (THROOP) LAKE

Location: T9S, R17E, S. 28 D
Elevation: 9,810 feet
Area: 11.8 acres
Maximum depth: 84 feet

North of Hidden Lake about three-quarters of a mile and up about 300 feet in elevation, is "call it what you want lake." Throop, a deceased resident of the Red Lodge area, was given recognition of his mountain travels by having a lake in the Lake Fork of Rock Creek named in his honor. Then, when the new Custer National Forest map was printed, Throop Lake appeared on Swede Lake's map location. Planted in 1980 with cutthroat trout and scheduled for an eight-year stocking cycle, good things are expected here.

235a. UNNAMED (5) (fishless)

236. GOLDEN LAKE

Location: T9S, R17E, S. 23, 26, 27
Elevation: 10,130 feet
Area: 48.9 acres
Maximum depth: 90 feet

Golden Lake was part of the original trout chain of lakes from Jasper to Hidden Lake (See Hidden Lake (#234) for details). Subsequent stocking of cutthroat in Jasper Lake after the demise of golden trout has now converted Golden Lake fishery to cutthroat trout.

Golden Lake has steep shorelines, deep cold waters, and no area in the lake where trout can spawn. The outlet is beautiful, with large deep pools flowing through large rocks; but again no spawning area exists. The inlet from Jasper, only 300 yards upstream, has nice flows but the substratae is cemented, too compact for fish reproduction. Cutthroat will be introduced at intervals to make Golden's fishery best when Jasper's is poorest.

237. JASPER LAKE

Location: T9S, R17E, S. 23
Elevation: 10,150 feet
Area: 54.8 acres
Maximum depth: 107 feet

Jasper is the hot spot of the Beartooths and for good reason. This lake produces nice, big fish. They are, however, less than easy to catch. Fish—in this case cutthroat of the McBride variety—grow extremely well, so for best action it should be fished the third and fourth year after stocking. Later years are good for very large fish but action is much slower. The last plant was made in 1982, and the cycle is every eighth year thereafter. Some natural reproduction is also occurring but not at a sufficient rate to satisfy the demand.

The route from Island Lake, Wyoming, to Jasper is via a trail over a 7.5 mile distance. A few little hills are along the route, but the biggest rise in elevation is at the Montana-Wyoming state line. Camping is best at Albino Lake which is sheltered and has limited fuel.

238, 239, 240, & 241. GUS AND UNNAMED LAKES (4) (fishless)

242. LONESOME LAKE

Location: T9S, R 17E, S. 35. B
Elevation: 10,050 feet
Area: 35.3 acres
Maximum depth: 38 feet

Lonesome Lake is an interstate water on the Wyoming-Montana border south of Lonesome Mountain. A long, slender lake, it is accessible by horse or foot traffic. No trail is next to the lake but trails in the vicinity are available. Good fishing for 6-9-inch brookies.

243. ABANDONED LAKE

Location: T9S, R17E, S. 26 CC
Elevation: 10,100 feet
Area: 10.5 acres
Maximum depth: 25 feet

Just up the inlet of Lonesome Lake is this scenic lake under the southeast face of Lonesome Mountain. There is no trail here, but travel is easy—cross-country from area trails—with or without horses. Trees are scarce, but not fish. Have a brook trout dinner.

244. ARCTIC LAKE (fishless)

245. ALBINO LAKE

Location: T9S, R17E, S. 25
Elevation: 10,000 feet
Area: 39.2 acres
Maximum depth: 149 feet

On the east half of the Gallatin National Forest, in a cold basin below the divide between the Clarks Fork and Rock Creek drainages, lies a steady producer of fat cutthroat 12-15 inches in length. Take the trail from Island Lake, Wyoming, for approximately 6.5 miles. The major elevation change is from the state line to Albino Lake, a .75 mile jaunt. Albino receives fish every four years and provides steady fishing.

246. LINE LAKE

Location: T9S, R19E, S. 34 BB
Elevation: 9,680 feet
Area: 4.7 acres
Maximum depth: 26 feet

At first one would assume Line Lake was located in the Rock Creek drainage, but in fact its outflow heads eastward via Line Creek to the Clarks Fork River. The lake rests on the Montana-Wyoming state line. The fast route is a quick hike from the gravel pile on the Beartooth Highway 212, eastward over Wyoming Creek to the head of Line Creek. There is a trail: not the maintained type, but one that is established from years of use. There used to be a 4x4 jeep trail to the lake, but it was closed some years ago.

Line Lake was rehabilitated in 1968 from a concentration of chubs and white suckers to cutthroat trout. The cutts went to work, consumed large volumes of food, and in turn converted themselves into large cutts. Fish averaged a pound per year during the late '70s and early '80s. The major detriment to good fishing is the wind that often howls through the area, causing poor catches. But when it's hot, it's hot.